Radiophilia

THE STUDY OF SOUND

Editor: Michael Bull

Each book in *The Study of Sound* offers a concise look at a single concept within the field of sound studies. With an emphasis on the interdisciplinary nature of the topics at hand, the series explores a range of core issues, debates and objects within sound studies from a variety of perspectives and within a multitude of contexts.

Editorial Board:

Carolyn Birdsall, Associate Professor, Department of Media Studies, University of Amsterdam, The Netherlands

Martin Daughtry, Associate Professor of Music, Arts and Humanities, NYU, USA

Michael Heller, Associate Professor, Department of Music, University of Pittsburgh, USA

Brian Kane, Associate Professor, Department of Music, Yale University, USA

Marie Thompson, Senior Lecturer in Popular Music, The Open University, UK

James Mansell, Assistant Professor of Cultural Studies, Department of Culture, Film and Media, University of Nottingham, UK

The Sound of Nonsense, Richard Elliott

Humming, Suk-Jun Kim

Lipsynching, Merrie Snell

Sonic Fiction, Holger Schulze

Sirens, Michael Bull

Sonic Intimacy, Malcolm James

Radiophilia, Carolyn Birdsall

Forthcoming Titles:

Wild Sound, Michael Pigott

Audio Paper, Sanne Krogh Groth and Stefan Östersjö

Radiophilia

Carolyn Birdsall

BLOOMSBURY ACADEMIC
NEW YORK • LONDON • OXFORD • NEW DELHI • SYDNEY

BLOOMSBURY ACADEMIC
Bloomsbury Publishing Inc
1385 Broadway, New York, NY 10018, USA
50 Bedford Square, London, WC1B 3DP, UK
29 Earlsfort Terrace, Dublin 2, Ireland

BLOOMSBURY, BLOOMSBURY ACADEMIC and the Diana logo are trademarks of Bloomsbury Publishing Plc

First published in the United States of America 2023

Copyright © Carolyn Birdsall, 2023

For legal purposes the Acknowledgments on p. xii constitute an extension of this copyright page.

Series design by Liron Gilenberg www.ironicitalics.com
Cover images: kumdinpitak/iStock and in8finity/iStock

All rights reserved. No part of this publication may be reproduced or transmitted in any form or by any means, electronic or mechanical, including photocopying, recording, or any information storage or retrieval system, without prior permission in writing from the publishers.

Bloomsbury Publishing Inc does not have any control over, or responsibility for, any third-party websites referred to or in this book. All internet addresses given in this book were correct at the time of going to press. The author and publisher regret any inconvenience caused if addresses have changed or sites have ceased to exist, but can accept no responsibility for any such changes.

A catalog record for this book is available from the Library of Congress.

ISBN: HB: 978-1-5013-7497-5
PB: 978-1-5013-7496-8
ePDF: 978-1-5013-7499-9
eBook: 978-1-5013-7498-2

Series: The Study of Sound

Typeset by RefineCatch Limited, Bungay, Suffolk

To find out more about our authors and books visit www.bloomsbury.com and sign up for our newsletters.

*In memory of Pat Picker (1930–2022),
who loved radio her whole life.*

CONTENTS

List of Figures viii
Acknowledgements xi

Introduction 1

1 Loving 13

2 Knowing 41

3 Saving 95

4 Sharing 147

Conclusion 189

Notes 199
*Bibliography (online at www.bloomsbury.com/uk/
radiophilia-9781501374968)*
Index 271

FIGURES

1 QSL card issued by 7MJ (Royal M. Howard) to 7AIB, dated 5 June 1924, Ketchikan (Alaska), United States, which was a remote settlement that had several thousand inhabitants at that time. 49
2 QSL card issued by an amateur radio group (VU2MA) in the context of a military academy in an independent and post-partition India, Indian Military Academy, Dehradun, India, dated 15 May 1951. 50
3 QSL card issued by VE2HI (Ethel L. Pick), who subsequently became one of the first members of the Young Ladies Radio League (YLRL), founded in 1939. Dated 28 December 1938, Montreal, Canada. 51
4 A 1949 cover of the magazine *Musen to Jikken* (無線と実験, or Radio Experimenters) depicts a young woman in school uniform working on a radio set. 53
5 One of the trade-exhibition-style halls with various stands at the International Radio Exhibition (Internationale Radio Tentoonstelling), Amsterdam, The Netherlands, 1925 64
6 A stand showing radio furniture during a radio exhibition at the Radio Salon, Scheveningen, The Netherlands, 1926. 66
7 A woman sits behind the wheel of a mock-up 'car' with a Blaupunkt car radio installed, German Radio Exhibition, Berlin, Germany, August 1932. 66
8 A radio-controlled robot was a sensation at the London Radio Exhibition, UK, 1932. 67
9 The Funk-Stunde Berlin radio station stand at the German Radio Exhibition, which depicted the events documented by radio reportage and the new broadcasting house, Germany, August 1931. 68

10	'AWA Tower from Wynyard St, Sydney', photo by Harold Cazneaux, in downtown Sydney, *c.* 1939.	70
11	'Humour Number', *Radio Times*, 9 October 1936, cover.	84
12	Argonauts Club membership badge issued by the ABC (Australian Broadcasting Corporation).	101
13	ABC radio Argonauts Club certificate with a badge attached, including the membership number (ship name and oar number).	102
14	Radio tower (ラジオ塔) in Nakamura Park, Nagoya City, Japan, 6 September 2017.	106
15 and 16	Photos depicting Martín Butera outside the 'A Noite' building, former headquarters of Rádio Nacional in Rio de Janeiro, Brazil.	108–109
17	'EKCO' Radiocorder device for recording radio programmes onto metal discs.	117
18	Membership card for the UK-based ORCA (Old-time Radio Show Collectors Association), issued in June 2017, front and back.	124
19	ORCA, Cassette Lending Library [Tapes 1 to 2099] catalogue, cover.	125
20	Ogden Oliphant, 'A Scrapbook for 1909', *The Radio Times*, 16 February 1934, 449.	136
21	T-Shirt for the 2SER community radio station, Sydney, Australia, which can be purchased or attained when signing up as a 'Passionate' or 'Lifetime' member.	151
22	Historical recreation of a radio dealer shop inside the museum display at the Nederlands Omroepmusem (Netherlands Broadcast Museum), Hilversum, Netherlands, *c.* 1993.	165
23	The exterior of the Japan Radio Museum, Matsumoto, Japan.	167
24	Tadanobu Okabe, director of the Japan Radio Museum, standing beside a display of historical wireless sets in the museum.	168
25	Exterior of the Taiwan National Radio Museum, housed in the former Minxiong Broadcast Station, built in 1940.	170
26	Transmission technology on display, with a screen for visitor information, Taiwan National Radio Museum.	171

27 Rachel Morton (RDU station) shows the radio journalist Yadana Saw the historical timeline within the space of the 'Alternative Radio' exhibition, Canterbury Museum, Christchurch, New Zealand. 173
28 A memorial plaque for offshore radio station The Voice of Peace in Tel Aviv, Israel, and the accompanying device through which historical clips of the station can be played. 175
29 Poster board promoting the Philips LP commercial release 'I Can Hear It Now: Winston Churchill', 1957 Radio Show, Earls Court, London, UK, printed in the *Evening Standard*, 11 September 1957. 181

ACKNOWLEDGEMENTS

This book has come into being with many helping hands. A host of individuals, organizations and institutions have been incredibly generous with their time and resources. The research and writing of this book were made possible by the support of the Dutch Research Council (NWO), as part of the project TRACE (Tracking Radio Archival Recordings in Europe, 1930–1960), with project number 016.Vidi.185.219. During this book's preparation, I was also kindly hosted by several institutions: the International Institute of Social History (IISG) in Amsterdam, the Goethe-Universität Frankfurt and the 'Epistemes of Modern Acoustics' group at the Max Planck Institute for the History of Science (MPIWG), Berlin.

At the University of Amsterdam, it is a privilege to work with a wonderful group of colleagues at the Department of Media Studies, as well as at the Amsterdam School for Cultural Analysis (ASCA) and the Amsterdam School for Heritage, Memory and Material Culture (AHM). In particular, I'd like to thank the Television and Cross Media team for their camaraderie and intellectual community. Our regular informal workshops allowed me to give this project a first 'temperature test' when it was in the starting blocks; I'd particularly like to thank Donya Alinejad, Joke Hermes, Misha Kavka, Jeroen de Kloet, Jaap Kooijman, Linda Kopitz, Vanessa Ossa, Toni Pape, Markus Stauff and Tommy Tse.

Special thanks to colleagues with whom I've had the pleasure to collaborate on a range of research activities related to radio, sound and media archiving, all of which has fed my thinking while working on this project: Alec Badenoch, Jeannine Baker, Karin Bijsterveld, Lauren Bratslavsky, Alejandra Bronfman, Elinor Carmi, Elizabeth Darling, Brecht Declercq, Friedrich Dethlefs, Simone Dotto, Anthony Enns, Erica Harrison, Anette Hoffmann, Jennifer Hsieh, Corinna Kaiser, Richard Legay, Anne MacLennan, Paulo Nunes, Lonán Ó Briain, Floris Paalman, Eszter Polónyi, Birgit Van Puymbroeck,

Pekka Salosaari, Lotte Schüssler, Senta Siewert, Marc Silberman, Kristin Skoog, Ewa Stańczyk, Jonathan Sterne, Alfredo Thiermann, Viktoria Tkaczyk, Shawn VanCour, Jennifer Vaughn, Joanna Walewska-Choptiany, Tom Western and meLê yamomo. I'd also like to thank those who hosted or responded to early presentations on this topic, or shared insights and encouragement as I started to prepare this research: Andrew J. Bottomley, Tim Crook, Michele Hilmes, Vincent Kuitenbrouwer, Kate Lacey, Philomeen Lelieveldt, Anya Luscombe, Carole O'Reilly, Nora Patterson, Seán Street, Neil Verma, Tim Wall, E. James West and Huub Wijfjes. Thanks especially to Bruce Johnson for his mentorship and support, and for leading by example in the study of popular music as global sound culture.

I am grateful to the libraries and archives that have opened up their collections to me. I would like to thank the BBC Written Archives Centre; the Deutsches Rundfunkarchiv; the British Library Sound Archive; the Netherlands Institute for Sound and Vision; the University of Maryland Library; and the Bodleian Libraries, Oxford University. Thanks to the Sheffield University Library Special Collections team, and to Jacob Kingsbury Downs for assistance in accessing the Radio Luxembourg collection. Thanks also to the University of Amsterdam Library team, in particular Fenna Geelhoed, Cecilia Kloppenburg and Alexandra van der Neut-Welling. For expert help with arranging image permissions, my deepest thanks to Anne-Elise Keen and Yumi Hasegawa. A special thanks also to the assistants within the TRACE project for supporting this research: Yuchen Chen, Lilli Elias, Mónica Baptiste Gouffray, Scarlett Lösch and Julia Neugarten. To the individuals who helped to provided permissions for images for this book, I'd like to thank, in particular, Bas Agterberg, Martín Butera and Ligia Katze, Po-Yi Chen and Shu-Ching Yang, Jo Featherston, Sally Garrett, Tadanobu Okabe, Thomas Roscoe and Graeme Stevenson.

It has been a pleasure to work with Bloomsbury Press. A warm thanks to series editor Michael Bull for his enthusiastic response to the initial idea and for encouraging me to develop it for The Study of Sound series. Thank you to Leah Babb-Rosenfeld and Rachel Moore at Bloomsbury for guidance throughout the review, revision and production process, and for copyediting, Ronnie Hanna. The present book has been much improved thanks to the constructive feedback shared by the anonymous reviewers of the book proposal and full manuscript.

ACKNOWLEDGEMENTS

A heartfelt thanks to Asli Özgen-Havekotte for her encouragement and astute comments on the first draft of the original book proposal, and to Alejandra Bronfman, Ayanna Legros and Laura Wagner for their feedback as I first began the writing process. In particular, I'd like to express my thanks to colleagues who read parts of the completed manuscript ahead of its final submission, and shared thoughtful feedback and suggestions: Tiziano Bonini, Ricarda Franzen, Matt Hills, Gascia Ouzounian, Toni Pape, Elodie A. Roy, Wouter Schreurs and Senta Siewert; along with a special thanks to Anthony Enns for reviewing the full manuscript.

To the friends who rallied from the sidelines while I was working on – but especially trying to finish – this book: A'na, Anna, Anette, Annette, Anoek, Beattie, Bożena, Bregje, Charlotte, Dagmar, Eef, Emma, Hendrik, Isabelle, Jana, Julia, Karin, Katherine, Maria, Mic, Natalie, Nic, Noa, Petra, Rachel, Sara, Toni and Yumi. Finally, I would like to thank my family in Australia and the Netherlands for their love and support, in particular my sister Bronwyn, who was an all-in-one editorial support team. And to Matthieu, for his support and encouragement, and for reminding me of all the love that exists above and beyond that felt for radio.

Introduction

It was the mid-1990s. I had my radio receiver on a clothes dresser and beside it sat a shoebox with cassette tapes. It was not my first analogue radio receiver combined with a tape player, but its dual cassette deck allowed for off-air recording (radio to tape), as well as copying (tape to tape). Having this combined device was key to what became a deeply-felt attachment to, and committed regular consumption of, radio. Radio had long been in my everyday environment, mainly listening via the home stereo, car radio and Walkman, but it was perhaps the first period in which I came to feel a strong attachment and emotional investment in particular radio programming. In this way, I gained access to new information and music recommendations from the presenters, which lay beyond what I could find myself in magazines, local music stores or via music television.[1]

I started to listen out for regular programmes, but also often explored up and down the analogue AM/FM dial to see what else was 'out there' on public, commercial, community or pirate radio. Being underage, listening to radio helped me 'peer in' to the world of going out, and feel briefly connected to it, even if that meant listening to second-hand stories while tuning in from my teenage bedroom. In particular I was drawn to the Sydney-based community station 2SER. During their programmes, multiple presenters would talk amongst themselves in a conversational tone, with a warm and inclusive address towards their listening audience, heightening my affection for these now-familiar voices, their choice of music and regular time slots on air, which I incorporated into my own weekly routine. In wanting to listen to the programme content again, I often stood close by with my finger positioned on the 'record' button. I then taped whole programmes and then 'retaped' excerpts onto new tapes, which became mixtapes I'd either play at home or on my portable cassette player while taking public transport, or occasionally copied for friends.

This personal narrative has been crafted from a set of personal experiences more than two decades ago, and might be a bit too neat. At the very least, I would need to further contextualize my own positionality at that moment, as a white, straight cis-gender teenager in a middle-class, suburban Australian home setting, with access to relatively-new or hand-me-down audio technologies.[2] Yet I share this narrative, firstly, as a self-positioning, as someone who has and continues to incorporate terrestrial radio listening in everyday life; although now in tandem with apps such as Podcast Addict on my smartphone that sends regular alerts for new digital audio available right at my fingertips. Secondly, this narrative can be included as one of the many intensely-felt attachments expressed towards radio across a century from early wireless and the start of the broadcast era in the 1920s through to the present. While the exact conditions, forms and media assemblages of 'radio' may differ across time and place, this study enquires into diverse possibilities for what *radiophilia* may be, defined in general terms as the love for, or strong attachment to, radio.[3] My personal story lends itself to observing the pleasures of radio listening, the desire to find and learn about new things via radio, and the effort to record, keep, relisten to and share radio. All of these will be key touchstones for this book, as the four central themes I have structured the chapters around: loving, knowing, saving and sharing.

As such, key questions that can be asked of this single case, and opened up beyond its particularity, include: what is the *love* of radio, and how do you enact or express this loving of radio? How do you *know* the thing you love? How do you *save* the thing you love? And how do you *share* your love of radio? These questions are embedded within the overall aim of the present book to survey 100 years of radio, providing the opportunity to investigate the major transformations in the medium and its renewal in the digital age, along with its place across societies and cultures. The overarching questions include: how is the love of the new and renewed medium characterized? How does it change over time, and what forms does it take in different national or regional contexts?

Departure points: literature, sources and selection

Given radio's initial rapid and sustained popularity over 100 years, it may seem surprising that media and cultural scholars have not yet sought to clarify the nature of a 'love' of radio, and the various dimensions of the attachments formed to the medium, its contents and material forms.

In radio studies, we find important recent groundwork with empirical scholarship seeking to clarify the significance of radio sound and its 'affective rhythms' for everyday acts of listening.[4] Such work has pointed to radio's content, predominantly based on music and the spoken word, and the imaginative possibilities offered by radio as a window to the 'magic' of the world, its cultural productions and politics.[5] There is also a strong tradition of research on the cultural history of radio that has been attentive to audiences, their diverse modes of listening and engagement with radio, as well as the formation of the 'intimate public' as a new social space, with its unseen voices provoking 'intense pleasure and anxiety' as new norms were established.[6] This scholarship has often focused on discrete periods or national contexts, and has not resulted in a broader account seeking to make sense of strong attachments to or investments in radio, or address how they may manifest in different ways across place and time. While the present study mainly centres on the love of radio, it's necessary to acknowledge its opposite: the aversion to radio, evidenced by the rejection or resistance to its use which runs through the century of radio; from 'haters', 'non users' and late adopters through to present-day forms of 'disengagement'.[7]

In the domain of digital radio and podcast research there has been an attention to radio as a 'social' and 'resilient' medium with 'enduring appeal' in the digital era.[8] The persistence of 'radioness' in the present, multi-platform media environment is evidenced by a major US station owner rebranding itself as iHeartRadio. While expanding to become one of the largest podcast networks that dominates podcast download lists, its 'I love radio' brand message continues to capitalize on the lingering appeal of radio, with the company also expanding its operations into 'brick and mortar' initiatives such as iHeartRadio theatres for fans to attend live events.[9] Across contemporary news reports, the industry and listeners, there has been a tendency to frame enthusiastic 'binge' listening practices in medicalized terms as 'podcast junkie' or 'podcast addict'; podcast research has since sought to offer nuanced reflections on the cultivation of 'sonorous intimacy' and 'affective engagement' of and by listeners.[10]

Digital radio studies, too, has explored how, in an era of 'sound on screen', listening experience and affective engagement with audio content via digital devices and interfaces is structured in ways that may differ significantly from terrestrial radio transmissions.[11] In particular, the activities of the networked listener in 'making comments, remixing media items, sharing media objects, producing user-generated or user-circulated content' have been identified as key elements in the production of radio's 'affective publics', for which commercial and public radio audiences produce 'different public displays of affect' via social media.[12] While radio has traditionally been understood as an ephemeral medium, other research has noted the expanded opportunities to record and archive radio, or maintain access to radio and podcast programming as 'content on demand'.[13] The era of digital audio 'plenitude' alters the audio media landscape, with the vastness of digitally-available content emphasizing the traces of past radio as 'scarce'. The present study therefore acknowledges how digital possibilities to listen again to programming have altered listeners' relationships with a once 'live' broadcasting system, and how the perceived scarce traces of radio's past traces serve as a trigger for nostalgic remembering of historical radio and its material cultures.

In the field of sound studies there have been significant efforts to account for how sound may invite particular affects or emotive states (e.g., joy, fear, boredom), and to explore how (recorded) sounds are incorporated into cultural practices of remembering and nostalgic recollection.[14] The interest in sound, embodied listening and affect has rarely translated into a specific theoretical attention to radio broadcasting, and, when it has, is mainly investigated in relation to specific practices or sites.[15] The adjacent field of popular music studies has developed an attention to a broader 'passion for music' in the modern era,[16] most notably in music fan and collecting practices, with the attachment to recorded music being approached in terms of a strong sensory and emotional engagement with its material forms. Here too we find key concepts about music fans defined in near-pathological terms, with 'gramomania' referring to a fetishistic collecting, or the 'vinylphile' who develops a romantic or nostalgic relation to the past through the vinyl record.[17] A more instructive account can be found in studies of 'audiophilia', a term that has been invoked for a male-dominated culture of music lovers preoccupied with 'high end' stereo equipment, who assert a distinct set of values and preferences towards sound that is at times in contrast to those of (professional) sound engineering.[18] Despite the tendency for the 'audiophile' to be reserved for a distinct group of individuals with specialized knowledge, this category is 'neither sharply bounded nor internally homogeneous; there are grades of audiophilia, and much difference of opinion within its ranks'.[19] In other words, while these existing categories may initially appear fairly narrowly defined, there is scope to broaden the critical understanding of a passionate consumption and collecting of a particular media beyond a select group of people. For the present study of attachments to radio, therefore, it is not necessary to limit the focus to passionate (super)fans or a discerning elitist group context, and as I will show, music fandom has frequently been an overlapping, if not a motivating, factor in strong attachments to radio and its programming.

In media studies, the fields of audience and fan studies have been attentive to questions of affect and emotional engagement with media products. In this context, researchers have called for an understanding of media fandom that affirms the role of fan 'attachments, emotions and passions' and exercises caution about separating fan affects/play from cognition/knowledge.[20] Departing from earlier characterizations of fan behaviour in either overly negative or positive terms, fan practice is generally treated as 'a spectrum in which a multiplicity of practices, groups, and motivations span between the polarities of the personal and the communal'.[21] Fandom is thus frequently a social resource that allows for existing personal affective investments to be reinforced and for the possibility of building connections with fellow fans. While a significant part of this field is concerned with questions of fan community and creativity, the present study builds on research that stresses how fandom may also be formed through the consumption of industry-led consumer culture, such as fan magazines or membership in official fan clubs. Particularly instructive for the present study is the acknowledgement of how objects, such as merchandise or memorabilia, constitute a material means for facilitating fan identification and affective attachments.[22] An attention to material culture's ties to memory and nostalgia is also consistent with an interest in how fandoms might change over time, across the individual 'life cycle'.[23] In keeping with such insights, the present study cites examples of fan creativity, performance and community formations, but situates these within a larger framework of how audiences come to love and know a medium, its forms and contents, and how they make sure it is saved and shared with others.

Aside from the growing literature on music-focused fandoms, the field of fan studies has generally not attended to questions related to sound, or to listening as affective engagement, let alone treated the specific case of radio.[24] Similarly, while histories of media fandom prior to the 1960s are rare, there have been a few important exceptions. For instance, between roughly 1840 and 1870, there are examples of music fans who developed private and public expressions of their fandom, with practices ranging across repeated musical concert-going, celebrity worship and collecting, such as gathering clippings in private scrapbooks.[25] Similarly, cinema scholars have studied the formation of cinema fan culture during the 1900s and 1910s in relation to film fan magazines and the creation of 'movie scrapbooks'.[26] Other histories of fandom in the US context have pointed to the origins of the term 'fan' in sport and theatre contexts around 1900, before being adopted by science fiction fans in the 1920s, while more recent impulses in the research field have emphasized the importance of considering fandoms in transnational and global frameworks.[27] In other scholarship there has been an interest in revisiting existing concepts, such as bibliophilia, or in coining telephilia, in order to address the love of complex 'quality' narratives or interactive TV audience practices.[28] Film studies scholarship on cinephilia is a significant precedent for the present effort to treat radiophilia as a historical and global phenomenon.[29] As a domain for viewer engagements with film culture, a vital insight is that worry, anxiety and fear, particularly about the loss of cinema, constitutes an important force for the 'historical' cinephilia of the 1920s through to the digital era.[30] Yet crucially, my approach differs from existing debates on cinephilia, in which a distinction is usually made between the cinephile's critical knowledge of the object and the supposedly emotional or passionate realm of fandom.[31] As mentioned above, my stance is that the study of radiophilia should necessarily treat 'ordinary' habitual listening as much as the activities of committed radiophiles or (super)fans.

A final concern relates to questions of focus, selection and periodization. In seeking to uncover diverse experiences and histories of the attachment to radio, I take up an approach that is conversant with recent work in feminist media history.[32] As the first chapter ('Loving') will outline, it is important to acknowledge masculinist accounts of radio and its history and to uncover the formation of male-dominated communities around radio, which frequently gained visibility and influence. Yet where possible, the chapters that follow do not only highlight 'master narratives' of broadcast radio – for instance, its domesticity, interiority or intimacy – but especially seek to challenge unitary historical trajectories, experiences or cultural practices around radio. For example, as part of the bid not to reinforce the accepted historical norm that most national radio systems were created in the 1920s, this study is attentive to the role of radio in colonial modernity, in anti-colonial struggle and in newly-independent nations. This study thereby highlights how strong emotive attachments to radio may be formed under fearful or fraught circumstances (such as authoritarian rule or conflict) as well as in nation-building projects taking place across the twentieth century.

As such, the study attests to the love of radio, in its plurality, dynamism, heterogeneity and open-endedness, but also underscores its radical situatedness, whether pertaining to individual biography or the influence of specific historical, socio-political or cultural conditions. Throughout this study, there is an effort to include non-Western and non-English media practices, while being aware, at the same time, of how media research retains its 'strong normative situatedness in Western modernity'.[33] Indeed, a significant portion of the cases discussed here are drawn from Europe, the Americas, Australasia and Asia. This choice is partly a reflection of my own orientation (coming from Australia, but situated in Europe). A further influencing factor was the writing of this study under pandemic conditions, which led to an increased reliance on sources accessible online, for which there is currently an overrepresentation of digitized sources for North American and Western European radio history. For example, the availability of digitized programme guides and magazines via the British BBC Genome site has led to an increased attention to examples sourced from British radio history.[34] Similarly, numerous magazines consulted during the course of this research were accessible via the archival initiatives AmericanRadioHistory.com and WorldRadioHistory.com.[35]

In terms of periodization, my own specialization in radio history has influenced this study's stronger emphasis on the first decades of radio until the 1950s, along with the most recent decades of terrestrial and internet radio since the 1990s, which coincided with my own coming of age as an 'independent' radio listener and, subsequently, radio researcher. While there is some discussion of developments during the 'transistor' radio era between the 1950s and the 1970s, there is certainly more scope for an expanded application of radiophilia to this period – and to the geopolitical conditions of Cold War-era radio cultures – than this study allows for. Similarly, digital radio, podcasting and the rise of the 'networked' listener are discussed, yet given a less detailed treatment than that of analogue radio transmission and reception.

An important insight is that audiences, fans and users tend to be more visible, or express their feelings or other emotional registers more explicitly, when a media technology is perceived to be 'new' and as the 'sociotechnical imaginaries' surrounding it are being established and negotiated.[36] As such, there is more media attention and debate in these moments of change, or during significant media events, than the realm of everyday habits or routines. For this reason, I have chosen to foreground certain everyday activities, such as fan scrapbook-making, which was practised widely yet only very few preserved examples can be found in heritage institutions or have been made accessible via amateur radio history initiatives. Despite devoting much of my research during the past decade to the study of (radio) sound, memory and material culture, and having encountered countless objects, recordings and other artefacts, the process of writing this study has served to further underscore how much more institutional and officially-published print documentation 'sticks' in the historical archive and online spaces than other materials. In particular, I was struck by the difficulties in finding sources and images of ubiquitous aspects of even very recent radio culture, such as merchandise like bumper stickers or t-shirts. Bearing in mind the archival absences restricting the available sources for documenting the affective engagements of audiences in diverse spaces and across radio's long century, this study nonetheless issues a clarion call for radiophilia as a new research agenda, as an invitation for more debate and further empirical fleshing out in future scholarship.

Book structure

The four chapters of this book are concerned with 'loving', 'knowing' and 'saving' radio, and, finally, 'sharing' the love of radio. The first chapter outlines the main theoretical embedding and contribution of this study, namely to establish a conceptual framework for understanding affective attachments and emotional investments in radio, and the forms that this love can take. With this departure point, the subsequent three chapters will pursue how the loving of radio takes shape in relation to practices of knowing, saving and sharing.

The main thrust of the first chapter ('Loving') is to consider loving as a site of action and practice, and acknowledge that loving not only pertains to the listener's one-to-one relationship to the medium, its contents or forms, but rather that a broader concept may include group practices or social moods, as well as changing intensities, durations and phases. The first part provides a broader historical canvas for the 'attractions of radio' since its emergence, and it offers categories for understanding the attachments to radio, in particular its ascribed medial qualities, content, material form and the social uses or needs it has fulfilled in audiences. The second part situates the present interest in the love of radio in recent scholarly discussions of emotions, affect and feeling, drawing productive insights about affective and emotional engagements with media from fan studies research, along with recent accounts of the history of the emotions that engage affect and emotions as socially-framed, relational and embodied practice. The third part addresses the experience of radio as taking place 'beyond the ears', as an embodied and multisensory encounter, which may also be produced at the interstices of multiple or cross-media engagements. This theoretical impulse represents a special attention to the haptic and other sensory domains in which the embodied experience of radio takes place, the framing functions of other media (e.g., programme schedules, fan magazines) and exchanges between radio and other media. While the chapter treats radiophilia as a particular type of attachment, it therefore acknowledges intersecting pleasures across media fandoms. It also identifies the significance of material culture, in tandem with heritage and memory studies, as a means of understanding how attachments to radio are not only associated with certain practices, but also take form in relation to particular objects or spaces.

The second chapter ('Knowing') takes up questions concerned with knowledge production related to radiophilia. It delineates three main concerns situated at the connections between loving and knowing, whether this pertains to learning, pedagogy or knowledge production. The first part of the chapter investigates early knowledge production (and know-how) emerging from radio as a technical hobby, a community formation and cultural practice in various national and regional contexts. The second interest is in the forms of epistemic authority claimed by regulators and industry, in the articulation of 'sociotechnical fantasies' of radio: a process that was negotiated, or 'co-produced', with audiences, broadcasters and other cultural workers. Here, the specific genres of the radio film, the radio exhibition and the radio encyclopaedia are identified as cultural objects that facilitate and perform 'knowledge work' around radio, its applications and its affective appeal for listeners.[37] The final part of the chapter will consider how knowledge and affect have operated in tandem with each other, focusing on how radio's 'perceived interactivity' fuelled letter writing, as well as the hands-on doing and learning encouraged in fan magazines, with the growth of a fan culture directed towards the radio medium, its specific programmes, content or stars. While some of these examples will initially be more historical, drawn from the first decades of radio, the chapter will also ask how certain knowledge formations and pedagogical practices might apply to other periods or settings.

The third chapter ('Saving') takes up an important domain for the attachment to radio, which is the desire to save, preserve or 'hang on' to radio. The first section explores the *non-sound* objects or traces that individuals or collectives seek to preserve from radio, whether in photographic or text-based records, personal souvenirs or fan scrapbooks used to hold various forms of radio-related ephemera, or efforts to save sites of past radio heritage, such as broadcast buildings. The following parts consider the radiophilic impulses in efforts to capture and save the 'ephemeral' *sounds* of radio transmissions, as pertaining to amateur practices and the formation of fan-based collector cultures. The final part considers how the radiophilic desire to 'keep' radio sounds has figured in professional archival initiatives and heritage discourses surrounding radio from its earliest period to the present, but can also include forms of radio archival activism in documenting radio perceived to be problematic, or in monitoring radio broadcasts by an enemy state. This treatment of professionals' rationales for saving radio as the site of emotional practice also takes into account how the first archives were bound up with national and imperial agendas. It will also consider the overall process by which the professional archivist's role as gatekeeper has been challenged in the era of digital preservation, and calls for archives to develop a more collaborative approach in how they co-curate radio heritage with community stakeholders. Covering a wide range of amateur and (semi-)professional contexts and analogue and digital practices, the chapter traces how these practices have continued to add cultural value to radio, and engages insights from studies of collecting, memory and material culture.

The fourth chapter ('Sharing') investigates how a love of radio is shared with others or put on display. The first part situates a longer history spanning 100 years of radio and digital audio in which radio listeners and enthusiasts have shared their attachment to radio as it pertains to particular content, practices and spaces. These examples range from forms of social performance with clothing or accessories, through to the organization of shared listening practices, whether these occurred in informal or personal settings or had a more organized character. The chapter goes on to examine the objects and built spaces in which the attachments to radio have been shared, from amateur and locally-oriented initiatives through to national media museums in which 'memory objects' are incorporated into physical exhibition practices. It starts with the earliest efforts to put radio and its history on display to audiences in the 1910s and 1930s through to present-day exhibitions that increasingly seek to engage visitors via the senses, embodied remembering and material culture, and include listener and fan collections in the narration of radio's public memory. The final part of the chapter closes this account of sharing and display practices by attending to various curation practices involving radio's audio content, such as the curated content included in radio programmes, the publication of radio sounds (on vinyl, cassette, CD) and acts of curation and display practices in online spaces that cater to consumption via digital devices. In attending to curatorial choices, it not only underscores efforts to share and display but also highlights the creation of selections and narratives that may overlook other, less conventional types of radio to which listeners may be attached.

The 'Conclusion' returns to the book's key concerns and themes: how to make sense of the attachments to radio, as demonstrated through the activities of loving, knowing, saving and sharing radio that have unfolded across the twentieth and into the twenty-first century. It stresses the broad range of ways in which radio has been embraced by its audiences and users across various times and settings, and translated their affects, emotions and passions into concrete practices, enacted by individuals and amongst collectives, across analogue and digital media materialities. It will close with a consideration of future directions for the study of radiophilia, and articulate what is at stake in critically treating the attachments to radio: to not adopt a position that laments such attachments, as a site for the manipulation of consumer desire to commercial ends, but rather treat them as a key component of radio's enduring potential as a flexible but binding social infrastructure.

1

Loving

> *The word 'love' is most often defined as a noun,*
> *yet all the more astute theorists of love acknowledge*
> *that we would all love better if we used it as a verb.*
>
> bell hooks[38]

This study is primarily concerned with making sense of the love of radio, taking into account its various emergences, related forms and practices. It offers an account that seeks to strengthen the understanding of how radio, over the past 100 years, invited the emotional and affective engagement of its audiences. When it comes to the love of radio, whether in the form of a general enthusiasm or a more pronounced fandom, a useful cue is the observation by the late cultural scholar bell hooks that it is productive to think of 'love' as not only a feeling or emotion, but rather an action and practice.[39] This understanding of love is also echoed in recent emotions research, which has sought to broaden an earlier scholarly focus on (romantic) love between (two) individuals to a more expansive notion of shared positivity:

> Seeing love as positivity resonance also blurs the boundaries that surround the concept of emotion. Many, if not most, scientific descriptions of emotions locate these affective phenomena within individuals, confined within one person's mind and skin. By contrast, the concept of positivity resonance aligns with perspectives offered within cultural psychology that position emotions as unfolding between and among people as they interact.[40]

This definition is productive for the present study since it creates space to understand the 'love' of radio as not only about the dyadic relationship between a single listener and radio, but rather as constituted through forms of co-presence between multiple individuals. The relational definition of love as positivity resonance can thereby be constituted through a joint activity or be generated as a shared social mood, but can also comprise various temporal spans, as 'a micro moment ... not necessarily an enduring or intimate relationship'.[41] This attention underscores positivity resonance as an event with multiple possible temporalities, from the fleeting to the sustained. It lends a crucial insight to the central concern of this book with the love of, or attachment to, radio as being constituted through situations that could span from ambient hearing of a snippet of sound (e.g., heard from a passing car) or other forms of distracted, incomplete or interrupted listening through to dedicated listening practices to a favourite programme or genre. Attending to the changing intensities of that 'love' over time aids us in developing a processual approach to not only treat radio sound as sonic events unfolding in time (and space), but also see the love of radio as a process taking various individual and collective forms, durations and phases. This insight serves as an invitation to further clarify the possible dimensions of the love of radio, and how this love reveals itself through particular habits, practices or materialities.

In response to the broader question of what the love of radio is, and how it can be approached or studied, the first section will first offer a broader outline of the 'attractions' of radio. This account will first outline the historical discourses framing the early users' fascination with radio, including pathologies of listeners as 'maniacs' or in the thrall of 'radio fever'. The early decades of radio are framed in terms of its relation to 'modern life' and considers how affections for radio were cultivated in exchange with pre-existing media and cultural consumption. The remainder of the section treats how particular qualities associated with radio prompted emotive attachments and how, in various appropriations of the medium, these attachments centred on radio as technology and cultural form, its content, genres and material form, or the social uses or needs it fulfilled in its audiences.

With this preliminary outline of the aspects contributing to the initial and enduring appeal of radio, in the second section I will draw on media fandom research and recent scholarship on emotions, affect and feeling, as a means of articulating a conceptual framing that may help to better understand aspects of the what, why and how constituting the love of radio. Media and cultural studies of fandom have increasingly endeavoured to revise 'pathologies' around passionate media fans and users, instead framing affective and emotional engagements with media in terms of practice and process. Meanwhile, the history of the emotions field has also sought to develop accounts of affect and emotions as a domain of practice that is embodied, situational and relational. Together, these accounts are helpful for my own approach to unpacking the love of radio – in line with bell hooks' account – as a domain of action and practice, thereby taking seriously individual experiences but also understanding their framing, conditioning and expression according to social and cultural scripts, and as articulated in practices.

Building on this attention to how embodiment, emotion and affective practice coalesce around radio, both past and present, the final section seeks to outline a conceptual understanding of the senses (and their interactions), connections between radio and other media, and of material culture. Treating the significance of multiple senses is crucial to the overall insight that the attractions of radio have been constituted as much via its 'look and feel' as its sonic components. Along with intersensoriality, the attention to intermediality is intended as a recognition of 'radio' as engaging multiple media and technologies, or aesthetic borrowing from existing media. And, in turn, the culture around radio has been and continues to be shaped by newspapers, magazines, recorded music, disc, tape and digital recording technology, photography, film, television, new media and smartphones. The final, intersecting concern draws on insights from the fields of material culture, heritage and memory studies, to highlight how attachments to radio have not only generated their own material expressions, but have also become attached to particular material forms or qualities of radio. This sensitivity to material artefacts, objects and other materialities (e.g., radio atmospherics) are recognized as crucial domains for the present study, whether pertaining to a radio set, paper ephemera related to radio, or the 'memory objects' incorporated in museum or exhibition spaces.

The attractions of radio

Wireless telegraphy was fundamental in the establishment of what Italian futurist Filippo Marinetti described in 1913 as the 'wireless imagination', predicated on the thrill and speed of modern technologies and their potential for new modalities of communication and creative expression.[42] In the early, amateur phase of radio, wireless was an object of fascination, imagined as an 'invisible, mysterious realm, somewhere above and beyond everyday life, where the rules for behavior couldn't be enforced'.[43] The novelty of 'fishing' the radio ether using Morse code, and later voice transmission, was a constituent element of early amateur radio practices, with an exploratory form of listening usually practised at night-time after work. These listening practices were part of a larger process in which users of radio accustomed themselves to the 'mediatization of the air'.[44] Amateurs cultivated their own self-image as radio 'maniacs' and shared enthusiastic accounts about establishing contact with faraway places, the sense of surprise in not knowing what they would discover, and the practice of noting down (and often boasting about) the stations they received, which prevailed more strongly than dwelling on the content of those stations.[45] At the same time, radio sparked cultural anxieties about too much affection for radio, with concern about amateur wireless users becoming 'mad', 'obsessed' or in the thrall of 'radio fever'. This was a gendered narrative that was initially centred on young male amateurs becoming socially isolated while holed up in attic spaces and removed from 'normal' family and social life.[46]

The tendency to strongly gender the figure of the obsessed radio listener continued in the context of broadcast radio's 'domestication' into private spaces of reception, yet it was primarily women during the 1920s who were reported to be at risk of becoming 'radio crazy' due to being overly excited or nervous when combining radio listening with other domestic duties.[47] This discursive framing of users of modern communications technologies as not only overly emotional but at risk of mental as well as physical illness is in keeping with the longer history of 'technopathologies' defining certain users as (ab)normal, spanning from the telegraph to the present.[48] Even with a host of diverse reactions – from affection, fascination and awe through to fear, suspicion or rejection – articulated in the early years of amateur and broadcast radio, the general cultural reception of radio was that it was a new feature of 'modern life' that promised to bring 'information and entertainment into the privatized home'.[49] In this sense, its arrival occurred in a mass culture context characterized by popular media, such as newspapers, magazines, recorded music, cinema and commercial advertising, and popular leisure activities such as sport participation and observation, and spending time in parks, fairs, dancing venues and shopping.[50]

Radio's links to modern culture also led to the association of this new technology with particular social groups, as can be seen in the case of Korea, where its introduction was connected to the 'Modern Boys' and 'Modern Girls', or in Soviet Russia, whose early radio enthusiasts were referred to as being the *radioliubiteli* (radio savvy).[51]

From the outset, pre-existing interests and pastimes acted as templates or 'mattering maps', guiding the affections developed for radio.[52] Early radio was also dedicated to existing spheres of modern life, such as musical, opera, theatre and comedy performance, lectures and literary adaptations, in addition to the development of radio-specific or 'radiogenic' genres and formats.[53] A common thread to the love of radio is this consumption of broadcast content, with the variety of cultural formats not only an attraction, but also a crucial democratizing aspect of radio, as a veteran broadcaster reflected upon in relation to his teenage experiences of radio in the 1920s:

> I first experienced a Shakespeare play through radio ... and Beethoven – I heard my first string quartet not in a concert hall, but in my living room ... [F]ortunately I was part of the first generation for whom sound broadcasting provided access to the cultural world beyond the family walls.[54]

Beyond cultural or light entertainment content, such as comedy-variety, live sport coverage has been a major attraction for listeners from the inception of radio. Its presence in radio schedules was strengthened by the widespread popularity of and participation in organized sports and exercise (such as calisthenics) practised in many countries during the period in which radio broadcasting was introduced. Religious programming, too, has been a significant factor in radio broadcasting, and an existing template on which a strong affective relationship to radio can be formed through regular programme slots or dedicated radio stations.[55]

The affection for radio has also been cultivated in other spheres of cultural production, since songs, novels, poems, films, and later television programmes, have explicitly reflected on radio and the experience of radio listening, while in radio, too, we can observe the historical development of crossover formats between various elements of the culture industry.[56] Particularly in relation to commercial stations, radio came to be associated with the cross-industry promotion of film, music and radio manufacturing industries, as well as advertising for other aspects of modern life, from medicine and toothpaste to cars and fashion. The design of radio sets was a highly competitive domain and had a strong significance in radio culture from the 1920s onwards, with the transition from headset-based listening to loudspeaker amplification. It became a key locus for the marketing aims of the radio industry, as radio sets were increasingly designed in line with domestic furniture, and considered part of the presence of the 'modern' in the home or in public life, such as restaurants, cafes and train travel.[57] As such, design can also be a motivating factor for radiophilia, since various periods of radio set design – from 'furniture-style' receivers in the 1930s to portable transistors or digital personal stereos – have been influential in shaping reception contexts for listeners, and their relationship to radio as a 'modern' medium, and in developing radio listening as a 'modernist practice' in its first decades.[58] Historically, this is suggestive of (valuable) radio sets as an emblematic sign of the modern, placed on display or shared with others, or in the present day, where the radio set may signify a piece of obsolete media that no longer functions but is kept as a personal souvenir or keepsake within a family.

The qualities associated with radio have been an important frame for affective responses by its listeners and users, who, in turn, appropriate radio according to particular social uses or needs. Early radio in particular was crucial in establishing a 'culture of liveness', which has been described in terms of the medium-specific qualities of *immediacy, intimacy, simultaneity, spontaneity* and *eventfulness*.[59] Immediacy can be understood in terms of a sense of events unfolding 'right now' in real time; intimacy can be seen in terms of the mode of addressing the audience in the domestic space; simultaneity refers to the situation of 'everyone' listening at the same time; spontaneity was the sense that 'anything' could happen during a live programme; and eventfulness refers to the prominence of special events, whether these be public events or well-known personalities performing or playing in concert.[60] These factors, together, have been identified as contributing to radio's promise of a sense of being included in radio's networks and communities of listeners. This sense of common listening activity with other audience members has been studied as a site of 'imagined community' formation, for which listening communities certainly hold the potential to be addressed or to operate as an 'emotional community'.[61] Other key factors attributed to radio broadcasting have included its *sociability* (in the communicative relationship between broadcasters and audiences), *sincerity* (as the 'projection and presentation of ordinariness') and *dailiness* (matching the temporal markers of everyday life, and in turn influencing the everyday rhythms of life).[62] While the above-mentioned range of aspects is certainly not characteristic for all types of radio, at all times or contexts, these qualities are also partially the result of promotional discourses and public narratives, which have proved to be influential and long-lasting sources of radio's appeal, and drawn on in podcast and digital audio discourse.

The attractions of radio have mainly been ascribed to its programme genres, style and types of content, which at the very basic level consist of voice/dialogue, music, sound effects and noise/ambient sound. To start with voice, the early period of radio has been credited with seeking to craft a 'radio voice' and debates about how to best achieve appropriate forms of vocal presentation, dialogue and style.[63] Such debates have often taken place in relation to finding standardized forms of national language and pronunciation, which may be the source of affection for a national broadcaster, or reflective of a language ideology implicated in the policing of belonging.[64]

Listeners fall for certain voices: how they sound as well as what they say. In the 1920s, broadcast radio listeners of the US radio performer and musical 'crooner' Rudy Vallée have been described as 'falling in love with a voice':

> Above all, I love to hear you sing, it seems to thrill me through and through. I have heard many singers, but none other has made me feel that way, cannot explain, can you? ... You sang 'Lovely Lady' the other night – that is me, that is the way I feel.[65]

The presence of a particular vocal style, accent or language may also be a key site for generating affection for radio, such as the popularity of the broadcaster K. E. Masinga in 1940s South Africa, whose presence is understood as pioneering the on-air presence of a Zulu 'radio voice' in a white-dominated radio system.[66] Similarly, achieving space for minority and migrant communities, as well as indigenous or Creole languages in radio, has also been identified as a crucial locus of pride and self-representation in hearing one's own language and being part of that radio listening community, but also potentially contributing towards linguistic preservation, community building and activism.[67] The attraction of particular DJs or star announcers was and remains an important locus for affective attachments to radio. In certain contexts, we find that fans not only consumed the visual appearance of 'personalities' via their photos in print media, but, as was the case of 1930s radio culture in the Philippines, were very active in trying to join studio audiences or gathering outside radio studios to watch their favourite announcers producing new programmes.[68]

While the reassuring or recognizable sound of an announcer's voice may be a source of radio's appeal, another key attraction is non-verbal sounds and their shaping, through sound design. The 'signature sounds' of the radio that attracted listeners included jingles, spots and idents, but also other evocative sounds, as suggested by the enthusiasm expressed about getting 'a kick out of' hearing the chimes of Big Ben on the BBC Empire Service during the 1930s and 1940s.[69] Similarly, recent audio research has found that Radio Luxembourg had a significant impact on UK-based listeners during the early decades of radio; the novelty of sponsor advertisements meant that 'a pre-war generation could still recall into great old age the theme song to *The Ovaltineys Concert Party* from an earlier incarnation of Radio Luxembourg, which may give this advertising jingle the greatest longevity of any British-known brand'.[70] Aside from sound effects and jingles, the enjoyment of radio has also been credited to the use of sound design techniques, such as the intimate 'audiopositioning' of listeners in fictional crime shows, thrillers or experimental drama, or in generating 'emotional conversation' through imaginative explorations of domestic space in soap operas between the 1930s and 1950s.[71] Such examples all attest to the suggestive qualities of radio: its ability to 'feed the imagination' of its listeners through sonic means.[72]

Among the attractions of radio since its early period has been access to information, whether that may be through news and reports on the weather, traffic, sport, politics, the economy, or agricultural markets, educational talks, panels and debates, and advice from experts, with themes ranging from 'household management' to health, relationships, sexuality and religious faith.[73] Aside from information, music has remained a key motivating factor in the everyday engagements of listeners with radio, since it constitutes the large bulk, both past and present, of much radio output. Radio, in turn, produced a constant presence of music, with its culture of 'ubiquitous' music and listening setting an important precedent for transistor and Walkman culture through to digital audio in the present.[74] It is instructive to think of music as having a structural similarity to radio in terms of how its content is drawn upon by listeners 'in the organization of self, the shifting of mood, energy level, conduct style, mode of attention and engagement with the world.... [M]usic's "effects" come from the ways in which individuals orient to it, how they interpret it and how they place it within their personal musical maps, within the semiotic web of music and extra-musical associations.'[75] The love or enjoyment of radio, in this case of its music programming, highlights how audiences actively adopt radio music according to particular needs and uses in their everyday lives.

The historical literature on how listeners made sense of radio and experienced pleasure by integrating listening into everyday life has focused on a range of aspects, including key modes of listening to radio, ranging from concentrated attention through to 'background' listening while performing other tasks in the home.[76] By incorporating radio into everyday life, listeners harness the 'affective qualities of radio sound and its capacity for mood generation'.[77] The 'love' of radio may precisely be fuelled by listening in spaces of the home, whether alone or with others. It may be heard intentionally, or incidentally, while travelling or commuting, for instance in a private car or while taking public transport such as a bus or tram, or in spaces of consumption, such as cafes, restaurants, shopping centres, airports and train stations, sport and gym facilities. The possibility of radio conditioning spaces of listening and thereby heightening the listener's affective relation towards the medium can also be found in other public spaces with loudspeaker systems, such as public squares, school classrooms or workplaces.

This strong public presence of radio, at particular times and in particular settings, means that the love of radio could be framed in terms of loving the ubiquity of radio. This enjoyment of its ubiquity could be constituted in public life, through the manner in which radio's presence participated in the 'technologizing' of public urban space.[78] The pervasiveness of radio also occurred within the home in some contexts; for instance, in the period around 2000, German households had on average six to seven radio receivers, of which roughly half were portable devices.[79]

The presence and integration of radio into the 'texture' of everyday life pertains to its temporal dimensions and spatial organization and also the micropolitics of the home, particularly within families.[80] In terms of time, the creation of a broadcast calendar of events, in particular, has been influential in marking the experience of days, weeks, months and the year, creating 'a horizon of expectations, a mood of anticipation, a directedness towards that which is to come, thereby giving substance and structure ... to everyday life'.[81] This has been a dynamic process in which radio programming became responsive to the domestic rhythms of its audiences, who, in turn, adjusted to the timekeeping produced by its 'scheduled time signals'.[82] In terms of space, there is an extensive literature about the accommodation of the radio set within the domestic interior, alongside the telephone, television, hi-fi stereo, home computers and gaming consoles; in several exceptional cases, the radio served not only as the impetus for a rearranging of furniture in living spaces, but for the creation of a separate 'radio room'.[83] The material qualities of the receiving device were a crucial focal point for listener affections, and radio listeners in their letters to stations or programme magazines discussed the emotive connection to the set, sometimes in terms of physical touch. The development of a familiar or intimate relationship with radio reception devices can also be found in a range of mobile media across the twentieth century, from the suitcase radios of the 1920s to the transistor culture from the 1950s onwards, and through to devices like the Walkman. This affection also manifested itself in terms of a personification, with the radio set figuring as a 'friend' and the broadcaster as a family member.[84]

While much of the literature has documented discourses about the comfort of the domestic 'hearth' and memories of group listening with family friends and neighbours, it is also crucial to acknowledge the gendered power dynamics of listening in the living room (and family car), with the male patriarch frequently presiding over programme choice, time and volume of listening. Such structures can have long legacies, with older women in the present day being found to 'limit their radio listening to times and spaces that do not bother their husbands', with radio listening mainly taking place during the daytime while 'doing other things' connected to domestic labour.[85] The desire to escape the strictures of radio (and television) consumption practices in the family unit has been a strong narrative articulated to explain the affections for the transistor radio in the post-1950 period, whose portability and increasing affordability were identified as an important means for teenagers and young adults to listen to radio separately from their parents, whether alone or with friends, in the bedroom or in public spaces like parks.[86] It is therefore important to maintain an intersectional sensitivity to the constitution of the attachment to (or disenfranchisement from) radio, underscored here in terms of gender, age and generation, but also extending to intersecting vectors of race, ethnicity, religion, class and ability.

A final key consideration pertains to how audiences appropriate radio for their own needs and uses and to acknowledge that the affective relation or attachment to radio may be cast in the context of a difficult, isolating or dangerous situation. There are historical examples that suggest that the overcoming of isolation, whether physical or social, via radio has contributed to a meaningful everyday existence, although this discourse of reaching the disabled or isolated 'shut in' members of society also constituted a powerful justification for the introduction of radio in numerous settings.[87] Nonetheless, listeners may genuinely feel heightened affection for radio as a 'lifeline' while experiencing a difficult work, home or personal situation, or as an antidote to loneliness in the context of physical or social isolation, as Chapter 4's discussion of talkback radio will explore. Having a 'love' for or attachment to radio is therefore potentially not only motivated by strong positive feelings towards the medium and its content, but also may be structured by a dependence on – or reassurance gained from – radio for news or information, or informed by feelings of fear or anticipation, such as in a context of war, conflict or occupation.[88] Research on the Second World War has shown that British and German civilians adopted a close physical proximity and intimacy with their radio sets during aerial attacks, for instance by taking the radio to bed or into shelters, and gravitating towards news and popular music programming but also the calming sounds of natural life.[89] Acts of illicit or 'enemy' listening have been a site of attachment to radio, whether in accessing information or a particular type of music, or for the threatened Jews in the Warsaw Ghetto in German-occupied Poland, for whom monitoring international news services became, as one man described it 'indispensable for life – simply an addiction'.[90] In other contexts, such as imprisonment or various forms of institutional confinement (e.g., hospitals or mental health facilities), radio may offer the means of facilitating 'acoustical agency' and 'fostering love', but also in helping those affected to emotionally cope with their situation.[91]

Such cases draw attention to the therapeutic potential of radio, as a site where individuals seek the means to cope with or work through difficult personal situations, or as a social infrastructure in contexts of national crisis and mourning. This insight about radio broadcasting has also been treated in recent podcast research that has considered the place of intimacy and emotions in podcast productions, with its 'nichecasting', for instance, identified as ideal for creating social spaces for difficult experiences, such as loss and grief.[92] While this present study will mainly consider 'positive' affects in relation to radio, such insights on the role of fear or anxiety are relevant to the discussion of 'saving' radio in Chapter 3, in which the perceived loss of radio due to its ephemerality has historically served as a crucial impulse for amateur collectors and professional archivists of radio sounds, often spurring their efforts to record and save radio sounds or other artefacts for posterity.

Overall, this section has aimed to sketch out some of the possible attractions of radio in terms of medial qualities, aspects of its content, genres or material forms, and especially the social uses or needs that audiences have developed for radio. While not wanting to delimit the affects or emotions underpinning radiophilia, the generally expansive definition is that it may pertain to a listener who experiences pleasure, comfort, distraction or a general 'shared positivity'. The love of radio therefore must be understood as invoking a range encompassing those who listen intermittently through to (super)fans who may be highly invested and develop intense emotive attachments to their object of affection. Similarly, it may even pertain to an individual who does not own a radio, actively listen to radio or necessarily like it, yet may be swept up in a collective mood facilitated by a media event, or experience affects while hearing radio transmissions in a public space. As such, it is crucial to acknowledge a diversity of listener and fan engagements and, ideally, to avoid presupposing who the listener is, or what fans' affective practices look like.

Love, emotions and affects

This section seeks a clearer understanding of how the love of radio can be treated in view of recent literature on emotions and affects. Here I will draw on media fandom literature that seeks to make sense of strong affections, attachments and investments in particular media and related objects. I will then outline recent accounts treating affect theory and the history of the emotions, particularly those 'pragmatic' strands that ask how we may connect affective experience and emotions to cultural and social practices. In turn, I will not seek to pin down a definition that would categorically distinguish emotions from affects, but rather see how practice and process oriented accounts can help to understand the love of radio being constituted (and maintained) in relation to the evolving radio medium, its material forms, sounds and the listener's embodied experience and uses of radio.

As noted in the Introduction, recent research on media fandom has generally not included the study of radio. Nonetheless, this research field offers instructive accounts for how to make sense of enthusiastic audiences, who may have strong emotional experiences or investments in specific media forms, contents, narratives, characters and performers/stars. In particular, this research has been crucial in forcing a shift away from pathologies of media audiences and fans. A key early intervention can be found in *The Adoring Audience* (1992), a collected volume that refuted the casting of fandom in a negative light as obsessive, disturbed or lacking.[93] In this volume, cultural studies scholar Lawrence Grossberg emphasized the need to theorize the affects underpinning fan attachments or investments:

> Affect is not the same as either emotions or desires. Affect is closely tied to what we often describe as the feeling of life. You can understand another person's life, but you cannot know how

it feels. But feeling, as it functions here, is not a subjective experience. It is a socially constructed domain of cultural effects ... The same object, with the same meaning, giving the same pleasure, is very different as our affective relationship to it changes. Or perhaps it is more accurate to say that different affective relations inflect meanings and pleasures in very different ways. Affect is what gives 'colour,' 'tone' or 'texture' to our experiences.[94]

This understanding of fan affect stresses its quality as a kind of felt intensity constructed in relation to a media object or text. While the fan relation to the object or text is established as a crucial concern, Grossberg also underlines the importance of devoting analytical attention to intersubjective processes taking place in the form of affective relationships and identity formations among fans themselves.[95]

Working in a similar vein, we find in later fan research, such as Matt Hills' *Fan Cultures* (2002), a call to treat affect as a central theme, and with it, the domain of 'attachments, emotions and passions'.[96] Hills' attention to affect in fandom cautions against Grossberg's earlier account as being marked by a strong social constructivism in which the 'mattering maps' of society and culture were emphasized over fans' subjective experiences. This earlier account of affect is criticized for its 'lack of playfulness; that is, for reducing affect to an effect of pre-existing structures or conventions'.[97] Hills instead proposes a stronger attentiveness to fans as engaged in subjective and affective play, as a means to better understand the formation of fan emotional attachments and the productive capacities of affective play that might not only follow pre-existing cultural scripts but also create 'new conventions' or 'biographical and historical resources' for the individual.[98] Hills' prioritization of affect also represents the attempt to challenge persistent 'moral dualisms' in fan research that have tended to treat fans as either inherently good (e.g., creative) or bad (e.g., pathological, irrational).[99] Rather than engaging in such dualisms, media fandom researchers have urged a more nuanced understanding of fandom:

> While fandom, evidently, has a social and psychological purpose for each individual in daily life, moral entrepreneurs portray it as

possession and fantasizing that poisons the social body. Fan practices are frequently more about comfort, relaxation and pleasure than they are about frustration with unavailable intimacy. Of course, admirers may wish to communicate their feelings or to meet their star – just for the thrill – but it is important to realize that they *already* feel boosted by their engagement.[100]

Such scholarship has therefore sought to critically reassess how fandom can be a social resource in connecting to other fans, but also suggests that fans are not always merely 'in love' with a particular object, but rather are experiencing their own pleasures in relation to it.

Most recently, media scholar Nicolle Lamerichs has offered a useful framework that builds on existing discussions of affect and media fandom, but further emphasizes the need for media researchers to foreground the 'affective and emotional lives of fans' as an embodied process.[101] In *Productive Fandom* (2018), Lamerichs suggests a stronger conceptual attention to the ways in which affect does not 'merely happen' to fans, but that they also play an active role in instigating or preparing themselves for strongly-felt affects. While affirming Hills' earlier interest in identity processes in fan communities as involving affects, Lamerichs proposes that a more expansive concept of 'affective process' is needed to approach affect in fan cultures. Affective process, as Lamerichs defines it, incorporates 'a range of emotional experiences that can lead to investments in the world through which we constitute our identity ... [A]ffective process develops over time, it has different entry points and objects of devotion.'[102] In other words, the focus of fandom may shift focus to other objects or forms of expression over time. I take my cue from this crucial insight that is also necessary for radio, since the community formations engaging listeners can take various forms and range in longevity and commitment across the individual 'life cycle'.[103] In the case of music on radio, the formation of a listening community may have a span that lasts 'from a few minutes ("my song" as listened to by thousands) to a lifetime (as a habitual listener to the national broadcasting corporation). The intensity of the participation might differ for the individual and among individuals. One can be an avid fan or just mildly interested.'[104] The value of this perspective is that it maintains that an analytical attention to practice remains crucial, yet a sensitivity to process is essential for understanding how fan affective attachments can take different forms or intensities over time.

With this emphasis on both practice and process in mind, I will now turn to two key frameworks that are instructive for the present study, namely a practice-oriented literature in the history of the emotions field, and a pragmatic approach to emotions and affect that develops the concept of 'affective practice'.

The history of the emotions field offers a helpful guide to working through questions related to affect and emotion. This field has generally sought to establish a humanities context for the emotions that mounts a challenge to an ahistorical or universalizing approach, as the behavioural sciences have sometimes been criticized for. By contrast, instead of treating emotions or affects as 'timeless as well as spaceless', Ute Frevert has argued that the contribution of historians is in taking up a critical and contextual approach:

> [The history of the emotions is] a genealogical and a critical endeavor: unearthing and unveiling the way in which people have thought, felt, expressed, and experienced emotions in history, while, at the same time, keeping in mind and emphasizing that emotions are themselves products of history, undergoing shifts both in content and shape.[105]

In this field, accordingly, one of the key approaches has involved the search for how 'emotion words' used in the past reflect particular worldviews or sociocultural scripts, and were embedded in historically-specific habits and practices. This is an approach to how emotion has often been used by historians as a means to distinguish affect and feeling from those experiences that have been explicitly labelled as emotion, such as fear or love.[106]

This take on the distinctions between emotion, feeling and affect is productive for the present account, as it serves as a reminder that listeners or users of radio may experience feelings or affective intensities without necessarily going so far as to connect these to an identifiable emotion. Some historians in this field have expressed concern that affect theory may be used to suggest that affective bodily experience can be separate from thought, rather than acknowledging how emotion and cognition operate together in shaping embodied experiences. In their reading, an attention to affect remains nonetheless productive for acknowledging those experiences that cannot be easily categorized or labelled, or perhaps not consciously registered by the subject.

The influential work of historian Monique Scheer has offered a practice-oriented approach to the emotions that insists on the emotions as located both in and through the mind and body. This concept of emotions stresses the 'mutual embeddedness of minds, bodies, and social relations in order to historicize the body and its contributions to the learned experience of emotion'.[107] In other words, practice theory offers a way for historians to consider 'emotional practices' as acts that help to produce the embodied subject, comprising 'not only habituated and automatically executed movements of the body, but also encompass[ing] a learned, culturally specific, and habitual distribution of attention to "inner" processes of thought, feeling, and perception'.[108] Nonetheless, Scheer takes pains to note that the history of the self in the West, as premised on notions of interiority, and the separation of thought and feeling, requires the scholar to remain sensitive to the specific social and cultural discourses that inform emotional practices.

Scheer develops her understanding of emotional practice by revising Pierre Bourdieu's theory of practice to take emotions as emerging from bodily knowledge.[109] For this, she revisits his concept of 'habitus' as bodily knowledge, as opposed to rational or conceptual knowledge.

> Like all practices, [emotions] are simultaneously spontaneous and conventional. The habitus specifies what is 'feelable' in a specific setting, orients the mind/body in a certain direction without making the outcome fully predictable. Emotions can thus be viewed as acts executed by a mindful body, as cultural practices.[110]

In underscoring the social and cultural underpinnings of the emotions, Scheer emphasizes how Bourdieu's take on bodily knowledge also serves to highlight the coercive manner in which habitus can be shaped, thereby demonstrating a sensitivity to the cultural politics of emotions.[111]

Overall, in treating emotion as a cultural practice, a practice theory approach to the history of the emotions invokes close attention to material bodies and social action. Scheer concedes that studying third-person observation may also give insights into emotional practices and related social discourses and norms:

> The history of emotions has traditionally viewed first-person accounts as the royal road to individual feeling, and as documents of emotives and the practice of introspection they remain important. But this method should not reproduce the assumption that 'real' emotions – the ones worth writing about – are necessarily internal and private.[112]

The benefit of the practice theory approach is that it offers a tool for researchers to overcome a persistent tendency to treat body and cognition as separate, instead understanding emotion 'as an act situated in and composed of interdependent cognitive, somatic, and social components, mixed in varying proportions, depending on the practical logic of the situation in which it takes place. From the perspective of practice theory, emotional arousals that seem to be purely physical are actually deeply socialized.'[113] In underscoring the socialized framework in which embodied affects take place, Scheer insists on an approach that treats emotions as enacted by the 'knowing body' and taking form as cultural practices.

Social psychologist Margaret Wetherell has similarly argued that affect theory has too optimistically read affect as non-conscious, as autonomous and demarcated from discourse. Wetherell has less of a stake in understanding historical practices, yet her astute treatment of the existing literature on emotion and affect offers productive ground for the present study. She similarly proposes a practice-oriented approach to emotion and affect for which recent empirical findings are used to inflect approaches in the humanities and social sciences. As Wetherell concedes, the study of affect is challenging, given that it can be understood as 'somatic, neural, subjective, historical, social and personal'.[114] The concept of practice, as she suggests, is:

> ... capacious enough to extend to some of the new thinking available about activity, flow, assemblage and relationality ... Affective practice focuses on the emotional as it appears in social life and tries to follow what participants do. It finds shifting, flexible and often over-determined figurations rather than simple lines of causation, character types and neat emotion categories.[115]

A key concept offered by Wetherell therefore is that of 'affective practice', which makes sense of how a given 'emotive body' actively participates in a given social setting or communal formation. Affective practice, as she understands it, invokes the possibility for practice to invoke action but also an established site or form of repetition, thus helping to capture how affect can be 'innovative and creative but also can be stubbornly lodged and painfully unmovable'.[116] The concept of affective practice, according to Wetherell, establishes:

> ... relations between subjects and objects through their intertwined formations and constitutions. But we also need to locate affect, not in the ether, or in endless and mysterious circulations, but in actual bodies and social actors, negotiating, making decisions, evaluating, communicating, inferring and relating. What creates value and/or capital is the direction and history of affective practice over time, and the history of its entanglements with other onto-formative social practices and social formations. The concept of affective practice, then, encompasses the movement of signs but it also tries to explain how affect is embodied, is situated and operates psychologically.[117]

This understanding invokes affective performance as being grounded in practice, and as situated and relational. Wetherell praises affect theory for seeking to establish a 'livelier' account of the social with a theory of becoming, yet she sees that a strict separation of affect from emotion and a rejection of discourse reflects a problematic and selective use of the hard sciences, whose empirical findings align with a practice approach. As such, it does not do justice to affect as a practice of meaning-making, as a 'relational and social event' involving performance and sociality.

This section has treated approaches to love, affect and emotion in recent literature that have drawn attention to the importance of treating media fandom, affect and emotions from the perspective of practice and process. While the present study uses the 'emotion word' of love, and the activity of loving, in reference to radio, the act of loving could comprise a potentially larger range of affects, feelings and dispositions of the embodied subject or collective formations; this is in line with fandom research that suggests a continuum that may comprise passions, affects and affections for radio. In turn, the chapters on knowing, saving and sharing will take up a broader definition of the love of radio beyond the (super)fan, with the potential to trace histories of radiophilia across various periods and settings, for analogue and digital media, and across amateurs and professional contexts.

Intersensoriality, intermediality and material culture

The previous section has underlined the embodied nature of affective practice, as a means to gain conceptual tools for thinking about the love of radio from its earliest incarnations through to the present. While this embodied dimension to the emotions, affect and feelings has been established as a theoretical departure point, this study acknowledges that there is no singular ontology of radio.[118] As such, the embodied subjects and collectives that engage with radio are subject to socially and culturally specific conditions and sensory norms, also conditioned by a historically-specific media landscape and radio's evolving position within it.

For this reason, the present section draws on existing conceptual accounts that have sought to underscore not only the embodied nature of a user's diverse engagements with radio, including radio listening, but especially to understand the experience of radio as taking place beyond the ears, as an embodied and multisensory experience. The multiple sensory registers involved in the broadest understanding of the 'love' of radio can variously involve hearing, vision, touch, taste and smell, but can also be cast wider to consider the sensing of body movement (proprioception and kinaesthesia), heat, pain, balance or atmosphere. The 'public senses' of hearing and vision have potentially been the most invoked and activated in relation to radio as wireless sound.[119] As such, the attachment to radio has therefore not only been constituted towards its sounds and atmospherics, but also the 'spectacle' of its material infrastructures (e.g., radio buildings, transmission towers) and visual appeal as a consumer object (e.g., radio design), and in the visual culture engaged in the overall promotional culture of radio and its potential to enhance popularity (e.g., via magazines, posters, postcards). The role of visual culture in 'learning to love' radio will be discussed in further detail in Chapter 2 ('Knowing').

With regards to the other senses, touch is a major component in the engagement of listeners with radio sound, whether at the level of its material conditioning of spaces of reception and the bodies of listeners with sound; tactile activities in relation to the receiver device (e.g., tuning); other tasks conducted alongside or in tandem with listening (e.g., reading, physical activities); or in the preparation of listening experiences (e.g., particular bodily poses or the adjustment of lighting). This perspective can bring about a nuanced understanding of skin as a primary medium of touch which is sensitive to sonic vibrations and atmospheric conditions.[120] In the case of mid-century radio design, the radio dial and its aesthetics – in visually depicting place names – has been understood as an essential 'mediating interface' in guiding the experience of radio for its listeners, where hearing, touch and vision came together as listeners tuned their radio sets.[121] From the perspective of haptics, 'the buttons and knobs on a radio are encountered through complex processes of touching, involving a dense network of receptors in the skin, joints, and muscles that work together to configure the experience of media both as functional and aesthetic objects'.[122] This sensitivity to the embodied sensory arrangements activated in a given use scenario for the radio has also been echoed in disability media studies perspectives on the radio set, which calls for scholars not only to underscore the radio sets as 'enabling' listening and forms of participation, but also to address how 'with its fiddly tuning knobs and often hard-to-read dials [the radio set] could itself be a disability technology for much of its history'.[123] This insight serves as an important caution against narrow generalizations of 'the 'listener' and how they responded to the various functionalities or 'emotional styles' in radio design.[124]

The sense of taste is an underexplored aspect of the embodied experiences of radio, and yet here too there is potential to consider how attachments to radio may be formed in relation to food-based leisure practices and routines, such as cooking in domestic and semi-public spaces or in consuming food or drinks at certain times (e.g., mealtimes or breaks), and in the 'gustasonic' discourses infused through commercial radio breaks and sponsor spots during the long history of radio through to podcasting.[125] Smell or the olfactory, too, has remained underdeveloped in existing approaches to radio, and its appeal, but could potentially be taken up in relation to interactions with other registers (e.g., taste and listening as per the previous example), and at the full spectrum of radio as a 'new' medium (e.g., the smell of a newly-acquired receiving device) through to its status as historical or related to the past (e.g., the dusty smell of antique receiver, programme magazines or other ephemera), and in relation to activities of collecting or in acts of remembering or nostalgia, as Chapters 3 ('Saving') and 4 ('Sharing') will explore in further detail.

While I will not elaborate on other potential sensory domains here, this book endeavours to attend to intersensoriality as a means to understanding the correspondences and conflicts between the senses, in keeping with the investment of sensory studies in 'the senses as interaction'.[126] In acknowledging the dynamic relations between the senses, and the world at large, I also take heed of the insights generated by the anthropology of the senses that it is crucial not just to develop a historicized multisensory approach, but one that avoids a singular, universal model of 'the senses', by operationalizing comparative and transnational perspectives, which also acknowledge fault lines generated in sensory differentiations of gender, age, class, ethnicity, race and ability.[127]

Overall, this theoretical impulse means a special attention to the haptic and other sensory domains in which the embodied experience of radio takes place. For instance, it sensitizes us to the fact that the 'attractions' to radio have not been, or remain, limited to its sounds and to auditory experience. An attention to other media can certainly be found in broadcast programmes discussing the latest modern design, fashion, cinema and art,[128] but the aesthetic appeal of radio was harnessed via its links to modern design, whether in the form of receiver sets or other consumer goods promoted by the global radio industry as 'objects of desire'.[129]

The second concern of this section is with intermediality. I posit that for the present attempt to chart the love of radio, a sensitivity is needed towards questions of intermediality and cross-medial processes underpinning radio and how audiences engage with it. Following W. J. T. Mitchell's critique of the term 'visual media', it remains instructive to highlight the 'mixed media' status of any given media technology, such as radio, telephone, cinema or phonography, and that even if one sensory mode, such as hearing, appears to be dominant, these media always necessarily invoke a mutual imbrication of the senses. In a similar vein, what I'm calling an 'intermedial' approach for the present study of radiophilia is based on four main insights. Firstly, that the medial aspects of radio (or its assumed functions) may in fact draw or build on existing sound media, or be adapted to suit a social or cultural need not fulfilled by other existing media (e.g., the privatized communication enabled by the telephone). Secondly, that part of the love of radio may be partly boosted or complemented by the reuse of media content deriving from other media, as 'nesting' or 'remediation', whether that be popular music or other intermedial crossovers of genre, performance styles or star performers.[130] Thirdly, the modern technological shaping of the senses means that, just as the senses should not be treated as 'natural' or a given, the embodied engagement with radio is dynamic and also inflected by existing 'audile techniques' or modes and habits in (un)focusing one's attention.[131] Fourthly, while the intermedial is usually reserved for questions of aesthetic style, genre or narrative, I take this term as a broader category that may also involve cross-medial dialogues or interdependencies, for instance in the development of radio programme magazines as a consumer good that had the potential to accompany or guide radio listener and user practices, as is discussed in Chapter 2.[132] An intermedial approach can therefore invoke the framing functions of other media (e.g., programme magazines, photography) or exchanges between radio and other media (e.g., music and film criticism on radio, radio sounds featured in music and film).[133]

By extension, it is also crucial to acknowledge intersecting pleasures and fandoms, since being a film, television or music fan does not exclude the possibility of a strong affection for or attachment to radio. The key insight is that affections for or a 'love' of radio is rarely an exclusive domain. The listener is always potentially also relating experiences of radio to other medial experiences of reading and viewing, and in some cases engaging simultaneously with radio and reading, for instance through a newspaper, magazine or novel. Media fandom research, moreover, tends to suggest that an individual's fandoms may be multiple in their focus over time, or take transmedial form, in following a particular story, character or performer across multiple media domains.[134] In relation to sound media like radio, it is thus equally important to consider certain pathways or habits of listening to and loving mediated sound that historically prefigured the introduction of radio.[135] In the case of the telephone and gramophone, Georgina Born has pointed to the consumption of sound media as operating according to 'a dual movement that is characteristic of this history: both *interiorising*, in the domestic provenance of early sound media and the inter-corporeal, prosthetic uses of telephony, and *exteriorising*, in those media oriented more to engendering collective forms of life and work'.[136] Making sense of the love of radio, therefore, should not only attend to the cross-medial dimensions feeding into the love of radio, but also this dual aspect in which the experience of radio has a 'pull' towards the interiority of the subject along with a 'push' towards social relations and collective settings.

The third theoretical axis that this section is concerned with is the domain of material culture, seeking a conceptual formulation that helps to attend to objects, materialities and practices bound up with the affection for radio. This broader domain helps to highlight the 'social life of things' and draws attention to the material environments and objects, their mobility and circulation, which help to co-shape the love of radio. This insight echoes the distinction that has been made in the study of media technologies between *media-as-text* and *media-as-object*, as a means to highlight the cultural signification generated by the material object, in this case a radio receiving device.[137] Building on new developments in research on love, this exploration also shares productive terrain with a recent theoretical attention to emotions and material culture that is committed to underscoring the 'materiality of love' in cultural practices, and, with it, tracing how affection, such as for radio, may take forms in material objects, practices, discourses or representational content.[138]

The attention to the material form of the radio receiver as (design) object has already been indicated in the previous section, but also constitutes an important potential site for user engagement across or between media, as indicated by combined radio and record players established around 1930, or between radio, tape recording and playback with personal stereos and Walkman devices.[139] Taking a close look at the material qualities of a radio set, its design and forms of signification can also help understand the imaginative worlds afforded by a particular feature, as has been explored, for instance, in the visual representations of city names on radio set dials from the early 1930s onwards.[140] Thinking about the materiality of radio is a process that can also be extended to questions related to the infrastructures of radio, such as radio station buildings and transmission towers, helping to understand them as designed built environments and also 'agents' to which broadcast publics came to 'attach' their understanding of radio, or as a focus of radiophilic behaviours of collecting images or memorabilia. Radio, in this sense, can be understood as a 'love object', as part of a larger recognition of the 'emotional potency of objects in our lives and the relationships that exist between people and objects'.[141] The materiality of radio, as has been emphasized, should be understood in terms of an assemblage, for which scholars need to be attentive to manifest differences, such as the status of radio as fixed in a domestic space with single ownership, or moving across multiple spaces and users.[142] This understanding is co-extensive with an emphasis on the need to 'remap' sound studies and take into account the multiple and various ontologies that (radio) sound may be in a dynamic relation with.[143] This posits a single radio set in a domestic space in terms of its relational positioning, proximity and interactions with various objects and subjects, also considering how the radio fits with the 'fashioning' of the spaces it may be placed in.[144]

In recent decades, an interest in the agency and biographies of objects has been particularly influential, leading to critical perspectives on their 'social lives' moving through their creation, consumption, and circulation, but especially the functions, values, meanings and 'identities' that objects may have.[145] Janet Hoskin's work in the field of material culture studies has been particularly influential in outlining the concept of 'biographical objects' as a means of understanding the complex exchanges that occur between objects and individual subjectivities, and stressing their place in how people narrate their lives, personal experience and memory.[146] As Hoskins points out, the stress on a concept of 'biography', drawn from literary theory,

> ... has provided new perspectives on the study of material culture, and prompted new questions about how people are involved with the things they make and consume. While anthropological research has expanded beyond the study of small societies to larger global contexts and connections, the emphasis on the individual agent and stages of the life cycle remains important in the discipline, and is perhaps a trade mark of even multi-sited fieldwork ... The agentive turn which has become prominent in various forms of practice theory requires attention to biographical frames of meaning and individual relations established through things with other persons.[147]

While such research suggests a close reading of the object, an 'interactionist' model for the material culture approach to 'technoculture' has emphasized not only the original intentions of the industrial designers or 'user scripts' articulated in advertising, but how multiple user interactions with the object are crucial to the historical meaning and significance of a given object over time. The presence of multiple devices in the 'media ensemble' of a particular user, and their domestic set-up, or of devices such as the radiogram with cross-medial functionalities, are important factors that have helped to shape affective engagements with radio. For the present purposes, this study will attend to the objects of radiophilia, while also remaining primarily human-centric in the analysis, by considering the uses, meanings and perceptions of objects by the people who engage with them, thereby treating 'object biographies' in a relational manner.

An important subset of material culture studies connects to the study of collecting and to museum and heritage studies. It encourages a sensitivity to how collectors seek to hold on to the ephemeral traces of radio through recording and storage media (paper, photos, audio recordings), but also according to the logics of collecting. The domain of material culture studies is helpful, moreover, for clarifying how an attachment or love of radio may relate to valuation, whether in response to a cultural esteem attached to radio at a given historical moment or social setting, or in the face of its devaluation. Practices of saving – for instance through collecting and archiving – can be seen as harnessing 'added value' to recorded sounds or other objects.[148] Nonetheless, it is crucial to keep in mind that heritage practices around radio have often privileged male technocultures, professional narratives and memories, which are not infrequently attached to national histories of broadcasting or dominant middle-class experience.[149] For this reason, it remains important to attend to less canonical spaces of heritage formation and practice, particularly those that create spaces for gender-specific memories, or of migrant, multicultural and diasporic heritage around radio.[150] Likewise, it is crucial to not only delineate professional practices of archiving or museum narration, but also those narratives emerging from amateur and fan collector cultures, who may serve as 'cultural intermediaries' with expertise in informal or 'grey' economic circuits.[151]

Memory is a social activity in which people actively construct the remembered past in present-day acts of remembering and it can be a key component in the formation and maintenance of social and collective identities, as people draw on memory to give meaning to the present moment. Radio can be a crucial 'memory object' in personal and interpersonal practices of remembering, whether in a small-scale setting or in actively-organized groups dedicated to 'old time' radio and its material heritages, as explored in Chapter 3. Regardless of the scale, a key contribution from the work of Maurice Halbwachs is the insight that memory dynamics involve a shared process of evaluating what is worth remembering or forgetting.[152] In heritage and memory studies, we also find instructive accounts on questions of attachment, site specificity and social memory that can be usefully connected to radiophilic practices.

Objects, moreover, have a particular status within radiophilia, given the strong attachments of radio memories to objects like radio receivers or other souvenirs that can serve as 'memory devices' in acts of remembering, or in prompting certain moods such as nostalgia. Chapters 3 and 4 will therefore take up a particular focus on the significance of material objects in radiophilia. Indeed, the perceived 'ephemeral' status of live radio is important in fuelling the desire to render radio sounds in tangible form, as recordings, and in cultural practices of collecting sets, recordings or other memorabilia. While internet radio, too, was initially framed in terms of the 'immateriality' of the digital, this erroneous assumption has been redressed in recent theorizations, which attend more closely to how digital media relate to questions of material waste, urban space, intimacy and embodiment. This sensitivity to the materiality of digital media is instructive for the attention in this book to digital archives for radio and podcast media (Chapter 3), and in digital curation of radio via online exhibition formats and display strategies (Chapter 4).

In popular music studies and investigations of the history of sound technologies, we can also find productive accounts concerning the relations between embodied listening subjects, sound technologies, consumer objects, (musical) sound, and processes of remembering and nostalgia. Karin Bijsterveld and José van Dijck, for instance, have stressed that sound technologies and recorded music during the twentieth century held a particularly meaningful role within memory dynamics between individuals and collectives.[153] This is helpful for our understanding of radiophilia, as we can locate the nostalgic dimensions to the love of radio, or how it figures in practices of remembering as taking place within a broader culture of popular music heritage practices, acts of memory and a culture of 'technostalgia'.[154] Popular music has featured prominently in recent heritage discourses, cultural memory and identity processes, as facilitated by museums, tourism, fandom and online archiving initiatives, including the rise of DIY community archiving.[155] Since the literature on radio-focused museum practices and collaborative community initiatives remains limited, such accounts are instructive for the analysis in the present book, particularly in Chapters 3 and 4. These perspectives are productive in acknowledging not only the disposition, tastes and subjectivity of fans involved in 'affective heritage practices',[156] but in demonstrating an awareness that the professional archivist may be a 'fan' motivated by a love of radio, or involved in informal collecting practices alongside their official work duties.[157]

Conclusion

This chapter has sought to establish theoretical insights for making sense of loving radio as pertaining to both action and practice. Taking bell hooks' influential account as its departure point, the three sections of this chapter established theoretical guidelines for the present study. The aim of the first section was to offer an account of the 'attractions' across 100 years of radio and digital audio, covering the various aspects of its potential appeal, but also how listeners and fans have harnessed radio for particular needs and uses. The second part delved further into how best to frame the love of radio with the aid of recent research on media fandom and on emotions, feeling and affect. Building on these insights, the final section outlined the importance of considering three key dimensions to the love of radio, namely, the senses (and their interaction), intermediality (within radio and in exchange with other media) and the significance of material culture (objects and practices). These insights in terms of theory and approach will serve as a touchstone for the subsequent chapters of this book, which are focused on knowing, saving and sharing.

2

Knowing

Broadcast listeners may love radio – or have loved it once – but the [amateurs] really love radio.[158]

Almost everyone is familiar with the Morse code emergency signal 'SOS' (save our ship). It's just one example of the widespread popular knowledge derived from early long-distance wireless communications that pre-dated and informed early amateur radio culture. It indexes the important role of wireless radio in coordinating information during a crisis, from the sinking of the *Titanic* in 1912 through to natural disaster relief and war intercepts today, a key function by which amateur radio enthusiasts continued to be relied on across the 'radio century'. This chapter delves further into radiophilia by asking how the enthusiasm or passion for radio takes certain shapes or forms in terms of acquiring, generating or imparting knowledge about radio. It builds on an insight, noted in the previous chapter, that fans' play, affects, emotions, pleasure and fantasies should not be seen as separate from or inferior to knowledge and cognition.[159] In a similar vein, this chapter will explore various ways in which radiophilia can be characterized by a 'thirst' for knowledge, sometimes verging on epistemophilia: as a passionate drive for knowledge. This desire for knowledge was not only present during the early years of radio, among amateurs, fans or the general public, but was also sustained (and renewed) across different periods and changing concepts of radio as a wireless technology and cultural form.

How do you learn to love radio after first encountering it? And how do you know the thing you love? These are the main questions this chapter will consider. Rather than start with a top-down or institutional perspective and end with listener practices, the chapter will begin by treating a broader category of amateur enthusiasts, tinkerers and 'hams',[160] and the types of knowledge and know-how emerging from radio as a technical hobby, cultural practice and formation of emotional community in various national and regional contexts. It is crucial to note here that participating in amateur contexts is not entirely separate from 'official' sites of knowledge production, and that radio as a technical hobby was often practised in tandem with, or became a pathway to, (semi-)professional employment in fields such as radio engineering or research and development.

The second consideration here is early knowledge formation in relation to radio, primarily linked to industry and regulators, but also 'co-produced' with other social groups. More specifically, the second section asks how specific cultural formats – the radio film, the radio exhibition and the radio encyclopaedia – presented authoritative knowledge while also allowing ongoing negotiation of 'sociotechnical imaginaries' surrounding radio.[161] These formats, which deployed multiple media for their respective knowledge dissemination and sensory engagement, highlight the various ways in which radio was popularized from the late 1910s onwards. These examples also support the claim, further developed in the final section of this chapter, that knowledge about radio was produced at the intersection with other media. Moreover, the process of experiencing affective attachment to radio involved multiple sensorial registers for audiences when engaging in often-simultaneous acts of viewing and listening, often in tandem with smell, touch and taste.

The final section will further delve into the rapid emergence of audience fan cultures around radio. It will enquire as to how writing and print-based formats and genres (via letters and magazines), along with radio programmes themselves, have been key elements in the intermedial pedagogy and practices of radio fandom. By invoking how both knowledge and passion were part of audience participation, play and engagement, this final section will posit knowledge as extending to forms of affective labour and practical 'hands-on' ways of doing and learning, whether that be through individual pursuits or in community settings. While acknowledging the risk of prioritizing (super)fans over 'ordinary' listeners of radio (and even its 'non-users'), the chapter seeks to sensitize the reader to the range of identities, dispositions and taste preferences underpinning the knowledge processes and practices created in the relationship between audiences and radio, whether that be directed towards types of programme content, or a particular star, station or network.

Amateur knowledge of radio

In French, the word *amateur* refers to the one who loves (as a lover of something), and historically came to have a meaning of pursuing or cultivating a particular interest or activity in a manner that is not professional.[162] Amateur radio enthusiast practices pre-dated formal or regulated broadcasting. Their activities have often been used to claim various national contexts as having the 'first' radio broadcast in the world. In the United States, for instance, licenses for amateur broadcast stations were issued from 1910 onwards, including for stations that started to regularly broadcast voice and music performances. Wireless Morse code messages, announcing the Irish Republican 'Easter Rising' in 1916, too, have been variously claimed as a first broadcast since these messages were intended to be emitted widely, rather than to a specific source.[163] This uprising serves as a reminder of the significance of the First World War as a context during which not only strict controls and censorship was enforced, but in which the conflict served as a catalyst for increasing training and access to wireless communication technologies among a large cohort of (male) military personnel.[164] More broadly, radio was associated with cultural modernity, with a rapid growth of amateur wireless societies in cities around the world, which also later in the broadcast era came to include 'radio clubs' in colonial metropoles such as Shanghai (China), Manila (Philippines), Saigon (now Ho Chi Minh City, Vietnam), Batavia (now Jakarta, Indonesia), Bombay (now Mumbai, India), Lourenço Marques (now Maputo, Mozambique) or Luanda (Angola), particularly during the 1920s and 1930s.[165] During this period, even as audiences grew in size, radio access remained limited, since 'outside of North America, north-west Europe, and a few other prosperous enclaves, individual or family listening in the home was a privilege enjoyed only by select members of a wealthy elite'.[166] Nonetheless, radio emerged as a site for expressions of technological nationalism, particularly for the rise or consolidation of national culture in relatively new nations, as was the case in the highly active amateur (*aficionado*) radio scene in Argentina or in the context of Soviet Russia, where an official Society of Radio Lovers (*Obshchestvo druzei radio*) was founded in 1924, dominated by young men from the urban working class.[167]

Radio amateurs in the decade prior to the First World War have been recognized as playing a significant role in developing wireless listening practices that contributed to the shifting notion of wireless communication from point-to-point to a one-to-many principle of radio broadcasting. During a phase of 'interpretative flexibility' for wireless, multiple new uses and applications for this medium were imagined and explored, and amateurs in Italy, for instance, started to engage in the practice of receiving messages (rather than engaging in two-way transmission).[168] Indeed, amateurs have been credited with playing an important role *prior* to the establishment of national broadcast frameworks, as crucial in popularizing and sharing knowledge across national contexts. Across Europe, radio hobbyists were actively involved 'in the discussion about radio technology, followed recent news by subscription to the international journals, exchanged knowledge with other hobbyists through publications and correspondence, and mediated their knowledge to the community and general public by applying the technology in their everyday lives before the First World War'.[169] The development of radio amateur activities points to how amateurs formed an identifiable community from the 1910s onwards, and how their active and experimental approach to radio helped to broaden the possible uses and interpretations of radio and its incorporation into everyday life.

In terms of a formal framework for radio enthusiasts, the 'radio club' emerged as a hub for early enthusiast and engineers, for instance with the Amateur Radio Club of America formed in 1909 in New York, along with the American Radio Relay League from 1914 onwards.[170] A revised edition of a US amateur wireless manual in 1920, for instance, included instructions on 'How to conduct a radio club', outlining the need for an organizational structure, with formal meetings and note-taking, in order to establish a community that is 'educational, instructive, and productive of advancement in wireless'.[171] Consisting of 'full members' (with at least one year of amateur experience) and 'students' (no prior experience), the manual explained that a newly-established radio club would need to rent a dedicated space as a 'club room' for installing an antenna, technical equipment and workshop, along with a library with the latest magazines and books, and maps depicting wireless stations across the world.[172] While this account does not provide further detail of the main activities, the assumption is that members would use the club framework to improve technical skills, exchange knowledge and make use of the facilities on site.

In the German-speaking context during the 1920s and into the 1930s, radio construction workshops – sometimes in the presence of professional engineers from the radio industry or engineering/ physics students – established the radio club as

> ... an important conduit of knowledge between universities, industry, and the general public. This exchange of knowledge was by no means one-way: technical innovation often came from the radio hobbyists themselves. Clubs held public displays of their latest products, and even held competitions for the best and most technically innovative home constructions. At a time when radio design and construction was literally being made up from scratch, workers in industry often gained inspiration or copied ideas which first came out of the clubs.[173]

In other contexts, we can find the activities of radio enthusiasts taking place alongside the establishment of official broadcasting. In the German-speaking context, radio clubs were formed in the tradition of local associations (*Vereine*) from 1923 onwards, and endorsed by the authorities as a means of popularizing the advent of the licensed broadcast radio system:

> [The radio clubs] gave classes, held talks, lectures and demonstrations, and brought people together with others to share knowledge. In short, they provided a social space within which people could learn about radio on their own terms. Not least, they provided work or 'maker' spaces within which people could build their own radios, a financial necessity for most new radio listeners in the 1920s and 1930s. The clubs also provided a wide range of social activities, many of which had little to do with the technology as such, but which were a very important

part of bringing people to the medium of radio. In a nutshell, people came for the parties, and stayed for the technology.[174]

The 'love' of radio was thus formed through radio as a hobby, as an activity that could be pursued in private, but that was largely shaped in the social environment of the radio club, which frequently created physical spaces for their meetings and activities. Crucially, the enthusiasm for radio technology must be seen in tandem with an ambivalence or outright fear circulating about the threat of modern technology. In this light, the hobbyist's desire to improve knowledge and skills about radio can also be read as seeking mastery over technology, a theme that remained predominant during the early 'domestication' of radio as a new technology in the home.[175]

The amateur radio club, association or society was a crucial node in knowledge creation and dissemination, and this took shape in the form of public events (such as lectures), mail order services for DIY kits and component parts, and producing 'how to' booklets and manuals, as well as member newsletters and magazines. In the United Kingdom, for instance, it was not only the formation of amateur radio societies or associations that proved to be an important conduit of knowledge for amateurs, as this occurred in tandem with a network of specialist magazines:

> Especially in the mid-1920s, news-stands and appliance shops witnessed a flood of wireless periodicals (up to 30 between 1924 and 1926). Equipped with step-by-step guides, notably on home-made assemblies, they conferred an even more popular appeal on craftsmanship. Publishing houses such as the respectable 'The Wireless Press' and its rival 'Radio Press' emerged as the patrons of ventures which served as a banner of consumerist material culture fostered by radio firms.[176]

British magazines, such as *Wireless* or *Popular Wireless*, served as important focus points for knowledge dissemination, as well as generating enthusiasm among those amateurs engaging in the self-building of receivers (for the further development of listener fan magazines, see the third part of this chapter).

While amateurs were commonly referred to as 'fans' up until at least 1930, most of the accounts of 'radio mania', 'radio fever' or 'radio madness' are used to refer to the first few years of regulated broadcast radio, which in many places occurred somewhere roughly between 1922 and 1927.[177] In most cases, 'amateur' is thus used as shorthand for the growth of a mass popular enthusiasm for radio, in the years when most listeners started to use headphones with crystal radio or super-regenerative receivers and, subsequently, models with loudspeakers with the advent of 'superhet' (superheterodyne) receivers with vacuum tubes from the mid-1920s onwards. This passion for broadcasting built on a pre-existing desire for distance signalling (DXing) or 'exploratory listening' already established by amateur listeners who sought to pick up signals from faraway stations in Morse code, and, following the advent of voice signals, formed a strong desire to pick up speech and especially music, whether far away or locally transmitted.[178] From the perspective of affect, we can identify this early phase of broadcast radio in terms of the thrill of the new, and the wonder associated with the feeling of real-time 'travelling' made possible by radio listening, allowing the previous concepts of space and time to be collapsed.

> For ordinary people, radio was the future. It was at the cutting edge of science and modernity, and it created a massive social movement the likes of which had never before been seen; a movement which was the direct ancestor of our modern enthusiasm for computers and the internet. Nothing about the new tool predestined it for success, and the social forms of its use were in no way pre-destined by the technology itself ... Some made it a business, others made it a career, and many more made it into a *hobby*, a new sort of mass free-time activity characteristic of industrial societies. For many, the frightening, exciting, and complex technology of radio became an obsession. For them and countless others, it also was fun.[179]

One of the major sources cited for the enthusiasm for amateur radio was the interest in practising a technical hobby, frequently centred on learning basic electronics in order to self-build a radio sets, as well as maintain and repair radio receivers and their components. Once in possession of a working radio set, one of the key attractions was to explore the possibilities of using one's equipment to make long-distance contact with other radio fans, which required an ability to use Morse code.[180]

Other aspects of the shared culture of amateur radio enthusiasts concerned the use of their own call sign, identifying them by country/location, and the ability to recognize other call signs. While often set up in a solitary attic, basement or office room, the participatory nature of 'ham' (two-way) radio practice in the United States has been appreciated:

> According to the standard procedures for initiating a dialogue, a call by licensee KB3DF requesting to talk with anyone available would be spoken as, 'CQ CQ CQ, this is KB3DF calling CQ. Kilowatt bravo three delta foxtrot, calling CQ CQ CQ'. The code for a general call ('CQ') might be modified to 'CQ DX' to elicit a response from a distant station ('DX' being radio jargon for long-distance operating) or be followed by the call sign of another hobbyist when answering a specific person's CQ ... A contact ended with sending 'best regards', couched in the code phrase '73', and declaring 'over and out' before recording the date, time, operating frequency and power, and the other party's license number in a log book that was subject to FCC [Federal Communications Commission] inspection.[181]

This description not only underlines such activity as a site of social interaction, but especially that a set of shared codes, conventions and practices formed around amateur radio.[182] The 'CQ' calling out for contact with anyone who would like to interact has been described as one of the key attractions, both past and present, of amateur radio, with the desire for contact described as having a certain anonymous eroticism, likened to a 'mating call'.[183] More generally, those who developed a passionate interest and active involvement in amateur radio had to invest time and gain skills and a knowledge of codified language in order to successfully engage in and enjoy the experience of radio.

Historically, the early culture of amateur radio can be said to have created a practice of 'keeping track' of radio through the sending of postcards confirming receipt of radio signals, which continues up until the present day amongst amateur radio communities. These cards, known as QSL cards, refer to the Q signal conventions developed in wireless radio, with QSL referring to the question 'Did you get my receipt?' and its confirmation.[184] Through this exchange of postcards, the amateurs participated in

FIGURE 1 *QSL card issued by 7MJ (Royal M. Howard) to 7AIB, dated 5 June 1924, Ketchikan (Alaska), United States, which was a remote settlement that had several thousand inhabitants at that time. Courtesy of Thomas Roscoe.*

a sociable interaction across distances, sometimes expanding on the basic technical information with the exchange of gifts or letters.[185] With its capacity to conjure up images of faraway places (see Figure 1), and as the basis for new long-distance contacts and sometimes even friendships, the QSL cards served as souvenirs of experiences of establishing contact, as well as opportunities for self-presentation and meaningful contact with others.

In some of these cards we see depictions of the geographical location or locale of the card sender, typical animal life or depictions of the amateur radio operator, sometimes shown in the context of their radio device or in the form of a portrait, not that dissimilar from the 'star' portraits circulated by radio stars from the 1920s onwards. There also appears to be a large number of cards produced in institutional frameworks, such as the military (see Figure 2) or other workplaces, with online galleries suggesting a high representation of colonial administrators or Christian missionaries in 'outposts' such as the Bahamas, Easter Island, Palau or Madagascar, which were controlled by European colonial powers such as the UK, France and Portugal.[186] The social nature of the

FIGURE 2 *QSL card issued by an amateur radio group (VU2MA) in the context of a military academy in an independent and post-partition India, Indian Military Academy, Dehradun, India, dated 15 May 1951. Courtesy of Thomas Roscoe.*

contact is suggested by the form of letter-style communication or in the marking of certain rituals, such as the Christmas sticker attached to VE2HI (see Figure 3). This underscores the emotional relations underpinning early radio practice, where the thrill of wireless communication was spurred on by the possibility of being in touch with fellow enthusiasts located both near and far away. This culture of cross-border listening and correspondence, established in the amateur radio era, was an important precedent for broadcast-era practices, as evidenced by audiences of international shortwave radio broadcasts, such as the Dutch PCJ station popular music programme *Happy Station* from 1928 onwards, which gained a large following of listeners across the British Empire, such as in Australia, South Africa and India.[187]

The love of radio as a technical hobby, moreover, appears to have served as a pathway to other associated interests. The advent of more advanced receivers created by the radio industry from the late 1920s onwards led members to develop adjacent audio technology interests within the framework of the amateur radio

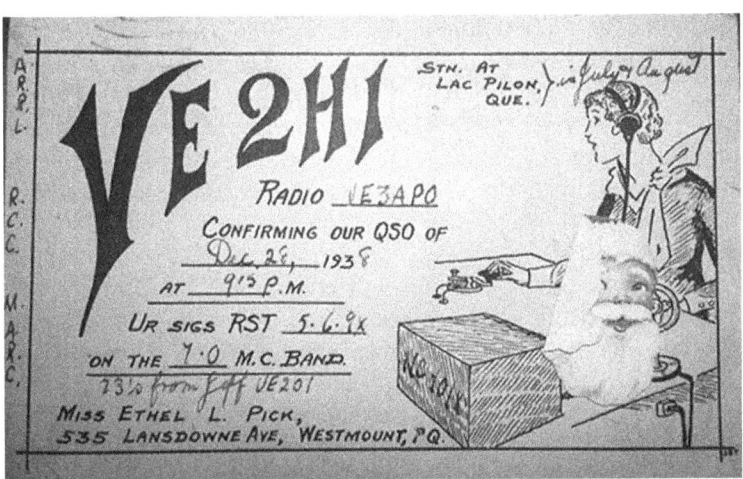

FIGURE 3 *QSL card issued by VE2HI (Ethel L. Pick), who subsequently became one of the first members of the Young Ladies Radio League (YLRL), founded in 1939. Dated 28 December 1938, Montreal, Canada. Courtesy of Thomas Roscoe.*

clubs, such as phonography, sound recording and sound film, or in tandem with the hobby of photography.[188] Amateur radio organization frequently took place at a local, regional or national level, but was also characterized by explicit international outreach, often framed in the spirit of post-First World War internationalism and a desire for radio to foster mutual understanding across borders. The first International Amateur Congress in Paris in 1925, for instance, conducted its proceedings not only in English and French, but also the international(ist) language of Esperanto.[189] The meeting in Paris led to the founding of the International Amateur Radio Union (IARU), as a key lobby group intended to petition the International Telegraph Union (ITU), and later the International Radio Union (IRU), for amateur access to radio frequencies.

In many countries, the radio hobby declined somewhat with the advent of the consumer market offering better quality and commercial receivers. In other contexts, such as National Socialist Germany from 1933 onwards, amateurs were subject to significant pressure, with political incorporation eventually leading to forced closure. During this time, German amateurs have been described as developing a 'tactical knowledge' by seeking to circumvent the restrictions on amateur access to radio frequencies, while the revival of amateur radio was initially limited to some self-building in the first few years after 1945.[190] However, the hobby went into decline in subsequent years due to the increased affordability of commercial receivers (following the 1948 currency reforms) and the advent of transistor radios that were more challenging to build than the previous vacuum tube models.

In other countries, the post-war era signified a boom in radio hobbyist practices and organizations grounded not only in self-building but also in the maintenance and repair of receivers. If we take the case of Japan, radio amateurs, tinkerers and semi-professionals actively started to build their own receivers from component parts prior to the launch of radio in 1925 (or commercial receiver production), and the launch of the national broadcaster NHK in 1926. The 'unofficial' activities of amateurs became a key driving factor in the growth of the national electronics industry.[191] Starting in 1926, the Japan Amateur Radio League (JARL), a voluntary association, represented amateur interests and was initially encouraged by professional and government bodies, with amateur stations gaining authorization in 1927.[192] Even though amateur radio activities were banned in 1941 and resumed only in 1952, a strong amateur and tinkerer culture persisted in Japan from the late 1920s to the 1950s. A key factor was that less technically-advanced regenerative models remained the standard, with the superheterodyne sets (with vacuum tubes, which were harder to self-build) coming into prominence with the advent of commercial radio in 1951, around two decades after many other nations.[193]

Under the US occupation government in Japan, there was a radio boom in the period 1945–53, despite depressed economic conditions. A key site of social interaction for young radio enthusiasts, amateurs and semi-professionals who sought to learn and share knowledge was a cluster of shops and informal sellers of component parts in Tokyo, which became known as Akihabara Electric Town.[194] Bound up with this, the huge popularity of self-building radio receivers has been described as being fuelled by magazines that had high circulations and served as a central node for knowledge dissemination. The radio magazines, which were enthusiastically consumed by Japanese tinkerers, encouraged their readers to experiment with building and repairing equipment:

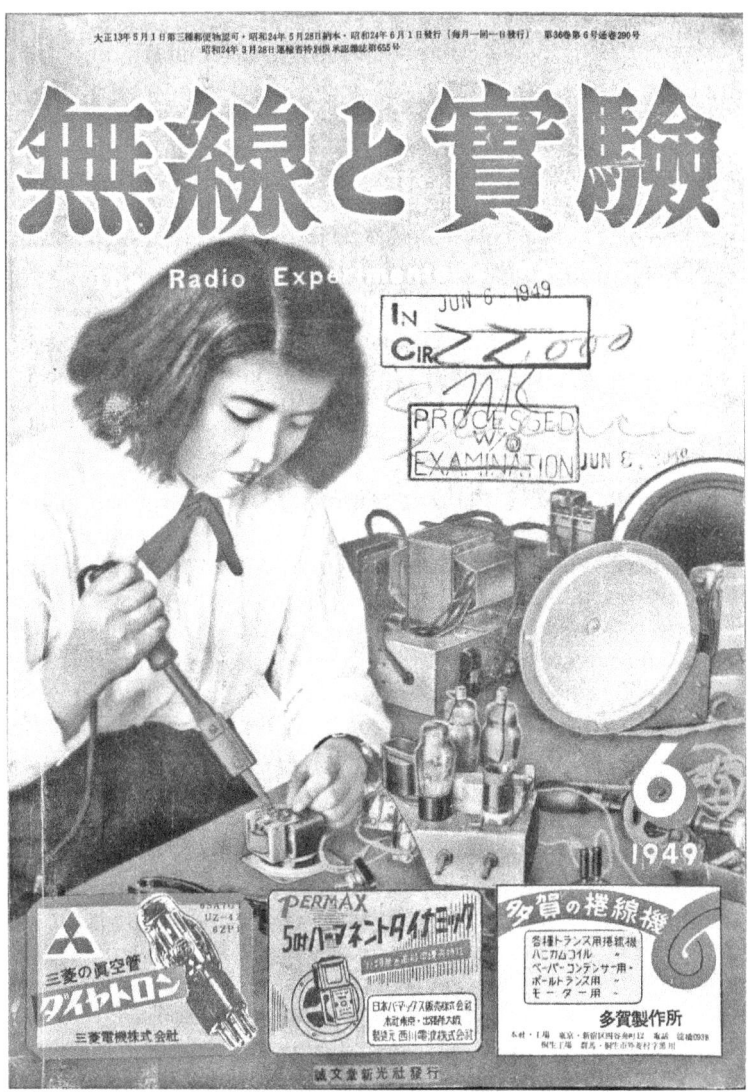

FIGURE 4 *A 1949 cover of the magazine* Musen to Jikken *(*無線と実験, *or Radio Experimenters) depicts a young woman in school uniform working on a radio set. Source:* Musen to Jikken *6 (1949). Courtesy of the Gordon W. Prange Collection, University of Maryland.*

The main topics of the magazines just after the war were how to repair old receivers, followed by how to rebuild radios using military components; as the postwar boom continued, the magazines expanded to include building superheterodynes, all-wave sets, and phonographs ... These magazines, connecting tinkerers and component manufacturers, played a pivotal role in the unofficial sector. Engineers with components manufacturers wrote articles for radio magazines to promote sales, component manufacturers placed advertisements in the magazines ... Contributors to the radio magazines included both university professors and professional engineers, who also produced a flood of books for tinkerers ranging from introductory texts to books for skilled semiprofessionals, among them many titles focusing on radio repair.[195]

While young women, students and military personnel had gained radio training during the Second World War, the tinkering culture in radio across the whole period was largely coded as a pastime for boys and men, and as a potential career pathway, with some exceptions (see Figure 4). Radio tinkering was encouraged through school clubs, training schools and correspondence courses, as well as an NHK radio programme devoted to the practicalities of radio receivers that ran between 1952 and 1957.[196]

Research on all of the above-mentioned contexts has underscored how the amateur technical hobby of self-building, tinkering and 'ham' radio has historically been heavily skewed towards a male demographic, and may even be read as, in part, a way to avoid engaging with emotional landscapes at home with partners and families. The default assumption that amateur radio practitioners are men has also established itself in the abbreviated language of hobbyists, who address each other as OM (Old Man) and refer to their partners as XYL (Ex-Young Lady).[197] Kristen Haring has shown how, in the United States, both the radio hobby and radio technology more generally was represented as masculine, and that, despite claims of democratic access, its members were predominantly (upper) middle class.[198] Their passion for radio, therefore, was coupled with a knowledge production in which certain values and traits were ascribed to radio, thereby also validating their own identities as radio amateurs:

As hams articulated, taught, and enforced expectations for behavior with regard to radio, they associated social norms with the technology. Hams routinely implied, and occasionally explicitly stated, that radio required operators who possessed traits such as precision, efficiency, discretion, rationality, attentiveness, political neutrality, and masculinity. Their logic was that these traits were technical demands of radio, following from the way devices were constructed and how they functioned. In the other step of the cycle, hobbyists took on a technical identity from radios. By personally identifying with technology and as radio operators, hams reflected back onto themselves the very characteristics they had imparted to radio technology.[199]

Haring has drawn attention to the key contribution of certain women to US amateur radio culture, and how they sometimes dealt with the dominant masculinist discourse by downplaying their own technical skills and framing their own practices through stereotypical notions of femininity and domesticity. In countries such as the United States or Germany, women's contribution to the amateur radio hobby was generally cast in terms of a limited visibility through 'behind the scenes' tasks in clubs, either related to social activities or in supporting roles such as that of secretary/treasurer.[200]

This is a necessary methodological challenge to keep in mind when treating the enthusiasm for radio in histories of amateur radio. It remains essential to amplify how, for instance, communication in Morse code was read as masculinist, while talk-based wireless communication was understood as feminized 'chatter'.[201] However, contemporary scholarship suggests that women amateur radio enthusiasts were sometimes misrecognized on the air as men, or were not actively encouraged in this technical pursuit either socially, by schooling or in (lack of) access to equipment. And yet recent work in feminist media history invites us to try harder to listen in and 'amplify' traces of women as actively interested and involved in the history and innovation of (amateur) radio.[202] For instance, to attend to contributions to infrastructure, such as the central role of women's technical labour in the professional field of telegraphy that led to radio, and in manufacturing radio equipment and component parts on factory assembly lines.[203]

Writing in a similar vein about male-dominated accounts in the history of electronic music, Tara Rodgers has noted the importance of acknowledging an enthusiasm among young women for analogue synthesizers in the 1950s:

> To be sure, gender was and remains a factor in whether technological enthusiasm and curiosity are encouraged and supported. In the 1960s and 1970s, while some men enjoyed the 'freedom' to tinker outside their formal engineering jobs, women were more likely to be discouraged from acquiring technical knowledge and pursuing those careers at the outset ... [M]any more women and girls may well have been poring over popular hi-fi and electronics magazines, imagining their own technological revolutions in sound, and helping, by their enthusiasm and amateur projects, to lay the groundwork for widespread acceptance of analogue synthesizers as the beloved, mass-marketable musical instruments that are still taking the world by storm today.[204]

Despite the scant nature of information about amateur enthusiasts who were not white or male, several images depicting young white women and Black people involved in amateur radio feature in commercial stock photography websites like Getty Images or Alamy, though often with unreliable source metadata.[205] Beyond these commercially-owned platforms, there have been recent US scholarly efforts to document the history of early Black wireless operators and the first Black radio club (the Woodlawn Radio Association, in Chicago) from the 1910s onwards.[206] One other exception can be found in documentation about the Young Ladies Radio League (YLRL), which was formed in 1939 following a call out to 'YL "key twitchers"' by Ethel Smith; in 1959 the organization was reported to have 850 members worldwide, while women were estimated as making up roughly 2 per cent of amateurs in the US (4,000 of the 180,000).[207]

Questions about the gender, race, class and visibility of radio enthusiasts in the historical record has been at the forefront of recent research on radio's history and its present, which has also uncovered the persistence of alternative knowledges of radio emerging and facilitating innovation, spanning pirate radio, low-power FM and micro radio movements,[208] as well as strongly emotive efforts to resist the apparent disposability of radio devices through the cultures of repair and maintenance (which will be explored further in Chapter 3). The sensitivity to the (in)visibility of some radio users and fans compared to others will remain a key insight for the remainder of this chapter, which considers how the love of 'radio' opened up from a narrow technical pastime (of amateur 'fans') to an expanded field of radio culture, with a broader domain of (mass) listening audiences, popular imaginaries and affective practices. We turn now first to institutional sites of knowledge production around radio and the initial popularization of broadcasting, and then, in the final section, to the intermedial dimensions contributing to the growth of radio fan cultures.

Institutional knowledge practices and the popularization of radio

In common usage, 'radio' is used in diverse ways, referring variously to the medium, its content or the production context in which it is created. One of the more overlooked aspects of radio is as a site of industrial research and development from the early twentieth century, particularly as imperial and settler colony nations recognized the benefits of military, government and commercial applications for radio. From the early 1920s onwards, many of these nations – including Japan, Germany, the United States and the UK – heavily invested in the development of long-distance shortwave radio through radio research in physics, acoustics and engineering. Underscoring the prestige afforded to radio research and education, Aitor Anduaga has stressed the importance of recognizing the multiple, vested interests in the generation of scientific knowledge relating to radio technology:

> [R]adio means not a simple entity but an utterance that comprises three interrelated applications: navigation, point-to-point communication and broadcasting (as it was used in the 1920s). These usually involve three generally interrelated processes: assembly, manufacture, and innovation. Each application results from specific procedures and developments, and the industrial incarnation of applications and of processes is the *radio industry*.

Broadcasting was thus one single aspect of radio industry and not its entirety.[209]

Clarifying this distinction, it is essential to understand that the expansion of radio during the interwar period was not as a neutral process, but rather the outcome of an explicit research and development agenda fuelled by the interests of the radio industry, government, military and universities. Moreover, European imperial powers often conceived of their investments in radio research in a competitive frame, with the German Telefunken joint venture from the 1900s onwards seen as a rival to British Marconi in the field of wireless communications, and seen also in imperial, military and government applications, as well as the development of radio and other electroacoustic technologies for consumers. Scientific research was a crucial site of knowledge production about radio, which also fed into popular discourses about 'important personalities' in radio, such as inventors Guglielmo Marconi (credited as the inventor of wireless telegraphy) or Lee de Forest (inventor of the triode vacuum tube).[210]

From the 1900s, acoustics became an 'imperial science' in Europe, while Japan's development and application of telecommunications proved to be a crucial 'tool of empire' in the imperialist military expansion into Asia.[211] This insight helps to underscore the connections between empire, communication networks and global markets prior to and following the advent of broadcasting.[212] It also helps to highlight the ways in which the widespread enthusiasm for radio not only resulted in discourses of internationalism, but was informed by public discourses of 'audio nationalism' and 'technological imperialism', in which 'the west's conception of itself as technological and modern [was] highlighted and reinforced by juxtaposing itself and its technologies against people without that technology'.[213] The love of radio, therefore, certainly gained traction in terms of enhancing a self-image of being a 'modern' subject, and in participating in a vibrant cultural moment. Yet it is also crucial to understand that this experience was not infrequently bound up with ideas about technological progress, racialized civilizational discourse and restrictive notions of the listener community.[214]

In what follows, I will now move from these more conventional sites of knowledge production around radio to key examples in which authoritative knowledge or epistemic authority are present, but often developed in an accessible way to engage or encourage the participation of the public in gaining knowledge about radio, namely through *films, annual exhibitions* and the *encyclopaedia*. Each of these formats pre-dated the advent of broadcast radio, yet we find in each one, distinct approaches to knowledge dissemination, visual communication and popularization that were well established by the time broadcast radio was introduced. In each we can also observe various knowledge strategies, including visual spectacle, pedagogy and multi-sensory appeal, particularly through the visual, tactile and auditory registers. This focus will also serve as a reminder of how, during the decades around 1900, colonial powers (and settler colonies) demonstrated a strong investment in both the exhibition and (non-fiction) film as opportunities to put modern technology on display, along with the perceived achievements of the imperial nation (and its colonies).

If we turn first to the genre of the 'radio film', a range of promotional shorts and documentaries through to feature films appeared that centrally figured radio as a crucial and attractive feature of 'modern life' from the 1920s onwards. In this context, cinema was used in many countries as a vehicle to demystify the workings of wireless radio transmission, to establish certain 'scripts' for the intended functions and uses of radio, or generate a pleasure in watching and learning about radio. One of the earliest examples of a film made about radio prior to the broadcast era is the US production *Caught by Wireless* (1908), in which wireless features in the plot as a means to catch a villain. In the broadcast era, films about radio have been described as reflecting

> ... both ends of [a] spectrum of public speculation: excitement that geographical distance and cultural difference might be abridged by radio, and fears that it would throw open the borders between white, Anglo-American ears and a heterogeneous mass composed of foreigners, the uneducated, and the uncouth who ... would exploit the new medium for their own ends. Whether the films were utopian, dystopian, or somewhere in between, they acknowledged radio's potential to revise the definition of media interactivity that the institution of classical cinema tried to defend.[215]

In the case of Germany, an early promotional film for the AEG company's radio receivers was *Spiel der Wellen* (The Play of Waves, 1926). Made by experimental filmmaker Walter Ruttmann, the animation short depicts radio allowing sound waves and melodies to travel through the ether, moving across city streets. A subsequent scene depicts a performance by a caricatured 'African' figure shown striking a drum, singing and playing a guitar, with transmission waves moving around the globe transporting exotic musical sounds to be consumed by a (male) German radio listener without interference.[216] Given the persistence of fears about the radio ether having magical or mysterious qualities, the film also reflects a commercial interest in presenting radio listening to music in the domestic home environment as an enjoyable pastime. This narrative is consistent with an overall trend in radio advertising from the mid to late 1920s, as high-end radio receivers came to be promoted as elegant furniture design in wooden casing, and for which parallels can be found with the promotion of gramophone players housed in cabinets and later in a combined form with the 'radiogram'.[217]

During the 1920s, in the lead-up to the industrial synchronization of the sound film, there was considerable fluidity between radio and film experimentation.[218] In turn, the 'radio film' or 'radio sound film' was among a multitude of concepts in circulation, and treated by the Soviet Russian filmmaker Dziga Vertov in his experimental films and writings during the 1920s.[219] In the sound transition period, radio was drawn on as a key tool for conceptualizing synchronized sound film in popular discourse. In turn, during the late 1920s, the Hamburg radio station introduced a 'film radio' (*Filmfunk*) technique for training reporters, who were tasked with narrating silent film footage in order to learn how to translate visual impressions into a 'radiophonic' style for live event commentary and reportage.[220] It was in this atmosphere of intermedial crossovers that Walter Ruttmann engaged in a new experiment titled *Deutscher Rundfunk* (German Radio, 1928), a promotional film commissioned by the German Broadcasting Corporation (Reichs-Rundfunk-Gesellschaft) and the Tri-Ergon Musik company.[221] Promoted both as a sound film (*Tonfilm*) and a radio play (*Hörspiel*), the film was presented to the general public at the annual German Radio Exhibition in Berlin in August 1928.[222] Featuring footage of live radio broadcasts and urban scenes, with a soundtrack blending field recordings, music and sound effects, the film depicted Berlin as the centre of a national broadcast culture and network, from which radio sound waves emanate and reach out to listeners across Germany.[223]

While the above examples are suggestive of an appeal to listeners to become part of a national listening audience, the radio films developed in the Netherlands between the early 1930s and 1950s responded to a media landscape in which newspapers, radio stations and even, to a certain degree, cinema-going was organized to reflect the 'pillarization' of Dutch society, with the liberal, social democratic, Catholic and Protestant radio organizations each given regulated allocations of airtime.[224] The earliest radio films (*omroepfilms*) of the 1930s, commissioned by the respective broadcasters, were intended to be educational and informative, in explaining the 'miracle' of radio broadcasting and in communicating the distinct identities of the stations and their imagined listening audiences. For instance, in a 1931 film, *De klokken luiden* (The Bells Ring, 1931), the Protestant station NCRV was keen to demonstrate the benefits of weather reports for farmers, and of church services on radio for the elderly, but an ambivalence about popular cinema meant that their film was only screened in the context of their own member association events held in church venues or halls. While the NCRV feature film *In Stormgetij* (In the Storm Tide, 1937) only used amateur actors, by contrast, the liberal AVRO station had 'glossy' films made by a feature film director.[225] This serves to illustrate how the imaginaries for the emotional communities formed around radio were often more discrete than national imagined communities, with the emotional appeal of radio presented in terms of social categories of belonging based on political orientation and/or religious affiliation.

In this same period, experimental films were also commissioned, such as *Philips Radio* (1931), in which the filmmaker Joris Ivens depicted the production of radio receivers in the Philips factories in Eindhoven, along with demonstrating the various ways in which radio had enhanced everyday life, from morning exercises, business reports, entertainment for housewives and evening entertainment for the family. This interest in showing audiences 'behind the scenes' of radio receiver production also extended to films depicting the production of programming. In the context of the Second World War, both the UK and Germany invested heavily in advertising shorts as well as feature-length films that offered an ostensible 'behind the scenes' gaze into broadcast production as part of a propaganda effort to highlight the significance of radio for the war effort and its importance in boosting civilian and military morale.[226] In the first post-war decade, 'radio films' returned in the Netherlands, as stations sought to redeem their reputation following their compromised role during the German occupation, regain their membership numbers (for revenue purposes), and trigger audience enthusiasm for radio programming through involvement in the activities of the member association.[227]

Along with the films mentioned above, the earliest radio films in Germany were not only premiered at the annual radio exhibition (*Funkausstellung*), but also include documentation of this event, such as the 'Opening Celebration of the 7th German Radio Exhibition' (*Eröffnungsfeier der 7. deutschen Funkausstellung*, 1930), which was produced with synchronized sound. This film is testimony to the centrality of the radio exhibition, in particular for large European nations such as Germany and the UK, not only as trade shows, but as promotional vehicles and showcases for a broader general public. While the trade exhibition has a long history, in the modern era, dating at least from the Great Exhibition of 1851 in London, technological advancements became a major feature of exhibitions in Europe and North America, with electrical inventions particularly foregrounded between the 1870s and 1920s. Electricity, during this period, was presented in exhibition displays as a crucial site of modernity, progress and connection, and has been described as having 'played a central role in the creation of a twentieth-century sensibility'.[228]

In tandem with the practice of putting new technologies on display, certain common features of the modern exhibition have been identified, such as 'displaying the skill and ingenuity of a nation; informing and educating the visitor; and entertainment or commercial influence, to which we might add in recent times the opportunity to express nationalism or to provide propaganda relative to a particular theme or culture'.[229] Indeed, the exhibition has been variously explored as an important site in which institutions of the new modern state – including museums, schools, libraries and galleries – strove to showcase the nation, heritage and culture. Such institutions and their practices have been described in terms of an 'exhibitionary complex', referring to the operations of discipline, power and knowledge in these new governmental assemblages.[230] A key parallel development was the establishment of the colonial exhibition from the 1880s through to the late 1940s. These exhibitions frequently featured wireless telegraphy and, later, radio broadcasting, as part of industrial technology displays emphasizing the assistance offered to colonial administrations and the contact between the imperial metropole and the colonies. The small anti-colonial exhibition in Paris in 1931 also featured radio broadcasts and recorded music playback during the exhibition and lecture programme.[231]

Radio was prominently featured in national and international exhibitions from the early 1920s onwards, with a particular concentration in the large (imperial) metropoles of the United States (New York) and Europe, such as Paris, London, Berlin, Vienna, Brussels and Amsterdam. One of the earliest reported radio exhibitions took place in March 1918 in The Hague. The Radiotelegraphy Exhibition was organized by the representative organization for radio amateurs and professional radio technicians, the Dutch Association for Radiotelegraphy (Nederlandsche Vereniging voor Radiotelegrafie), one year before the first official broadcast of a radio programme made by inventor Hans Idzerda. A later account of the exhibition described how its main aim was to showcase devices sent in by amateurs, companies, government organizations and military representatives. The exhibition was described as a sensation, with 7,500 visitors each day, including the Dutch Queen Wilhelmina and government ministers. In keeping with the general public's appetite for new inventions, one of the main attractions for the visitors was a display of the radio receivers with valves, whose glass lit up in a warm 'blue glow' when put into use:

> You can't begin to imagine how the crowd thronged around the stand [owned by] Bal, who, just by turning a tuner, managed to conjure up every imaginable station signal from his simple shelf unit; granted, they were Morse signals, but with countless stations playing every imaginable musical tonality. This was all the more impressive if one compared it with the demonstrations of military receiving stations with valve amplifiers, which were housed in impressive black boxes, but for which the interiors could not and were not allowed to be seen; or compared with the amateurs' jittery, fiddling attempts to make [simple] receivers work to make anything audible at all with their crystal detectors.[232]

This observation highlights the visual attractions of radio for the throngs of visitors, for whom the sensation of hearing stations from far away was coupled with a view into the workings of the radio receiver, with its glowing valve. An example of another visual attraction at the exhibition was by the Dutch state postal and telegraphy company P&T, whose head engineer gave a demonstration of a beam coil (with a Marconi antenna) connected to a spark emitter with the high voltage causing one-meter lightning sparks to shoot up into the air.[233]

The notion of the radio exhibition as a site for acquiring new knowledge about radio through accessible demonstrations, lectures, displays and forms of visual spectacle remains consistent across the events of the interwar period up until 1939. Some radio exhibitions started with a predominant trade show focus, such as in the UK and the Netherlands, both of which initially catered strongly to the amateur self-build market for component parts (see Figure 5).[234] In Berlin, too, the annual German Radio Exhibition had a strong

FIGURE 5 *One of the trade-exhibition-style halls with various stands at the International Radio Exhibition (Internationale Radio Tentoonstelling), Amsterdam, The Netherlands, 1925. Courtesy of Nationaal Archief/ Collection Spaarnestad/Het Leven.*

presence of commercial representatives from the radio industry, but also included displays by scientists, individual radio stations and government organizations. From the first exhibition in 1924 onwards, displays of the best home-built radio receivers by regional associations of amateur clubs were put on display, and served as an important source of inspiration feeding back into radio receiver design and construction for the commercial industry.[235] This is an important reminder that the production of new knowledge about radio was never merely driven by industry, or in a top-down relationship from science and business to the grassroots level, but that innovation and new ideas also emanated from the hands-on 'maker' contexts of the radio clubs and associations, attesting to the 'co-production' of knowledge in early radio culture.[236] Nonetheless, the exhibition was frequently a hub for a professional elite involved in radio and for the convergence of the music, film and radio industries in the period around 1930, with presentations of film sound, electro-acoustic musical instruments and experimental music.[237] From the early 1920s through to the last pre-war exhibitions in the late 1930s, there was a concerted effort to present the diversity of radio's applications, and to introduce visitors to the latest technical developments in radio (and television) broadcasting technology.[238] For instance, the effort to promote radios built into luxury cabinets was emphasized in a 1926 Dutch 'Radio Salon' display in which the receivers were placed in a mock-up of a bourgeois living room replete with flowers, plants, statues and carpets (see Figure 6).

The experiential mode was expanded with later exhibitions increasingly prioritizing hands-on and interactive experiences, as can be illustrated, for example, by the 1932 Berlin radio exhibition in which visitors were invited to try out sitting at the wheel of a car with a built-in radio (see Figure 7). While a large portion of exhibition displays showcased new radio models and applications, a strong emphasis remained on future-oriented imaginations of radio, as was the case with the sensation of the 1932 London Radio Show, which was a robot (with an in-built microphone and loudspeaker) that was able to sit and stand, and speak multiple languages, for exhibition visitors (see Figure 8). The intense nature of the radio exhibition as spectacle also drew criticism, with the 1925 Amsterdam radio exhibition restricting stand holders from playing music, since the chaos from simultaneous music playing had created too much chaos and did not serve as good 'advertising

FIGURE 6 *A stand showing radio furniture during a radio exhibition at the Radio Salon, Scheveningen, The Netherlands, 1926. Courtesy of Nationaal Archief/Collection Spaarnestad/Het Leven.*

FIGURE 7 *A woman sits behind the wheel of a mock-up 'car' with a Blaupunkt car radio installed, German Radio Exhibition, Berlin, Germany, August 1932. Courtesy of Nationaal Archief/Collection Spaarnestad/Het Leven.*

FIGURE 8 *A radio-controlled robot was a sensation at the London Radio Exhibition, UK, 1932. Courtesy of Nationaal Archief/Collection Spaarnestad/Het Leven.*

for the radio'.²³⁹ Such complaints continued to be aired well into the mainstream establishment of radio, as can be ascertained by a 1930 review of the British Radiolympia exhibition, which complained of the 'din' caused as 'all the speakers were blaring the same tune from the BBC's transmission' in the exhibition halls, as a way for stand holders to demonstrate the loudspeaker strength of their latest radio receiver models.²⁴⁰

At exhibitions, architectural models were one of the forms of visual depiction of new developments in broadcasting, and also in radio programming, as was the case at the 1931 Berlin radio show, which displayed an architectural model accompanied by a collage signposting the innovation of using sound recording to create news compilation programmes (see Figure 9). The collage, in the shape of a round window connected by cable to the newly-built Berlin broadcasting house, emphasized the notion that audiences were being given access – via radio listening – to the latest forms of actuality reporting, from political and commemorative events

FIGURE 9 *The Funk-Stunde Berlin radio station stand at the German Radio Exhibition, which depicted the events documented by radio reportage and the new broadcasting house, Germany, August 1931. Courtesy of the Bundesarchiv, Bild 102-12189.*

through to car races and horse racing. Indeed, this depiction reflects an overall process by which the visual appearance of transmission towers and broadcast buildings became a crucial part of the image of radio as modern, urban and internationalist. While an identification with purpose-built radio buildings from around 1930 onwards was enhanced by 'behind the scenes' reportage in newspaper, magazine and films coverage, it is significant to note the high circulation of postcards emphasizing the 'wireless monumentality' of broadcast buildings and transmission towers (see Figure 10).[241] Similarly, from the 1920s onwards, a strong cultural imagination developed linking cities and their broadcast towers, as in the case of the former Warsaw Radio Mast, the Tokyo Tower or the CN Tower in Toronto. This association was already to be found with the installation of a wireless radio transmitter on the Paris Eiffel Tower in 1914, a development that led to the tower – described as a 'precious and legendary ornament on the skyline of the capital' – being used as a radio transmission tower attracting the 'pride of the Nation'.[242] The formal development of radio in the 1920s and 1930s cemented the notion of the Eiffel Tower as generally synonymous with radio from the capital city of Paris. The concept of the transmission tower or broadcast building as a visitor attraction is also suggested by postcards of the JQAK transmission station building in Dalian, China, built in 1936 in the context of the Japanese puppet state of Manchukuo (Manchuria), with the caption description – 'Grand Sight of Dairen Broadcasting Station' – emphasizing the pride in the building as an attraction for visitors, based on its modern, futuristic appearance.[243]

We can understand the Berlin radio exhibition as a prominent 'media event' for generating and communicating knowledge about radio, which was highly anticipated for its audience of radio professionals and industry, scientists and inventors, the general public and dedicated radio fans, as well as German and international journalists.[244] The 'mass' character of these events are indicated by the high visitor numbers, with the event attracting between roughly 100,000 and 200,000 visitors during the Weimar Republic years (1924–33) and an average of 350,000 visitors for the significantly expanded exhibitions held until 1939 under National Socialism.[245] Across the interwar period of the German radio exhibition, from 1924 to 1939, we can observe the persistence of multiple formats for engaging the public in knowledge about radio, ranging from

FIGURE 10 'AWA Tower from Wynyard St, Sydney', photo by Harold Cazneaux, in downtown Sydney, c. 1939. Courtesy of The National Library of Australia.

radio history exhibitions, statistical overviews and infographics through to architectural models, photographic displays and stands featuring radio magazines and books. We can also find a full programme of events with live broadcast transmissions of musical and light entertainment programmes, screenings of 'radio films', scientific technical demonstrations and memorials for recently-deceased figures, such as important inventors or announcers.[246] For visitors, learning might therefore have taken the form of looking at an organigram for the organization of German radio, or a historical timeline display showing the set design of radio receivers. Yet interactive participation was a crucial component of the radiophilic desire to see how things worked, with popular exhibition features including 'The Speaking Wire' microphone with which visitors' performances were recorded and judged by a jury, or disc recorders allowing visitors to create recordings of their own voice or from live radio transmission.[247] These interactive features not only facilitated the love of radio, but allowed for one's own voice recording or public performance to be recognized in the context of an official site of radio culture, perhaps even with the promise of being discovered for a future career as a radio announcer or performer. An exhibition display of listener letters to radio stations at the Berlin radio exhibition in 1928, for instance, also served to put listeners 'on display' and suggests that their input was important to radio stations, thereby giving additional prestige and affirmation of the radio listener's fan practices, which the following section will outline in further detail.

Overall, the German case explored here has served to demonstrate how a significant political-economic investment was created around the annual radio exhibition as a context for displaying national prestige, achieving commercial aims and engaging the broader public in both radio and a wider audio culture, and in which strong ideological overtones were evident during the National Socialist era, with radio's media publicity and 'exhibitionary complex' further incorporated into governmental assemblages. In the post-1945 era, radio exhibitions tended to focus on new proliferations of radio technology, with transistors and other portable devices, through to the combined home stereo and sound recording systems – and in the first post-war decades, in tandem with television exhibitions. Looking at documentation of radio exhibitions in London, the exhibition format remained a space for visitors to learn about radio technology and its history; to see the latest developments; and to handle equipment themselves, push buttons, watch demonstrations and performances.[248] Yet it increasingly gained the visual appearance of a fun fair, and promoted the exhibition as an opportunity to get close to radio stars and hear their voices in live performances, thus facilitating a collective experience – and affective practice – of the love of radio.[249] The predominance of the transistor also led to the creation of a renamed, dedicated event, the International Transistor Exhibition, which was held in London in 1959 and featured exhibits from Japan, France and Russia.[250] Other countries also started to host their own radio (and television) exhibitions as a way to put new developments on display. For instance, the archives of the British Marconi Company show how, in the 1950s and 1960s, they contributed exhibits to events spanning the UK, as well as Australia, Canada, Ghana, Kenya and Taiwan.[251] The international character of exhibitions and fairs was reinforced during the 1970s and 1980s, particularly with the global significance of Japanese consumer electronics manufacturers, centring on hi-fi stereo systems and portable stereos including the Sony Walkman (1979–80).[252]

The final example of the popular knowledge and pedagogy around radio is the radio encyclopaedia. In the first years of broadcast radio, while programme makers tried to search for cultural content that would be suited to radio, one of the common 'programme fillers' was lectures by prominent university professors and researchers.[253] Due to complaints about the rather staid approach to communicating 'science on radio', calls were made to develop better strategies for making scientific knowledge accessible to radio audiences, as well as imparting information about radio itself.[254]

While the handbook or manual was a common feature of early (amateur) radio culture, radio quickly grew from the early 1920s onwards into an extensive field of public interest, for which it would have been increasingly difficult to gain an overview. This sense of there being many rapid developments was responded to in the form of radio 'yearbooks' created by (national) broadcasters to give an overview of the previous year's programming developments, highlights or technical achievements, or in radio magazines, which frequently offered readers historical timelines or gave overviews of a 'radio year' in review.[255] The production and sale of radio calendars had a similar function of keeping listeners informed of the important dates in the 'radio year', and photo books of radio announcers and 'stars' were also created, so that listeners could keep track of the names of those involved in their favourite radio programmes.[256]

An encyclopaedia usually deals with a topic that is too large and has too many facets to establish an easy, straightforward description, requiring a mapping of knowledge that would help readers to gain an accessible overview and easy grasp of a wide range of aspects of radio. One of the first general encyclopaedias about radio was by the British journalist John A. Hammerton, who worked for the press magnate Alfred Harmsworth from the early 1920s onwards on illustrated popular education series. Released in twenty-four fortnightly instalments across more than 2,000 pages between 1923 and 1924, the publication was named *Harmsworth's Wireless Encyclopedia: The Only ABC Guide to a Fascinating Science-Hobby*. The subtitle already pointed to an intended amateur and 'experimenter' readership, while the opening editorial, by the consultative editor and wireless radio pioneer Oliver Lodge, further stressed that radio hobbyists were no longer 'content with merely listening-in and making demonstrations to their friends and relatives; they want to understand more seriously the principles underlying this great and remarkable development of human powers of communication'.[257] This turn towards a more 'serious' approach is further underscored by Lodge's observation that the rapid popularity of radio had sparked the need for a synthetic reference work, while the editor Hammerton stressed that the publication had been conceived along similar lines to his previous popular works, which had strongly relied on the 'instructional value of the photograph'.[258]

In the wake of this publication, and following the establishment of regulated broadcast systems, several other encyclopaedias were published with an amateur or technical reader in mind, including *Radio Encyclopedia* (1927), by prominent United States-based radio magazine editor and author Sidney Gernsback, and *Encylopédie de la radio* (1928), in which French radio technology professor Michel Adam offered 1,300 entries with a strong focus on technical terms, abbreviations and symbols and their English and German translations, which was a reflection of the significant presence of international radio market players in France at that time.[259] The radio encyclopaedias of the 1920s were generally devoted to the accessible presentation of technical and general information via text and image, and we can observe by around 1930 a parallel growing interest in the possibilities of creating intermedial resources, such as 'audio books' consisting of text, image and sound recordings, which I will discuss further in Chapter 4.

The radio encyclopaedia does not appear to have been a prevalent genre after 1930, with the technically-oriented publications such as described above no longer pursued. However, roughly a decade later, we can find two striking radio encyclopaedias – one in the Netherlands (1939) and the other in Hungary (1944) – both of which aimed to be a useful resource to a broader readership of radio listeners.

When turning the pages of the *Encyclopaedie voor radioluisteraars* (Encyclopaedia for Radio Listeners), completed in May 1939 by Dutch radio journalist J. J. L. van Zuylen, it is striking to note how this compilation seeks to give an explanation of the current situation of radio, as related to aspects of new technology and musical knowledge, as well as the organization of radio domestically (the Netherlands), regionally (in Europe) and internationally.[260] The encyclopaedia promised its readers the essential knowledge on radio in the late 1930s, with accessible descriptions of the 'expressions, names and terms' in current use in national and international radio programming.[261] Furthermore, the richly-illustrated text revels in the latest developments in modern audio culture, spanning entries for new musical styles, hit songs and jazz musicians through to 'behind the scenes' information on radio studios and recording technologies and their uses for creating new genres, such as the radio play or actuality programming. While still providing certain basic information about the history of radio, important inventors and technical problems (such as interference or Morse code), the entries, graphic portraits and photo inserts are oriented towards the popular culture of radio, featuring the names of musicians, composers, musical repertoire and sounds known from radio (such as entries for interval signals or for 'Big Ben', whose bell chimes were featured on the BBC).[262]

Even though this book was banned by the German occupying forces one year after its publication, van Zuylen noted upon producing a second edition in 1949 that it was created in response to a strong demand for an update among Dutch and Belgian listeners who kept the first edition 'next to the radio set' at home.[263] Thus, unlike some of the earlier encyclopaedias in larger print formats, the A5 size of van Zuylen's book made it an easy reference guide for listeners to keep at hand and help answer questions they might have while listening. This accessible style of informing and instructing is in line with various efforts up to and during the early twentieth century to exploit the potential of the encyclopaedia for sharing knowledge beyond elite, educated audiences.[264] Yet it also reflects the classic understanding of the encyclopaedia as a tool for knowledge organization and visualization, thereby also asserting an implicit textual authority to its readership.[265] So while its contents demonstrate critical insights into diplomatic tensions with National Socialist Germany in the lead up to 1939, its overall scope reflects a limited view of radio as largely confined to Europe and North America, with the exception of some basic information on Dutch radio services to the Dutch East Indies (now Indonesia) and the kroncong (*krontjong*) music instrument and style.[266]

The effects of European fascism and the Second World War are even more pronounced in the case of *Rádióhallgatók Lexikona* (Radio Listeners' Dictionary), a two-volume publication that was completed in January 1944, whose foreword was written days before Germany's military occupation of Hungary in March 1944.[267] Its subtitle indicates a broad scope that, while intended for radio listeners, went beyond radio and its technology by naming other popular areas of interest, including literature, music, theatre, the gramophone and sport. In contrast to the largely solo effort that characterized van Zuylen's encyclopaedia, the Radio Listeners' Dictionary prominently features a list of over fifty contributing authors, and each entry is clearly credited to an author. This makes for a polyvocal publication, reflecting a diversity of expertise, opinion and (political) orientation.[268] The contributing authors span local writers, journalists and employees of the Hungarian radio through to international radio figures employed in Basel, Paris, Brussels, Warsaw, London and Rome, who most likely delivered their contributions prior to the outbreak of war.[269] The stakes in completing this publication at this tense political moment – just before the mass deportation of Hungarian Jews from May to July 1944 – are highlighted by the presence of several Jewish contributors (including co-editor Géza Falk). Moreover, the completion of this documentation of radio and mass culture for the general public in Hungary took place at a moment when the other major radio programme magazines had been discontinued and against the background of several new political appointments in Hungarian radio's management during 1944.[270]

The radio encyclopaedia is established not just as a site for knowledge dissemination and strategies of popularization, but also for political contention and an effort to document aspects of radio perceived as facing the threat of erasure from the official record in the context of fascist repression. At the same time, the cases of the encyclopaedias from the Netherlands and Hungary also confirm a general trend in which a dominant technical culture of radio had come to accommodate a broader domain of radio and mass culture (e.g., music, film, photography, magazines), which were included as essential knowledge for radio's listening audiences. In the post-1945 period, the overall pursuit of encyclopaedic exhaustiveness in the attempt to 'save' an object of affection against the threat of disappearance has developed into a predominant strategy in fan communities, in producing 'encyclopedic media [which] ... generally take the form of discographies (of records), filmographies (of films), episode guides (of television shows), and similar indexes',[271] a field of practice that will be discussed further in Chapter 3. In the context of contemporary fandoms, the radio encyclopaedia has either been produced for fans of 'old time radio', most visibly in the US context since the 1970s,[272] or, in the case of more recent publications, as historical encyclopaedias intended to help scholars and other interested readers navigate national radio histories,[273] which has also contributed to the prestige accorded to radio as a field of scholarly study with its own readers, handbooks and journals.[274]

This section has covered the exhibition, film and encyclopaedia as facilitators of knowledge production about radio, but also in terms of establishing emotional relations with their (imagined) viewing and reading audiences, whether they were new or established fans of broadcast radio. In some cases, such as film and the encyclopaedia, we've observed a rather unilateral flow of knowledge dissemination, but in the case of the exhibition, we've observed how this format allowed for more interaction between the various overlapping groups that attended these events, including the mass public of visitors. The interactions and sensory engagement of listeners have aided not only top-down pedagogy but also a negotiated domain of radio culture, as audiences have engaged in acts of knowing and affective play.

Intermediality, print and audiovisual culture

As noted in the previous section, the first broadcast systems were established during the early 1920s, a decade that has been credited with the development of an 'intermedial' culture, for which technological experiments were tried out in the fields of recorded sound, broadcasting, cinema and print media. In each of these fields, we can find examples of crossovers and exchange between media, and efforts to approximate (and sometimes imitate) each other's aesthetic conventions and norms.[275] This section turns to the historical emergence of radiophilia with the advent of radio broadcasting systems globally, and the increasing popularity of radio, concomitant with the mass consumption of cinema, recorded music, newspapers and magazines. The main claim of this section is that it is crucial for scholars to understand radio's appeal to its listeners as not merely a 'sonic attraction' but as something generated in tandem with activities such as letter writing and the consumption of print forms, such as radio programme magazines and newspapers that printed radio programme listings. In this manner, various 'paper knowledges'[276] of radio took shape with the participation of readers, and the significance of print cultures for establishing and legitimating fan attachments to and practices around the new medium of radio. Indeed, already during the course of the nineteenth century, newspapers and popular print formats, including serial novels, often employed direct address or a conversational style to heighten a sense of intimacy with their 'dear readers'. Following the advent of modern print culture and the impact of increased literacy, newspapers were a crucial site for the formation of a reading public, who all performed a simultaneous act of reading, contributing to their self-image as participants in a 'mass ritual' shared by an imagined community of readers.[277] While not all listeners of radio were necessarily readers (or literate), as this section will emphasize, acts of writing and reading were crucial factors in the formation of radio's 'listening publics',[278] but especially in terms of the knowledge and information practices developed in tandem with the formation of a strong attachment to radio.

As mentioned previously, the first periodicals directed towards radio enthusiasts that emerged were strongly connected to the 'amateur' culture of radio hobbyists and had a strong focus on new technical developments and inventors. In the context of the United States, we find a subsequent development in which two types of new radio fan magazines developed during the 1920s, with glossy magazines for middle-class audiences released alongside cheaper editions for lower-income listeners. These titles entered a publishing landscape in which popular film magazines had already been established since the 1910s, with the 'pulp' publishing industry issuing titles such as *Photoplay*, *Modern Screen* and *Screen Guide*, along with science fiction, romance and detective magazines.[279] Such popular magazines have been described as generating a 'discourse of empowerment' during the 1910s and 1920s, positioning their readers not only as consumers but as active participants in film celebrity culture and fandom. Film fan magazines encouraged reader interactivity, invited them to engage in a range of activities in which they could 'demonstrate mastery of knowledge about films and stars, to writing letters to ask questions, offering opinions, and even making contact with the stars themselves, to, on occasion, trying to become a star through fan magazine contests'.[280] As such, the magazines trained their readers not only to feel knowledgeable but also gain the sense that their input was valuable, a dynamic that also served to drive sales, with magazine advertisers engaging reader participation by sending in product testimonials and taking part in quizzes and contests.[281] Fan involvement in film culture – and investments in film stars – was encouraged, with various official activities positioned as 'within reach' of its readers, which had concrete economic benefits for the film industry as a whole.

The pre-existing magazine cultures related to both film and amateur radio – with their emphasis on reader interactivity – presumably informed broader expectations among broadcast radio audiences. For instance, many fan letters, preserved today in collections from the early 1920s, demonstrate that even the very early listeners in the US to a station like the independent WGI, outside of Boston, were in response to stations' requesting the listeners' opinions of their programming, and listeners were clearly willing to share information about reception quality and their listening preferences, including music requests.[282] In turn, for early radio stations, prior to the development of audience research methods such as surveys, such listener letters provided a means of estimating, also for the benefit of sponsors, the popularity and reach of their transmissions. In the context of a colonial-government-controlled All India Radio (AIR) during the 1930s, we find examples of listeners writing in as self-professed members of the 'radio-loving public':

> I am exceedingly pleased to congratulate you on the remarkable success that you have so far achieved in placing before the Radio-loving-public [a] varied programme of wireless entertainments from time to time from the Delhi Station ... The reproductions are quite distinctly audible and hence more intelligible than what we receive from other well established stations of India, such as Bombay and Calcutta ... [O]ur deep sense of appreciation may kindly be conveyed also to the officer responsible for such nice entertainment.[283]

This letter, along with those from other listeners in India and internationally in the same 'Our Listeners' section of *The Indian Listener* magazine, sought to praise the reception quality of AIR station transmissions, while also acknowledging the various attractions of the broadcast programmes, from the voice of individual announcers to the music, light entertainment and language choice (Urdu), along with requests for more international programme listings in the magazine.

Even though broadcast radio operated on a one-to-many principle, rather than a two-way exchange, its audiences perceived fan mail as a means to engage in interaction with radio, via its stars, producers, stations or networks. This 'perceived interactivity' via letter writing was often prompted in response to having listened to a programme, and then generally took the form of offering feedback (e.g., compliments, criticism, suggestions and corrections), making requests (e.g., for scripts, factual information, photos) and providing content input (e.g., answers, poems, factual information).[284] These activities are suggestive of the experience of listeners in learning and gaining knowledge via radio, but also an emboldened sense – at least for those who sent letters – of their ability to share feedback and give input, but also make requests and sometimes demands of radio stations.

Letters written to other programmes and stations during the 1920s and 1930s have been shown to similarly use the opportunity to contact performers with intimate modes of address, such as the standard 'Dear Radio Friend' used by fans of WLS Chicago's 'National Barn Dance' programme (starting in 1924), which was intended for Southern migrants and their families, but whose stars received individual letters from the young and old, urban and rural.[285] While the individual letters often expressed private thoughts in the style of correspondence with a friend, from 1935 onwards listeners were also encouraged to contribute letters to the station's fan magazine *Stand By!*:

> [These] letters addressed a broader, more public audience. They included not only the performer, the editors of *Stand By!* and station broadcasters, but also fellow readers and subscribers. Writing, in this case, connected listeners to like-minded people and created an imagined community among reader/listeners, though they did not know each other. The original intent of letters differed, of course. Some writers wrote to announce their favorite artists, others to criticize a program, but their primary goal was to announce themselves as listeners.[286]

Indeed, in the vibrant culture of listener participation in US radio of the 1920s and 1930s, fan magazines were also crucial in how listeners came to terms with the new 'network system' of radio broadcasting. During this period, a number of film magazine editors switched over to working for radio titles, such as *Radio Stars*, *Radio Mirror*, *Radioland* or *Radio Guide*. 'The visual style and print content of the new radio periodicals,' as media scholar Elena Razlogova notes, 'extended the sensational and vivid styles of movie fan and pulp magazines of the period.'[287] Along with a variety of glamorous star pictures on glossy paper, the new radio fan magazines followed the lead of film magazines in prioritizing sensational stories and interactive elements, which were skewed towards a lower-income readership. The film magazine editors who came to lead the new radio magazines during the 1920s and early 1930s introduced 'numerous popular interactive features … audience interviews, quizzes, contests, popularity polls, and expanded letters to the editor departments'.[288] A good illustration of such elements can be found in the rubric employed in answering the questions of listeners, as seen in a *Radio Mirror* series entitled 'What do you want to know?', in which listener questions about certain facts were answered, such as the marital status of stars like popular singer and radio star Rudy Vallée, the full names of radio actors or musical performers, the location of studios, or the correct postal address for fan letters to stars.[289]

Overall, radio magazines were crucial in facilitating audience negotiations with network producers over programmes, and the magazine copies were often consumed – along with radio itself – in sites of sociality and interaction, from public libraries and educational institutions to waiting rooms, cafes and local clubs. However, there was also friction in the exchange between US commercial networks like NBC and the radio fan magazines, who at times worked together in promoting particular network programmes and stars but on other occasions saw a refusal by the networks to facilitate magazine requests for information or involvement in their activities, such as contests. In some cases, broadcasters themselves initiated competitions: for instance, the BBC Arabic Service during the 1930s and 1940s offered poetry and radio play competitions for listeners based in the Arabic-speaking world, with the intention of attracting larger audiences and promoting British interests in the region, but also in order to produce 'user generated content' to help fill the schedules of the service.[290]

While the first broadcast stations in some countries, like Argentina, had been developed with the involvement of newspaper owners and publishers, in other places a strong sense of competition emerged, as was the case in the UK with the establishment of the British Broadcasting Company in 1922 (and later, British Broadcasting Corporation, or BBC).[291] The newspaper industry viewed the new medium with distrust, and took measures to have the new broadcaster restricted in its coverage of news. It was not just that newspapers were wary of the BBC as a competitor for their news coverage, but also that the broadcaster was circumspect about how its activities were covered by the press.[292] From the 1920s to mid-1930s, UK national newspapers started to offer coverage of radio to their readers, leading to the emergence of radio criticism, which had a role in establishing radio as a popular cultural form. The main form of coverage was programme listings and previews, which were modelled on theatre previews, but with the distinction that radio programmes during the 1920s were rarely performed more than once, and those writing previews had to do so without having heard the performance.[293] This press coverage, and in particular, the listings and preview highlights, not only encouraged listeners to consume a national culture of radio, but increasingly, during the 1930s, to become aware of European programmes, mainly in the form of musical concerts and operas. This trend is indicative of how audiences came to rely on newspapers and magazines to guide their listening, with those writing such pieces serving as 'cultural intermediaries, helping the public to understand, evaluate and value radio'.[294] Regular radio columns by UK newspaper critics were common by the early 1930s, with serious or 'quality' newspapers reserving dedicated pages to radio previews, reviews and listings, whereas more popular newspapers tended to combine radio with other popular entertainment such as cinema, with an 'impressionistic textual focused criticism' similar to that found in music, theatre and book reviews at the time.[295] Increasingly, however, newspaper critics started to develop columns that were not only dedicated to programming but also larger questions about the BBC organization, the radio industry, cultural policy and media regulation. This points to an increasing critical attention to radio as a popular medium, with reviews, at least in the popular press, increasingly written in an entertaining manner, seeking to respond the needs of an ever-larger radio listening audience, without excluding the views of broadcasters and cultural elites at the time.

On the whole, the BBC's management, itself holding a public monopoly on broadcasting, did not generally welcome press attention, even if its producers sought various forms of publicity for their work. Yet the BBC did facilitate the establishment of two programme magazines, *The Radio Times* (from 1923) and the more highbrow *The Listener* (from 1929). *The Radio Times* programme magazine was under the jurisdiction of BBC management, who held exclusive rights to print its daily schedule and remained for decades the leading radio (and later television) schedule magazine.[296] Nevertheless, this magazine was the locus of a more popular and interactive relationship with its readership, with popular features, such as a listener letters pages, crosswords and also humorous sketches and cartoons, filling its pages.

An illustrated column entitled 'Both Sides of the Microphone: Radio News and Gossip by "The Broadcasters"' was a regular feature from the late 1920s onwards, and mainly focused on industry news, often related to star announcers.[297] To take an example from the 9 October 1936 edition, the column promoted upcoming programmes with extra 'titbits' about radio feature narratives and the BBC announcers who worked on them, gave updates on BBC television tests with Marconi and EMI, recalled an item from the magazine from 'Ten Years Ago', advised readers on which page the crossword could be found, and noted that the next magazine issue would be an early autumn 'Book Number' issue.[298] The general tone of 'Both Sides' is one of intimate and informal address, in which readers are informed and reminded about 'radio news' and upcoming developments in both the programming schedule and forthcoming magazine issues that they should keep in mind. It demonstrates the pedagogical impulse of such a magazine for its reader by indicating which forms of knowledge they should retain as keen radio listeners, but also fuels the desire of readers to stay 'up to date' and learn more about the 'behind the scenes' of radio production.

Aiming for a popular, approachable and visually-appealing style, *The Radio Times*' editor Maurice Gorham wrote in 1934 that they sought to develop an intimate relation with their readers 'to make what they read there help them to understand and appreciate their broadcast programmes', while also avoiding 'being highbrow'.[299] Its strong emphasis on visual art and graphic design has been noted as a major drawcard for radio fans. A popular account of the publication cited the 9 October 1936 'Humour Number' as capturing the imagination of its readers (see Figure 11). The cover image, created by illustrator John Gilroy, depicted a large Cheshire cat-like face, with an oversized grin, closed eyes and movement stripes on either side to indicate convulsions of laughter. In response, readers were described as having 'carefully cut out the cat face and pasted it to office walls, school [notebooks], and even bits of cardboard to produce cat masks'.[300] This type of fan appropriation is indicative of a broader participatory engagement of readers, who felt encouraged to cut out pages of the magazine; it also reflects the intentional affective appeal of the magazine insofar as the visual images lent themselves to display in homes and workplaces, also

FIGURE 11 *'Humour Number'*, Radio Times, 9 October 1936, cover. Courtesy of Immediate Media.

creating playful objects such as masks to be worn or held up against the face.

If we take a look at this same October 1936 issue of the magazine, now with the shorter title of *Radio Times*, we find a weekly schedule of BBC radio programming for its national and regional services, with no reference to European programme offerings. While the British newspapers had arranged for the magazine's advertising content to be limited to a quota that helped facilitate operating costs, we can find a popular style that addressed readers as consumers not unlike that of the US radio fan magazines noted above. For example, one ad for Lux soap featured the Hollywood film star Bebe Daniels, who had moved to London. The advertisement asks 'Is Coarse Skin spoiling YOUR loveliness?', and shows three shots of Daniels, noting that 'Her beauty fascinates on the screen ... and in private life star Bebe Daniels is just as lovely', with a testimony from Daniels that she uses Lux soap 'at home and in the studio, too'.[301] Overall, there is an emphasis on various forms of knowledge acquisition and self-improvement that would be facilitated through consumer purchases, most of which invited listeners to submit coupons.[302] We find advertisements for radio sets (and batteries), from Ultra Electric, Philips, Every Ready, Philco and Murphy, almost all of which invited readers to clip out and mail coupons for further information. A similar trend can be found with other consumer products, as illustrated by an advertisement by the Cadbury chocolate company with a mail coupon for a free cocoa whisk that could be received if the label from one of their tins was submitted with the coupon.[303]

Many of the feature articles in *Radio Times* are in line with the focus of this issue on humour, and an author gives an overview of over twenty 'favourite radio comedians', written in the reportage style of a radio announcer, and tries to emphasize the style – in writing – of each comedian (in monologue or dialogue style), interspersed with small ink sketches (or photogravures) of each comedian and full-page comedic sketches.[304] In addition, the programme pages are interspersed with cropped photos of popular announcers and musical performers, and programme preview highlights. Such examples suggest the manner by which the *Radio Times* took up a design aesthetic in line with popular illustrated magazines, with readers engaged in a mode of address that sought to be fun and interactive. Unlike the commercial ethos of both magazine publishers and radio networks in the US, however, the *Radio Times* was restricted in its advertising content and subject to BBC management approval and financial control.[305]

From January 1934, BBC publications were faced with a competitor in the popular magazine market: *Radio Pictorial*, a glossy colour radio fan magazine, which covered BBC programmes but soon also included programme listings for its offshore rivals, the commercial popular music stations Radio Luxembourg and Radio Normandy.[306] *Radio Pictorial*'s editor, Bernard Jones, was well known for editing the early amateur magazines *Amateur Wireless* (from 1922) and *Wireless Magazine* (from 1924). In anticipation of *Radio Pictorial*'s launch in January 1934, Jones included a two-page advertisement in *Amateur Wireless*, which promised to 'bring to life the unseen artists and personalities of the broadcasting world ... 40 pages of intimate stories – by and about famous stars – exclusive articles and fascinating photographs'.[307] *Radio Pictorial* was marked by the absence of technical articles with diagrams typical of the male-oriented market of amateur and science experimenter magazines, and this development has been understood as reflective of a shift to addressing the growing domestic audience of radio by the early 1930s, by which time the self-made receiver had become 'a comparative rarity'.[308] From the first issue onwards, *Radio Pictorial* offered readers crayon portraits of key radio personalities, starting with BBC dance band leader Henry Hall, with the second issue featuring 'radio DJ' Christopher Stone, subsequently praised in a listener letter, which explained that they had cut it out and placed it in a photo frame, noting that 'by now [Stone] seems just like one of the family'.[309] The listener, from the working-class East End of London, compliments the magazine for including a 'simply splendid' free portrait, while also noting the emotive attachment to the presenter, who was well known for his accessible presentation style and popular music programming, as Chapter 4 will discuss in further detail. As part of the strong emphasis on the attractiveness of stars, *Radio Pictorial* readers were also encouraged to purchase postcard-size photographs of (mainly British) radio stars from the magazine, along with albums to hold these portraits in.[310] The more 'commercial' approach in the magazine was also reflected in the content of stations like Radio Luxembourg, which not only featured advertising spots but also programmes with competitions and money prizes.[311]

Jones's editorial for the first issue of 'Radio Pic' – as it immediately nicknamed itself – in 1934 further stressed the inclusion of prominent 'radio names' as contributors and that it would aim to give a visual supplement to radio's 'great invisible world ... now made visible for your eyes to dwell upon and to add pleasure to your listening'.[312] The magazine targeted a (female) lower middle- and working-class market, although it probably drew a wider pool of readers, given its unique status in the UK as a radio 'fan' magazine and in sharing European programme listings. For the roughly five years of its existence, until 1939, *Radio Pictorial* featured a significant amount of non-radio content in line with women's magazines at this time:

> [It] was launched as a twopenny, in addition to the instruction and knitting patterns, it carried advertisements for dressing on a budget, for example '"Smartwear" How to dress well on 10/ or £1 per month', and sold itself on romantic escapist fiction. ... Unlike the BBC magazines, which saw their role as guiding public taste, *Radio Pictorial* set about catering for the public's wants and ministering to its desires. Variously sub-titling itself 'The Family Magazine' and 'The Magazine for Every Listener' ... *Radio Pictorial* was inclusive and gave its readers what they wanted: fashion tips and etiquette advice, lots of glamorous, smiling photographs of the stars, romantic stories, and plenty of views 'behind the scenes' and backstage gossip.[313]

The publication was the first of its kind to attend to British radio listeners as fans and address their popular preferences: from the earliest months of its publication, *Radio Pictorial* encouraged reader participation in the form of letters to allow readers to 'voice' their opinions about radio programming and possible improvements, thereby marking a departure from, and occasional opposition to, the highbrow aspirations of the BBC.

The BBC's more highbrow title *The Listener* has been examined by a number of scholars who have pursued an 'intermedial periodical studies' approach, considering the relations between radio, film and magazines.[314] Launched in 1929, *The Listener* appeared in weekly instalments that usually included a number of edited texts from talks aired on the BBC, and after its first year of publication, had a stable yet smaller circulation than *Radio Times*. Under the leadership of editor Richard S. Lambert, who was similarly invested in the BBC's mandate to facilitate public education and cultural uplift, the magazine was involved in a series of booklet publications, *Aids to Study*, intended as an education support for BBC programming.[315] To take an example of the 14 October 1936 issue of *The Listener* (the same period as the *Radio Times* example discussed above), we find the 'Early Autumn Book Supplement' alongside regular items such as poetry, lecture transcripts, crosswords, letters from listeners, and a weekly programme guide. The publication was somewhat restricted in being subject to BBC official approval of its content,[316] although there is evidence of a more popular style of content, such as a regular photo series entitled 'Radio News-Reel', which used photo collage and a reportage style to cover recent local and international news, and diverse advertising content, ranging from radio headsets and furniture to medicine and cosmetics, book series and educational courses. Its content reflects an engagement with readers by soliciting their participation in filling in crosswords and writing in with their opinions about radio programmes, enabling them to amass an up-to-date knowledge of cultural developments in music, cinema and literature and participate in contemporary consumer culture as recipients of advertisement content. Despite such participatory features, the magazine's educational impulse was in keeping with fears of cultural elites at the time about dominant values being threatened, and reflected a highbrow, if not top-down, notion of knowledge transfer to its readership.[317]

The Listener operated at the interstices of the press, broadcasting and the film industry, with its weekly publication responding to the rhythms of broadcast schedules but also to the release schedules of new films appearing in local cinemas.[318] The magazine's film criticism during the period 1929–35, led by editor Richard S. Lambert, also linked to the formation of the British Film Institute and the quarterly film journal *Sight and Sound*, for which a 'serious' or 'intelligent' cinephilia was encouraged, which focused on film as an art form, educational aid or an industry,[319] rather than emphasize Hollywood star culture and gossip, as was typical of the more popular US-based fan magazines, noted above. Nonetheless, by the mid-1930s *The Listener*'s film criticism devoted a growing attention to film narratives and star actors. Magazines such as this thereby served as 'mediators' in their engagement with broadcasting and film, remediating and adapting the content of non-print media that was combined with other forms of content, such as advertising, within the magazine framework.

The above accounts are in keeping with a study led by Austrian sociologist Paul Lazarsfeld, who led the Radio Research Project in the mid-1930s, first at Princeton University, then at Columbia

University in New York. In his 1940 book *Radio and the Printed Page*, Lazarsfeld reported on the results of his recent audience survey about the relationship between radio consumption and reading practices in the home. In his discussion of the results, Lazarsfeld reflected on the possible negative impacts of radio on listener's reading habits, seeking to assess which factors (such as formal education) also played a role, for instance in the preference for particular content (e.g., serials) in radio as opposed to in printed form.[320] This research has been described as discovering that 'the experience of listening to radio was impossible to bracket completely from the experience of reading printed texts, and [arguing] that the growth of radio (and later television) broadcasting took place within the context of a vibrant reading culture'.[321] Lazarsfeld's research did not attend to intermedial relations, nor did its concept of reading fully take into account radio listening in tandem with radio-specific magazines; however, it does reveal a scholarly interest in radio listening taking place in conjunction with other forms of media literacy and consumption.

In the European context, the rise of film fan magazines in the 1920s and 1930s was strongly intertwined with the birth of a participatory cinephilic culture. With a similar attachment to the 'picture personalities'[322] from the emergent star system in the United States, building on a culture of theatre stars before it, European film magazines have been read as adopting a pedagogical project for cinemagoers to 'learn how to love' the cinema, in their urging of readers to become experts on cinema, to understand its workings, to gain a hands-on knowledge of (amateur) filmmaking, to develop evaluative skills, to establish film clubs and to correspond with film stars. 'The pleasures of knowing' the magazines modelled for its readers therefore centred upon 'interactions with film technology and aesthetics, the look "behind the screen," the unveiling of technical secrets, as well as the loves of film stars'.[323] Play was posited as an essential part of filmic education, and during the 1920s magazines increasingly adopted a 'playful' style, in particular the layout used for photo reproductions and collages. Among the many types of participatory rubrics, film puzzle contests served as means of eliciting reader participation, affective processes and pedagogical instruction of 'learning to love' the cinema. This is in keeping with a notion that readers' development of a love and knowledge of cinema was not a solely individual pursuit, with magazines urging readers 'to love film art and to *share* that love with others'.[324] Such features have been considered from the perspective of audience interaction and the participatory culture of early radio magazines, although more could be said in that literature about the particular look and feel of these magazine elements, or the haptic and affective engagement with such objects of consumer culture.

This individual and intersubjective dimension to the facilitation of radiophilia was indicated in the previous discussion of radio magazines, although with a stronger attention to not just the visual gaze and photography, but also the engagement with a modern auditory culture. We find a similar trend in the connection between the visual, haptic and sonic in early film cultures in Japan, which has been treated in tandem with early anime fandom, which served as an important bridge between graphic novel reading and cinematic viewing.[325] In studies of modern Japanese culture, the thick traffic between film and visual culture, particularly for the early 1920s to 1945, has been described in terms of a 'promiscuous' media, as located in 'intermediality (intersection and interaction between film and painting, between live-action film and animation, and among film, photography, painting, and radio) [and] cross-genre fluidity (between documentary and dramatic films)'.[326] Significantly, while early Japanese film magazines foregrounded the *benshi* (live narrator) as an attraction for audiences, by the mid-1920s – following the advent of radio broadcasts in Japan – their performances also were in demand in radio, for commercial gramophone recordings and in the theatre.[327] This emergent cross-medial stardom had a distinct influence on the early aesthetic development of radio in Japan, since film-related programmes featured prominently in radio broadcasting schedules, along with news, entertainment and cultural programming. In the 1920s and 1930s, a significant genre of radio emerged called *eiga monogatari* (film stories, narrated by the *benshi*), and subsequently in the *eigageki* (film dramas) in which film actors performed dialogue from upcoming film releases, with the accompaniment of musical and *benshi* narration. In the period prior to synchronized sound film, radio significantly 'diversified the cinematic sound space', allowing for the voices of actors, narrators, musical songs and themes to be heard by audiences of silent cinema. However, with the transition to synchronized sound, there was an overall shift in which the 'sonic attraction' shifted in cinema 'from the benshi's voice to theme songs and the actors' voices'.[328] The participation of newspapers in the extensive coverage of radio drama narratives, theme songs and lyrics (and star images of *benshi* and actors) was already significant from the launch of radio in March 1925, as within a few months the *Nikkan Rajio Shinbun* (Daily Radio Times) had started, and all major newspapers had radio sections initiated within the first year of radio. However, these early film genres in radio gradually disappeared following film sound synchronization, along with *benshi* narration, and radio stations instead opted to have live broadcasts of imported 'talkie' films (*talkie chūkei*) from the mid-1930s. Nonetheless, this cinematic sound space, developed outside of cinema, facilitated a significant space for creative sound production and allowed for new forms of audience participation in the consumption of storytelling across cinema, radio and newspaper radio sections, as well as via commercial phonograph records.

The cross-medial practices developed by fans in connecting their listening experiences to reading and writing practices continued well into the post-war era of radio, gaining significance with cross-border listening in a Cold War Europe after 1945, and, in other places, such as Australia and Indonesia, up to the 2000s.[329] What is striking is that there has been a strong representation of listeners from rural or regional areas, rather than urban ones, engaging in postcard- and letter-writing practices.[330] In the Indonesian case, the integration of the on-air reading of handwritten or typed paper messages presents 'a complex multidirectional interchange of messages', intended as greetings issued to the letter-writer's 'own radio-centred social network', often using pseudonyms.[331] The act of writing to radio stations, as demonstrated in the All India Radio (Vividh Bharati) station in Mumbai, India, from the mid-1950s to the mid-1970s, served as a crucial interface between film, radio and audition, since the majority of *pharmaish* (request postcards) were almost all focused on Hindi film songs.[332] Having first been heard via Radio Ceylon (Sri Lankan Broadcast Company), due to a ban on broadcasting film music between 1952 and 1957, listeners subsequently returned to All India Radio stations that started to regularly play this repertoire, and developed a host of request-oriented programmes at the Mumbai station. While the musical register of film love songs had a strong pull for listeners, the attraction of writing requests was to then listen out for one's own name, insofar as 'the intensity of the desire to hear one's name on air was a desire for recognition'.[333] The reading-out of the *pharmaish* brought with it the potential for regional listeners and listening communities to experience a sense of recognition, of being 'on the map', but having the announcer read out a listener's name and message also served to connect the listener to the same space as the announcer, generating a sense of closeness and intimacy. The *pharmaish* situated the request writer at the interstices of the love of radio and that of cinema, with fan magazines guiding this practice with 'best practice' guidelines, thereby affirming and codifying this affective practice into appropriate contours, to some degree trying to contain its excess of affect.[334]

Conclusion

This chapter has covered various aspects of how a strong attachment to, or love of, radio was bound up with knowledge practices. The first part focused on the forging of an amateur culture of radio from the 1910s and 1920s, which established particular practices and cultural norms around radio as a technical hobby, as well as a spirit of radio enthusiasm encouraged by early wireless magazines. In particular, it examined forms of self-organization, such as radio clubs, initiated within amateur circles that provided a framework for amateur radio communities, including workshops for hands-on building and repair of radio sets and access to publications, manuals and events facilitating knowledge acquisition around radio. At the same time, it drew attention to the process by which wireless operators who were women or non-white have frequently been underrepresented in the historical narrative of amateur radio, and who, despite radio's ethos of egalitarianism, were often not actively encouraged to participate in amateur radio culture.

Maintaining this critical insight, the second section further investigated institutional or 'authoritative' knowledge practices in tandem with the popularization of radio broadcasting among a broader audience in the 1920s and 1930s. Having first acknowledged the significant state and commercial investment in radio research and development from around 1900, this section investigated three domains of knowledge production that sought to guide a growing affective attachment to, and understanding of, broadcast radio: radio films, radio exhibitions and radio encyclopaedias. The examination of radio films primarily focused on the early promotional films about radio, which tried to promote radio listening as a pleasurable, and especially domestic, activity. These films various sought to explain radio's technical principles, encourage radio receiver sales, show 'behind the scenes' of production and create intermedial experiments between radio, sound recording and film. In the German case, as shown, some radio films were created for, shown at or documented the annual radio exhibition held in Berlin between 1924 and 1939. The radio exhibition itself, while originating from, and maintaining a strong link to, professional industry and amateur communities, has been shown to provide a key infrastructure for popularizing radio and making knowledge about it accessible to a larger public via forms of interaction, display, pedagogical strategies and sensory appeal via the auditory, the visual and the tactile.

While helping to fuel the popular attachment to radio, the radio exhibition can also be understood as to be part of the 'exhibitionary complex' of the 1920s and 1930s, bound up with expressions of national pride, imperial power and, in National Socialist Germany, fascist ideology. This section also drew attention to the knowledge generated by radio publics around the world in connection with the postcard image of broadcast buildings and transmission towers as highly-circulated icons of radio modernity. This attention to the knowledge produced, circulated and negotiated via the print culture of radio is maintained with the final case of the radio encyclopaedia, which considered the form, address and organization of this print-based genre, beginning with the amateur wireless era and guides intended for a wider audience of radio fans in the broadcast era, through to its use for 'old time' radio documentation and more recently, facilitating historical scholarship in radio studies. It highlighted questions about authorship and textual authority, but also knowledge politics related to radio encyclopaedias that were banned or had a fragile existence in the context of the Second World War, as their authors sought to preserve a vision of radio's creative and popular cultures threatened by fascism and military occupation in Europe.

The final section took up the question of knowledge and the love of radio by further delving into the role of writing and print media for popular engagements with radio. The first part zoomed in on the 'perceived interactivity' experienced by audiences through letter writing from the early broadcast period onwards, which was, in turn, encouraged by broadcasters. Letter writing offers a sense of how audience members engaged with radio, its content and its performers, as their object of affection. It also showed how fan letter writing – especially to magazines and radio stations – functioned as an act of knowledge gathering and sharing, and variously provided a space for private emotions and public recognition, for instance in the case of contests or music requests. The second part devoted further attention to the emergence of radio coverage in print media, and the rise of the radio fan magazine, in the case of US and UK, as a crucial site for facilitating – through text and visual image – the popular engagement with fan-oriented knowledge cultures of the 1920s and 1930s onwards. It also took note of the phenomenon of the listener letter addressed to a station, to those involved in their programming (both announcers and performers), or to radio fan magazines, from the earliest period of radio until at least the 2000s. The huge volume of listener letters spanning the decades since radio's advent signals the letter not simply as a site of communication, exchange and knowledge in the affection for radio, but especially its ephemerality as having been largely discarded after its immediate use had passed.[335] It is precisely these dynamics of discarding and neglect and the impulse for saving the 'ephemeral' traces of radio that will be the central topic of the next chapter.

This chapter has considered various sites, practices and media forms in which knowledge production and dissemination took place in tandem with the affection for and engagement with radio. Read here as affective practices, these processes were crucial in facilitating emotional communities related to radio. The chapter has primarily attended to examples drawn from the early decades of wireless and broadcast radio, while acknowledging the legacy of certain objects, genres or practices related to the love of radio for the post-war era. The remaining chapters of this study, on 'saving' and 'sharing', will cover a longer period, up to the present, and will include consideration of how radiophilia has fared with the advent of narrowcasting and digital culture, and how individual and collective practices of memory, nostalgia and preservation deal with radio's status as an 'old' and yet 'resilient' and renewed medium.[336]

3

Saving

I strongly wish that after their invention of the radio the bourgeoisie would make a further invention that enables us to fix for all time what the radio communicates.

BERTOLT BRECHT[337]

Professional broadcast archivist Laura LaPlaca started acquiring broadcast memorabilia at a young age, starting with a pair of shoes belonging to a famous presenter and growing to a collection of over 3,500 pieces by the time she finished high school. In 2015 she described the process:

> As I accumulated each one, I polished it, and labeled it, and learned its story. The history of broadcasting, as I knew it, grew wider and deeper along with the piles on my bedroom floor. The material relationship I developed with broadcast history as a collector and, eventually, as a media archivist in more formal settings, leads me to balk a little bit when I hear the radio and television archive referred to as 'ephemeral' ... [W]e tend to emphasize ephemerality to such a degree that we do not discuss the broadcast archive's extraordinarily expansive physicality at all. Its size and weight, as well as the infrastructures – both physical and intellectual – that support it, too often go unremarked upon.[338]

LaPlaca reflects on her own process of taking care of her newly-acquired items (often purchased via eBay), labelling them according to her own system and trying to find out more about their origin. This intimate, hands-on ritual performed in the act of acquiring each item for her personal collection can also be read as an act of preservation, in seeking to save and care for objects of broadcast history. In objecting to the use of the term 'ephemeral' in reference to broadcast archives, LaPlaca suggests that this undue emphasis comes at the expense of recognizing the vast and substantial material traces that can be found in archival spaces, as well as circulating beyond formal institutions.[339] This observation, moreover, points to the predominant sound-focused understanding of 'radio heritage' as limiting and that it may even obscure other types of radio-related objects and their histories.

As noted earlier, the love of radio has generally been expressed through a regular, sometimes daily, practice of listening to radio. The routine quality of broadcasting was established 'in order to produce and deliver an all-day everyday service that is ready-to-hand and available anytime at the turn of a switch or the press of a button', and achieved via the 'routinization of programme schedules and the serialization of production'.[340] However, this regular consumption of radio, with a certain uneventful, quotidian quality, might be understood as a pattern of forgetting and then consuming once more, rather than of saving. This relationship of renewal is perhaps best illustrated by long-running programmes such as *The Archers* (BBC, 1951–present), which in its persistent presence enacts a process of *not* losing an attachment to characters and stories. The structure of 'continuous serial' programmes – due to a strong sense of anticipation since the storyline events continue to unfold – certainly invites a certain forgetting or dispensing with the past on the part of its listeners. Nonetheless, there is still a strong investment by producers and audiences in memory practices centred on the series, as illustrated by the series' recent seventieth anniversary, for which a collection of seventy objects were curated, including fan creations such as a cardigan listing key names and locations in the series, and a collectively knitted map of Ambridge (the fictional setting of the series).[341] While a self-organized fan culture exists for the series, its producers, too, have embedded additional content on their website, such as clips, podcasts, character lists, a blog and features, including a summary of 1,500 Twitter answers from listeners to the question 'Why did you start listening to *The Archers?*'[342] So, even when a long-running serial has a future-oriented structure as its narrative unfolds each day, its listeners' attachment to the programme is narrated and filtered through their own memories, and its cult status also elicits active forms of saving amongst its fans and those involved in its production.

Across much of the radio century, we can observe a radiophilic desire to find ways to capture the material traces of radio. The present chapter will delve further into how social and institutional actors have sought, in various ways, to keep or save radio. The central question addressed concerns how to 'hang on' to the thing you love, which is, in this case, radio. This impulse is often sparked by the perception of radio's sound transmissions as being ephemeral, and sometimes in reaction to the threat of destruction, devaluation or neglect. A radiophilic impulse may prompt acts of saving at the time a programme is made, yet the desire to save radio may develop over time as both listeners and makers start to look back and cherish past radio. Theoretically, the chapter is interested in how the desire to save radio for posterity underscores the temporal dimension of radiophilia and, in turn, notions of history, memory and heritage value. It takes into account the 'life cycle' of radio's traces, whether this pertains to analogue or digital recordings, documents or physical objects, and asks what kinds of dynamics of neglect, decay or discarding are at work, and how the 'loving' acts of saving are bound up with revaluation and legitimation.[343]

Even though the terms 'radio collection' or 'radio archive' are generally taken to refer to sound recordings, we will start here instead with a first section that considers *non-sound* objects or traces of radio. In this domain, we often find attachments to 'memorable' radio events, objects or devices, with a range from dedicated practices of creating various forms of documentation via photography, QSL cards and inventories through to scrapbooks, diaries, letters or fan authorship. The second and third sections will attend to efforts to record and preserve the *sounds* of radio transmissions. The former will examine amateur and non-institutional practices that have emerged over the past century, as radio lovers became radio sound collectors by storing and circulating radio sounds, with the aid of recording technologies, and acts of organized collection, selection and curation. As the analysis will show, these practices materially connected radio consumption to sound recording, editing, storage and distribution, ranging from private spaces to organized settings, from the sporadic to the dedicated, and across analogue and digital media cultures. The third and final section will attend to the forms of collecting or recording practised within the institutional framework of broadcasters or related organizations, with a radiophilic desire to 'keep' radio by making off-air recordings and establishing archives for facilitating both programme production and historic preservation. Overall, the chapter is interested in how practices of saving serve to bestow value and significance on radio, thus sharpening our consideration of the radiophilic impulse to keep or preserve radio with insights from studies into collecting, memory and material culture.

Saving non-sound traces of radio

This section will examine various efforts to save paper-based traces (or small souvenir objects) related to radio, before turning to the saving of built structures and finally to technological devices, primarily receivers, with reflections on the online activities devoted to acts of saving radio-related heritage.

LaPlaca rightly emphasizes the material traces of the institutional broadcast archive, and when we consider the private collections of listeners, we may consider their personal nature, especially when strongly related to a love of radio. The personal collections amassed by individual listeners often reflect a specified fandom or attachment to radio, whether that be a particular programme, announcer/performer, station or type of object, such as a radio receiver. Indeed, some collectors develop specific taxonomical interests, whereas others collect guided by a broader scope of 'anything related to radio'.[344] The emergence of radio during the 1920s and 1930s overlapped with the idea that collecting as a hobby could be a form of 'serious leisure'; against this background, some radio fans kept related objects as children or (young) adults and only later came to see them as worth 'saving' in a more formalized manner within personal collections.[345] While collecting has been seen as removing objects from their usual setting and function as consumer goods, its historical emergence coincides with that of modern consumer culture:

> [C]ollecting is an act of production as well as consumption. Collectors create, combine, classify, and curate the objects they

acquire in such a way that a new product, the collection, emerges. In the process they also produce meanings. More precisely, they participate in the process of socially reconstructing shared meaning for the objects they collect.[346]

This observation points to the manner by which collectors develop ways of ordering their collections, subjecting the objects to 'ordering rules' based on individual preference and in dialogue with others.[347]

In turn, a life cycle perspective emphasizes collecting as often taking place at a younger age, as well as in later life since, for instance, retirement-age radiophiles potentially have more time (and resources) to take up an active engagement in collecting and preservation. In this context, the personal collection, in some cases acquired during youth, often serves as a springboard for developing broader collections related to 'radio history', including materials actively sought out from others, or via flea markets, antique shops or (online) auctions.

While some collectors may intend to acquire radio-related objects with the intention to resell them, one of key factors motivating much radio collecting since the post-war era is a belief in radio as having a crucial socio-political and historical importance, and thereby cultural value, which serves as an important justification for acts of 'saving' radio through collection. In a similar vein, book collectors, or bibliophiles, have been found to seek acceptability for their collecting by emphasizing the importance of their collections based on their serious content and interest to scholarly researchers, thereby trying to gain legitimation for their attachment and 'highly-involving passionate consumption' based on the rationale of 'forming a collection that may be of real value to the scholar of the future'.[348] However, while the book or art collector may take advantage of the social validation of 'high culture', the objects collected in tandem with radiophilia can potentially come from a broad range of collectibles spanning announcer signatures and car bumper stickers through to 'highbrow' magazines and publications. Another motivating factor for collecting may also be the (perceived) disinterest of formal heritage institutions in certain aspects of the material cultures of radio history in their collections, whereby a perceived neglect and loss can motivate individuals to establish a collection devoted to the general history or a particular aspect of radio, such as local, regional or language-specific radio.[349]

QSL postcards remain one of the prominent and popular early souvenirs from personal radio collections, and they have gained a strong online prominence, with digital galleries and tributes created by amateur radio history organizations (see Figures 1–3 discussed in Chapter 2). Yet there are many other objects that were saved and invested with personal meaning across the century of radio. The 'Australian Old Time Radio' website, set up by a group of volunteers, recently offered an account of the main categories of memorabilia in the Australian context, as divided between 1) 'Advertising memorabilia' (merchandise or giveaways to listeners); and 2) 'Radio station or radio people' memorabilia that had previously belonged to a station or its employees. The website's author explains that there are some overlaps, but that the majority of these objects are print-based materials made of paper or cardboard, its wide range suggestive of the scope of items collected for early Australian radio history.[350] The webpage includes a photo gallery with several examples of items collected by the author, which all provide insights into particular key moments of the first decades of Australian radio and the involvement of listeners in radio.

The author points out that the two main categories noted above are a contrast to the official items issued by the Australian stations' radio clubs, such as pins, badges or membership certificates, which are also sought-after items for radio collectors. Websites created by collectors and amateur radio historians are replete with stories about the treasured souvenirs of childhood membership of the Argonauts Club, linked to a radio programme of the same name aimed at the under-eighteen age group, which ran between the early 1930s and early 1970s. For the cost of a stamp, children and teenage listeners could send in a request for membership, after which they received a metal badge with green enamelling and a certificate (see Figures 12 and 13), with their signed pledge as new members read out by the presenters on the programme.[351] Additional souvenirs could be acquired, since 'as a reward for sending in drawings, stories and poems that were marked and could be read out on-air, they would earn points to be admitted to [the] "Order of the Dragon's Tooth" and then the "Order of the Golden Fleece"'.[352] In some cases, these narratives link the ownership of these items to their radio fandom, while other accounts explain the anguish of having lost these prized possessions. Despite an estimated membership of at least 100,000 at its peak, it is likely that only a fraction of these

FIGURE 12 *Argonauts Club membership badge issued by the ABC (Australian Broadcasting Corporation). Courtesy of the State Library of South Australia.*

radio fan souvenirs were kept or saved, while others were discarded or passed into the antiquarian circuit, as evidenced by one institutional acquisition of radio badges in 2019 which had been found at an illegal rubbish dumping spot in Australia.[353] The badges had been arranged together by a previous owner on a piece of cardboard; and yet they may have subsequently been perceived as worthless by the person who discarded them, which is suggestive of a general logics of waste and devaluation, often as the original owners pass away.

This phenomenon generates a broader insight that radio badges, issued in a commercial media landscape alongside newspaper,

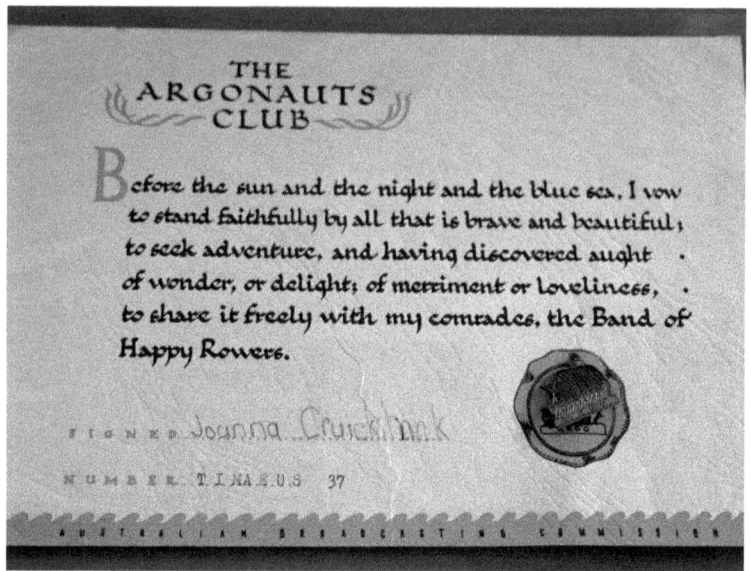

FIGURE 13 *ABC radio Argonauts Club certificate with a badge attached, including the membership number (ship name and oar number). Courtesy of Jo Featherston (Cruickshank).*

cinema and television badges, served as souvenirs for special events, prizes, fundraisers or club membership, and sometimes as advertiser giveaways, which were coveted for a time (sometimes a lifetime) but also often discarded as the owner lost interest in club membership or as time elapsed since the original relevance of the pin, which – along with their ubiquity – also serves to explain their prevalence in collector circuits.[354] We find a similar interest in ephemeral media connected to radio with the strong focus on radio programme magazines both in amateur radio history circles, which are extensively curated on websites like World Radio History, and as prominent features of collector circles and online auction websites like eBay. Those passionately invested in collecting often set themselves in a heroic role as saving radio from loss or neglect, a tendency that will also be discussed in the final part of this chapter on archivists in professional contexts. This investment has been considered as reflecting two different types of collector, demonstrating either an 'agapic' love for the object, which can take the form of an altruistic 'selfless love' of dedication to the object, or an 'eros' attachment, in which a particular interest, belief or desire of the collector is projected onto a particular theme: in this case, radio history.[355]

An important dimension to radio fan and audience practices is not just how they collect paper-based items, but how they appropriate them into new forms as part of a (self-)identification as fans of radio, or of particular stations, types of programming or stars. In recent years, attention has been drawn to the practice of scrapbooking as part of modern fandom, particularly on the part of young women as fans of theatre and cinema in the period from around 1900 onwards.[356] In this period, scrapbooks were encouraged in media discourse as an ideal way for girls and women to record their cultural interests and experiences, and prompted them to exchange items with each other such as postcards and newspaper cuttings.[357] The scrapbook allowed individual fans to 'save' their individual emotional experiences, also shared with friends, and reveals the scrapbook as a memory practice that documented passionate attachments to particular stars and cultural forms. In the case of radio, there is scant evidence remaining today, but the earliest scrapbooks appear to have overlapped with the logbook documentation of early amateurs, with a strong presence of QSL card collections as paper ephemera that needed to be organized and which serve as souvenirs of amateur radio correspondence. For example, a scrapbook from an amateur radio enthusiast held by a university library in the US state of Maine was mainly comprised of 1930s and 1940s QSL cards, but also included some other souvenirs and a transmissions log.[358] Another early scrapbook covering the period 1914 to 1945 was created by amateur radio enthusiast Lyndon Seefred in San José, California, the first half of which is a handwritten log of all transmission for an eighteen-month period in 1914–15, while the other half is a scrapbook of news clippings, postcards and other mementos related to radio, with some more personal and family documentation mixed in.[359]

In the broadcast era, radio employees often kept scrapbooks about their own press coverage or with letters and art from their fans, but there are examples remaining today of scrapbooks made between the 1930s and the 1990s, many of which have been preserved thanks to the efforts of radio history initiatives or amateur enthusiast circles.[360] For instance, it is possible to examine a radio fan scrapbook on the Radio Heritage website, originally made by teenage listener Elsie Orams (from Auckland, New Zealand) using a stationer-issued 'Public School Scribbling Book'.[361] In this fifty-page scrapbook, there are cut-outs of newspaper portraits and sketches of New Zealand radio personalities, organized between radio stations (1ZM, 1ZB, ZB), along with whole pages cut out of programme magazines, and news items about particular stars as they created programmes, got married or visited sick listeners.[362] A later example of a radio scrapbooking practice can also be found in New Zealand, with pre-fabricated scrapbooks with titles such as 'School Project Drawing Book' or 'Cuttings Book – News Scraps' for the period covering 1988–97.[363] One amateur radio website describes the discovery of a scrapbook by a fellow radio enthusiast from the Isle of Man, UK, in terms of saving heritage: 'The scrapbook should be in a museum, instead of being thrown out or ripped apart, I am very grateful that I managed to grab it before it got lost forever.'[364] As this and the above examples indicate, scrapbooks have a scarce presence, mainly preserved by radio history groups such as Radio Heritage, or by heritage institutions, such as university libraries, where the scrapbook was incidentally included as part of a personal papers acquisition rather than as an intentionally gathered cultural genre. Yet they offer a resource for observing how radio enthusiasts and fans assembled paper-based ephemera associated with, for instance, their involvement in amateur radio, or their attachment to particular radio stations and their stars, using paper, scissors and glue to assemble and reassemble information and souvenirs that they had access to and found relevant.

In tandem with efforts to save or keep radio via print materials and objects possessed, one of the strong attachments of radiophilia and the desire to 'keep' radio has been related to the built environment. Over time, some early radio infrastructures – like radio buildings, transmitter towers or public loudspeaker systems – were reused by new political orders following war and occupation, such as in the case of the present-day city of Wrocław, Poland (formerly Breslau, Germany), whose radio building has been in almost permanent use since it was first established in 1925.[365] Indeed across radio culture, radio infrastructures such as large-scale towers, offered a monumental scale when contrasted to that of the private radio receiver, whether a domesticated piece of furniture, a transistor or a self-build kit:

The miniature was domestic, it was the contrast to the tower – the miniature was personal and private to the tower's public, authoritative position. To continually miniaturize the wireless receiver was to make it blend with the home. And the smaller the wireless and the less 'towering' it seemed, the more it resembled everyday life, ever-increasing its apparent necessity.[366]

Here the process by which the monumental towers of the 1920s and 1930s gradually became eclipsed in the modern metropolis is considered against the process of miniaturization, which can be found in the transistor radio from the 1950s onwards, and personal stereos (e.g., the Walkman) from the 1970s, through to the present-day mobile phone as a portable wireless receiver. In this sense, the gradual obsolescence of the historical radio tower can be read against miniaturized wireless technologies that have displaced its previous authority; meanwhile, a heritage perspective is often applied to remaining media infrastructures, whether they are situated at the (former) heart of urban 'media capitals' or on their outskirts.[367]

A useful illustration of the effort to save and revalue radio's built structures can be found in the remaining 'radio towers' installed in public parks and schools in Japan during the 1930s and early 1940s that have been read as 'overlooked and sometimes misconstrued pieces of public heritage' (see Figure 14).[368] These concrete radio towers have now begun to gain the attention of local organizations who have started to explore possibilities for their preservation and reactivation of their previous use for radio calisthenics in the present day. A 2017 article about this initiative included of photograph of two older men looking admiringly at the radio tower, with one of them touching the concrete structure in a gesture of affection for these previously ubiquitous features of public radio integrated into everyday spaces like parks, which were bound up in the politics of the public exercise routines in pre-1945 imperial Japan.[369]

Amateur radio enthusiasts contributing to online websites frequently offer accounts of the history of past radio buildings. A good example can be found in a recent article by radio enthusiast and alternative radio founder Martín Butera, who is based in Brazil. Writing for the Radio Heritage website's 'Co-operative Global Radio Memories' project, Butera's historical account focuses on the Joseph Gire building, the historical home and headquarters of

FIGURE 14 *Radio tower (ラジオ塔) in Nakamura Park, Nagoya City, Japan, 6 September 2017. Photo by Mr Chikurin.*

Brazil's Rádio Nacional in Rio de Janeiro, which in 2020 was sold by the state to a private investor and currently has the status of 'a colossal abandoned building'.[370] The article describes the discarding of this important site by state authorities, given its significance in Brazilian media history as first the location for the *A Noite* newspaper, then host to the national radio. It also acknowledges its status as architectural heritage, having been the highest and most 'modern' skyscraper in Brazil at the time of its unveiling, a tourist attraction which was given 'national heritage site' status by the Federal Heritage Office.[371] This history is accompanied by several photos of Butera standing outside and looking at the abandoned art deco building, along with another photo in which he is shown touching a plaque (see Figures 15 and 16). This affective gesture, of touching the plaque, which he notes is 'the only [remaining] memory that shows that a station existed there',[372] is suggestive of the desire to physically reconnect with the history of the building. Against the disappointment at the abandonment and neglect of the building, the article reflects an attempt to reinscribe significance and meaning to this radio building, through offering examples and photos of historical programming innovated in the station's studios, such as soap operas or musical performances, and sharing images of the station's afternoon concerts that were eagerly attended by radio fans.[373]

We can find two other striking examples of the passionate commitment of audiences and fan communities to the preservation of built infrastructures of past radio, which attest to the strong emotional dimension to practices of radio preservation and how such impulses relate to the material physicality of past radio production spaces. The first example is in Brussels, Belgium, at the former headquarters of the national broadcaster INR-NIR, commonly referred to as the 'Maison de la Radio' (house of radio).[374] While this modernist, purpose-built building had been widely praised upon its unveiling for its architectural design, by the mid-1990s it was empty and run down, having been abandoned following a gradual migration to a larger facility completed in the mid-1970s.[375] A campaign by a group of cultural and heritage professionals – using posters, letter writing and a listing on the World Monument Watch – succeeded in convincing local authorities to rescue the building, which ultimately led to the facilities being restored as a new cultural venue and café.[376] Yet, as has been argued,

FIGURES 15 AND 16 *Photos depicting Martín Butera outside the 'A Noite' building, former headquarters of Rádio Nacional in Rio de Janeiro, Brazil. Courtesy of Martín Butera and Ligia Katze.*

FIGURES 15 AND 16 *(Continued)*.

the strong emotional value attached to the iconic building by Brussels citizens is an overlooked aspect of this heritage process:

> In the middle decades of the twentieth century, radio broadcasting tapped into, transmitted, and created a wealth of emotions through the news, concerts, and dramas it broadcasted to eager audiences. Given the vast reach of public monopolies like the INR, individual listeners tuning in each day heard the same sounds, voices, and music, curated around the institution's mission to educate the mind and elevate the soul... The emotions felt by radio listeners marvelling at the new technology in the 1920s, nervously anticipating the occupation in 1940, or rejoicing in the liberation of 1944 were not the same as the emotions experienced by those who contemplated the elegant profile of the deserted building in 1999, worried by its possible disappearance. Though not responding to past radio broadcasts themselves, it was the continuity between these emotions in the present and the memory of emotions surrounding the building's previous functions that defined it as a significant site of collective remembrance and feeling.[377]

In other words, the ability of the campaigners to generate support rested on a legacy of shared emotions and memories of radio associated with this building and in the civic identity of Brussels' inhabitants as it has developed from the 1930s onwards. The heritage professionals involved in the campaign were most likely primarily motivated to rescue the building as a piece of architectural heritage rather than as a site of radio heritage. Nonetheless, this case highlights the role of place-based radio memories in such processes and the emotional value attached to the building in Brussels that was marshalled in the rescue campaign.

A second striking example of preserving the memory of past radio in built environments can be found in the case of the radio fandoms associated with pirate radio stations like Radio Caroline established in the UK and elsewhere from the mid-1960s onwards, whose highly-popular rock and new music broadcasts were transmitted from ships off the British coastline in international waters. Given the reluctance of the BBC to play pop music on air, stations like Radio Caroline gained an enormous following during the 1960s and 1970s, particularly teenage and young adult listeners, who from the outset were able to join fan clubs like the Caroline Club, while station presenters gained a cult status amongst listeners. A focal point of the culture of offshore stations like Radio Caroline has been the ships on which the programmes were made and from which they were transmitted. This was illustrated in the logo and graphics used for the station, for instance in the very earliest booklets sent to fans in the 1960s[378] through to more recent releases, such as the 2009 feature film *The Boat That Rocked* or the memoir *Radio Caroline: The True Story of the Boat that Rocked* (2014).[379] The importance of the boats associated with Radio Caroline to fans was demonstrated after the sinking of the *Mi Amigo* during a storm in 1980, which seemed to heighten the attachment to the subsequent boat, the *Ross Revenge*, used between 1983 and 1991, when operations ceased in the wake of a high-profile police raid in 1989 that ended offshore transmissions.

Most recently, the commitment of a group of listeners and former DJs to restore and maintain the *Ross Revenge* since it was brought back to dock in 1991 has been examined as a site in which the nautical atmosphere of offshore radio transmissions, their sounds, embodied memories and the built materiality of the ship come together:

> [The volunteers] are armed with needle guns, paint brushes, and tool boxes. Affected over the many years by what they've heard – years of struggle, oppression, hardship, resistance – they now hope to elicit new affects through their action in renovating the ship and enabling broadcasts from its decks once more, even if just from the shore. The affects sparked through a unique, atmospheric radioscape that is remembered and recalled have compelled listeners to participate and to join Caroline and its cause on land and in dock. Those affected listeners are in turn affectual in seeking to engineer a new atmospheric from the ship, now, in the twenty-first century. The desire to 'engineer' an offshore atmosphere lingers on, through senses of nostalgia and loss and the bonds of friendship that were built through an invisible tether that tied listeners on land to communities at sea.[380]

This attention to atmosphere in sustaining the love of radio through acts of maintaining the material container of a past station provides an opportunity to consider the activities of the emotional communities formed around Radio Caroline. Those participating seek to maintaining the ship in a collective spirit that brings both fans and former employees together and which invests value and meaning in a radio culture that was ultimately targeted and disrupted by government authorities. This act of 'keeping' radio via the restored boat has been reactivated during anniversary broadcasts from its on-board studios, but also complemented by online activities around the memory of Radio Caroline, exemplified by fan merchandise featuring the ship symbol to raise funds for the ship restoration project.[381] Since the infrastructures of pirate radio have often been in flux – with changes to stations names, locations and frequency use – several initiatives continue into the present day to keep track of the ephemeral lives of the stations and to help listeners continue to find stations in the radio frequency spectrum, which in turn is a form of community documentation and memory work.[382]

Finally, I will end by considering the keeping or 'saving' of technological devices, primarily receivers. The earliest accounts of radio equipment being 'saved' is in relation to industrial equipment that was discarded and circulated in consumer markets after the First World War, for which in some countries, such as Germany, the circulation of former military equipment was the origin for many amateur hobbyists being able to initially acquire affordable parts to construct self-made receivers.[383] In terms of institutional sites for 'saving' radio sets, the first radio museums were already appearing in the 1930s, often inspired by or working with technology museums, which in some countries had been founded in the years around 1900; radio museums and exhibitions are discussed in more detail in Chapter 4.[384] As noted in the previous chapter, national radio exhibitions during the 1920s and 1930s were also a site in which historical displays of radio receiver devices 'over time' were presented to the public, already underscoring the notion of obsolescence in the consumer market, as well as encouraging listeners to acquire new receiver sets (with the implication to discard or sell on old sets).

Many of the amateur collector societies with a substantial public profile are concentrated in North America, UK/Europe and Australia/New Zealand.[385] In the United Kingdom, for instance, the British Vintage Wireless Society (BVWS) was formed in 1976 by a group of radio enthusiasts who felt frustrated by what they perceived to be a lack of interest among museums and academic researchers in their commitment to 'the preservation and restoration of vintage radio and related equipment'.[386] The website indicates that their main activities revolve around the publication of a member's bulletin focused on receiver restoration and historical articles, managing an online discussion forum and organizing public meetings with 'swapmeet' and auction components.[387] To get a sense of these activities it is instructive to view a professionally-made video of one such event in 2004, which offers the viewer a sequence that alternates between close-up shots of radio receiver designs and the auction and swapmeet, in which members of the BVWS, mainly white men who appear to be mainly in their sixties or older, gather around the stands and talk to other stallholders, in search of component parts, sets or restoration tips.[388]

Despite the wide remit of the BVWS, little is said on their website about what attracts their organization and its members to radio itself. However, nostalgia has been recognized as an important motivating factor in popular culture fandom and for collector culture in general.[389] In China, for instance, nostalgia serves as a key impetus for older-age radio enthusiasts involved in large historical radio associations engaging in the collecting, tinkering with and repair of old and discarded radio sets, enacting a saving of radio. These collaborative activities are not just a pleasurable or nostalgic pastime but are in line with past public discourses about self-reliance from the 1950s to the 1970s. This practice reflects not just an individual passion for radio, but as a collaborative activity it connects to past personal experiences with a particular national imagination in the Cultural Revolution era in which technological 'making do' despite limited resources was understood as contributing to the social order. The present-day recovery of old radio models from that era reflects a 'memory practice' that serves as 'crucial way to "save" and record China's history of technological development for the younger generations'.[390] For the participants, who are mainly men, this engagement with radio also has significance in their own life narrative, since their 'hacking' skills bettered their employment and financial situation during their working lives.[391] It signals an effort to rescue the past significance of radio sets as a valuable consumer item but also reflects a past identification with repair and maintenance in contrast to the 'disposable' culture of technology in the present day.[392]

The US-based website ChildhoodRadio.com, hosted by Ron Mansfield, focuses on transistors and acknowledges the importance of 'childhood' nostalgia as a motivation for many enthusiasts. In a section of the website entitled 'Becoming a collector: What do you like, and why?', Mansfield explains that many collectors tend to specialize in particular periods or specialty models of transistor radio, with this focus extending from the 1950s through to the 1980s. Mansfield's account offers a classification of 'boomer-aged radio collectors' (born roughly between the mid-1940s and the 1960) into seven categories:

1. Period collectors (i.e., collecting a few radios alongside mid-century furniture, toys or posters);
2. Lovers of vintage electronics (collectors of tube and transistor radios, hi-fi and stereo);
3. Specialists (focused on a particular niche, such as crystal sets, shirt pocket transistor radios or ephemera; sometimes former employees of electronics companies);
4. Historians (those who are keen to catalogue and preserve details about radio sets and their documentation, and often want to publish and share this information);
5. Restoration hobbyists (those who are keen to open up old devices and get them working again);
6. Perfectionists (collectors who seek pristine items with only original parts, and are less concerned with them working);
7. Insatiable shoppers (those who seek to acquire and stockpile items, sometimes as parts to use for repairs).[393]

Mansfield explains that he himself is a 'restoration hobbyist', with a tendency towards becoming an 'insatiable shopper'. As a fan of transistor radios, Mansfield takes pains to validate a wide spectrum of collecting interests, yet elsewhere on vintage radio forums, there have been complaints about 'collecting snobs' or 'bullies' who value only pre-1945 valve models and who denigrate collectors who are keen to restore transistor models.[394]

The by-line of Mansfield's website, 'make them look and sound like new again', highlights a central interest in helping other collectors to use new parts to try to restore receivers.[395] This emphasis on getting sets to work is stressed elsewhere in collector circles:

I have met radio collectors with marvelous collections of sets, all dead, incapable of uttering another sound ... [O]ld radio sets give more pleasure if they work. Why, I'm not sure. It may be the enforced delay and anticipation while you wait for the valves to warm up, perhaps the mingled smell of burning dust and wax capacitors, or else the mellow sound of the speaker in a decent-sized cabinet.[396]

This statement, drawn from a radio collectors' handbook from the late 1990s, posits that much of the pleasure in collecting and restoring vintage sets is derived from the enjoyment of their analogue sounds, along with the smells and slower operations of the device. It also underscores the observation in fan research that the engagement in collecting practices allows individuals to 'reconstruct memories of youth' via present-day acts of engagement and remembering.[397] In the case of Mansfield, his commitment to restoration for operational use means that he points readers to his own eBay profile, which sells reworked parts as 'hacks' to get older devices working again, and gives tips on how to buy and sell on the large online auctioneer eBay.[398]

The prevalence of eBay, founded in 1995, has been seen to have noted effects on the British vintage radio community, as they became 'virtual radiophiles' with their collector culture undergoing changes in its forms of knowledge exchange and ritual, concentrated as they were on swap meets, fairs and car boot sales.[399] Initial complaints focused on the negative effects of online trading, such as price fluctuations, and the perception that it reduced the chances of finding rare 'gems' or 'nuggets' at organized events. Yet eBay also arguably expanded information about radio receiver types and their availability, offering new opportunities for knowledge acquisition:

> Some radio collectors find 'spaces of unknowingness' on the eBay site. Although eBay is qualitatively different from the swap meet or boot sale, UK radio collectors project back onto eBay analogies between finding virtual spaces of unknowingness and finding them physically in the geographic 'hunt'. Poor descriptions, misspellings, and wrong categorizations on eBay are the virtual equivalents of the liminal items that fall between swap meet stalls and the boxes on the floor.[400]

In response to this new situation – with individual collections often accelerated by the 'addictive' qualities of the speed and ease of acquiring new collection items online, often across national borders – participants in online discussions saw the mistakes made in eBay listings as an opportunity to assert their own expertise and (shared) knowledge in contrast to 'unknowing others'.[401] Nonetheless, the risk of damage to vintage radio sets sent through postal systems and an ongoing attachment to the collective ritual of coming together at an organized event have retained a meaningful quality for those radiophiles who are invested in saving radio sets. As one radio collector noted, 'There still [is] something about queuing up on a Sunday morning . . . I don't know, it's the fun of it, it's the event . . . That feeling of community.'[402] Indeed, despite criticisms of the tendency for some buyers to attend swapmeets only for the purposes of finding items for online reselling, meeting up in person at events remains a key collective ritual of trade exchange with peers, facilitating an emotional community, their knowledge exchange and the process of value adding. Moreover, it is the anticipation and promise of a serendipitous discovery that maintains an ongoing attachment to events within the UK radio collector community, and it is such a 'hunt' for new acquisitions that will be treated in the next section focused on the creation, collection and trade of radio sound recordings amongst amateur communities.

Amateur efforts to save the sonic traces of radio

Shortly after inventing the phonograph in 1877, Thomas Edison speculated on its possible commercial applications, primarily in relation to voice recordings, spanning audio letters and dictation, audio books, speech training, language preservation, educational instruction and musical performance.[403] At this early stage, he also envisaged the recording's potential as a keepsake or 'souvenir',[404] later summarized by Edison as 'The "Family Record" – a registry of saying, reminiscences, etc., by members of a family, in their own voices, and of the last words of dying persons.'[405] Edison emphasized the idea of a framework of family memory for collecting voice recordings, even arguing that the phonograph would 'outrank the photograph' as a means of collecting important moments of the family.[406] This notion of a 'family sound album' was conceived as a companion to the pre-existing popularity of photography for documenting the family from the 1840s onwards, and was again deployed in the promotion of tape recorders during the 1950s and 1960s.[407]

While home recordings of radio transmissions in the US date back to wax cylinder recordings from the 1910s, media reporting in the late 1930s referred to bootleggers using home recording devices to record off-air or to make copies of transcription discs. Such radio collecting was rare since 'at that time obtaining recordings was prohibitively expensive and access to original transcription discs or copies was restricted to a small social network of radio collectors'.[408] In the UK context, various models of acoustic and electrical 'home recorder' devices, such as the 'Mivoice Speakeasie', 'Fay' or 'EKCO Radiocorder' (see Figure 17), were being marketed as both voice

FIGURE 17 *'EKCO' Radiocorder device for recording radio programmes onto metal discs. Courtesy of the National Museum of Scotland.*

and radio (music) recording devices at radio exhibitions in the early 1930s, although most other remaining private radio recordings in the UK context derive from collections that had been owned by musicians and were off-air recordings of their own performances made for them by local recording studios.[409] In amateur radio and phonography circles in Germany, there was a similar interest during the 1930s, with publications devoted to questions of creating your 'own recordings' (*Selbstaufnahme*) on gramophone disc.[410] Most of these publications had a strong technical component, with instructions and diagrams, with one of these produced by the editor of an amateur photography periodical, who wrote in 1932 that self-made sound recordings would potentially appeal to fans of radio, phonography and amateur sound film.[411]

In Germany, a 1938 publication, titled *Schallplatten-Bastelbuch* (Records-Scrapbook), explained to its readers the appeal of self-recording, as an exploration of the possibilities offered by the 'unknown record' in contrast to the familiar sounds of commercially-available recordings.[412] The author also alluded to the massive collection of radio recordings held by the sound archives of the Nazi-controlled national broadcaster in Berlin, suggesting their attraction to amateur recordists: 'the whole world wishes to be able to share in these treasures'.[413] An amateur enthusiasm and interest in recording radio does not seem, at least with the technologies available in the 1930s, to have led to the creation of large private collections among listeners; this despite the proliferation of tape recording in professional settings expanding significantly during the 1930s and in the context of the Second World War.[414] The private collections of radio recordings that have emerged from the war period are quite rare, and are often linked to those with professional skills and access to scarce sound recording resources. Examples include a private collection of a German sound studio owner who recorded radio reports and speeches on 2000 Decelith discs during the Second World War, and recordings of the Dutch government-in-exile's 'Radio Oranje' and 'Herrijzend Radio' programming created by audio engineers situated in German-occupied Rotterdam.[415] In the US in the early post-war period and afterwards, wire recorders were the primary means by which individuals, especially young white men, started to record a variety of radio programming, which offers a particular selection of historical recordings but also highlights 'a specific, widespread practice of recording broadcasting programming that has gone unremarked in most academic and national histories'.[416]

The limits on private collections changed in the 1950s with the advent of (relatively) affordable reel-to-reel tape recording, with regular improvements made to portability, sound quality and recording duration.[417] This development led to an increase in the popularity of sound recording as a hobby, which included but also expanded beyond the recording of radio content to interests in outdoor field recording. The increasing portability of recorders allowed for 'sound hunting' to emerge as a popular hobby from the early 1950s onwards, with French and Swiss broadcasters hosting radio programmes featuring the collections of sound recording amateurs as early as 1948, and national contests with categories including everyday sounds, self-created radio plays, interviews and reportage.[418] The growth of the sound-hunting hobby led to the formation of an International Federation of Sound Hunters (FICS), with members including the UK, the Netherlands, Germany, France, Switzerland and former Czechoslovakia.[419] In the latter, sound hunters were known as 'phonoamateurs', with their organization, Český Fonoklub, established in 1966, whose activities from the outset included a national competition and radio show.[420] In the context of Cold War-era restrictions on cross-border radio, one of the active members of Český Fonoklub later noted that his main motivation when taking up this hobby was to access Western music via radio broadcasts:

> There was a late-night programme in which they played ... also the music from the West. Usually just one in a programme. So I was sitting there, headphones on, a finger on the record button. It would take me more than a year to collect about one and a half hour of recordings of such music. But then I could throw a kind of party.[421]

In other words, while the sound-hunting community has been studied for their development of a sound aesthetic that was largely distinct from that of professional radio programme content,[422] this example points to the manner in which the effort to keep or save radio, by recording its music, could serve as a pathway towards other forms of engagement with sound recording. Moreover, in keeping with the envy expressed in the *Schallplatten-Bastelbuch* from 1938 towards the sound collections amassed by (Nazi) German national broadcast institutions, we find that amateur recording associations had already begun assembling their sound archives during the 1950s,[423] demonstrating an interest in building up sound libraries that could be used in radio plays, reportage and audiovisual presentations, with a certain similarity to radio production archives for which sounds are often 'saved' with a view to future reuse in the creation of new programmes.

The 'heyday' of sound hunting in Europe has been identified as concentrated in the period from the early 1950s to the mid-1960s, in parallel with the popularity of the reel-to-reel recorder prior to the compact cassette player. However, in other contexts, such as Japan, it was precisely the early 1970s when this hobby had its boom, as radio and tape recording technology expanded for young Japanese consumers, whose interest in 'home recording' (*Takuroku*) of radio and music records gave way to an interest in outdoor or live recording (*Namaroku*), conceived of as distinct from 'the dubbing of FM radio, records, and tapes'.[424] Nonetheless, a 1977 guidebook cited audio recordings of radio and television as possible areas of interest for *Namaroku* enthusiasts, noting a typology of eleven types of sound recordists including the figure of the 'air-check specialist', who was focused on recording radio music and programmes from Japanese FM stations and sometimes foreign broadcasters.[425] In a subsequent period, with the onset of the Walkman, in Japan and globally, the practice of 'saving' radio by taping music and programmes became part of 'mixtape' culture, which strongly aligned with (and was informed by) hip hop and DJ vinyl mixes recorded onto tape, which in turn fed into the aesthetic of popular radio from the 1980s.[426]

In the radio fan cultures of the 1970s through to the 1990s, cassette tapes remained a crucial means of holding on to radio, and even though technically illegal in many countries, it lent itself to relatively easy reproduction and distribution. In the 1970s in West Germany, for instance, manufacturers promoted cheap radio cassette recorders as being ideal 'for the young hit-hunter'.[427] An intensity of fan recording activity might concentrate on a particular band or album release, as evidenced by the archives for the cult band Grateful Dead in the US, which included significant amounts of 'bootleg' recordings created by fans that were derived from radio transmissions.[428] In other cases, it was the popularity of a particular presenter and music programme that produced a surge of fan taping activity, as in the case of the late BBC Radio 1 broadcaster John Peel, who gave rise to an online Yahoo group that has, for over two decades, discussed his programmes (covering the period from 1967 to 2004) and 'digitally reconstructed more than 1300 otherwise lost radio shows presented by Peel, by ripping, sharing and combining listeners' collections of fragmentary off-air cassette recordings'.[429] Such listener-driven, crowdsourced archiving has been accompanied by a growing receptivity within heritage institutions to a more participatory model of the archive, conceived in terms of decentralized curation, increased user agency and co-created meaning.[430]

A strong motivation for many listeners is not only their own attraction to the content of radio programming, but their sense at the time that they were capturing something of importance. For instance, Kimberley Peters' history of the UK offshore pirate radio station Radio Caroline notes how she first came to listen to a fan's private cassette tape collection in 2010:

> Prior to this, my only direct audio engagement with the station had been through CDs of selected key moments of the station's history which had been opportunely captured, packaged and made available for sale on a fan website. Hearing these tapes was an altogether more unadulterated listening experience. The recordings were far from perfect. The stop and start of the cassette recorder interrupted the flow. The sound quality was rough and raw. The tapes lacked a logic or order to an outsider. They were just the recordings of a young man. I asked my research participant why he made and kept so many of them. There were boxes upon boxes of tapes on the table around me . . . He said he had a sense he was listening to something special.[431]

The recognition that these transmissions by offshore radio stations were valuable, and constantly at threat of shutdown by authorities, heightened the sense of the need for the fan to save programmes by taping them off-air. In the description above, the souvenirs of Radio Caroline take their shape in the content of the self-created tapes, but also in the materiality of the format of the cassette tape and the device of the Walkman as an intimate personal stereo device facilitating audio playback of the individual's taping of past radio consumption.⁴³² These mixtapes not only invoke the desire to save something treasured but also the emotional charge produced by engaging in the process of lifting a favourite piece of music and tuning in to pirate radio, both of which had a certain illicit association.⁴³³

We can find the development of an affective practice in the collecting and trading of particular radio programme recordings. From the 1970s onwards, the collective activities of the 'Old Time Radio' (OTR) scene, dedicated to programmes from the 1930s to the 1960s, took the form of clubs, newsletters, fanzines, conventions, and so on.⁴³⁴ Chuck Seeley is a key figure, having authored one of the early guides to the hobby of collecting radio recordings on cassette tape in the US context. His brochure *The Old Time Radio Collector's Handbook* (1978) gives an overview of how to engage in the main activities of radio collecting, including acquiring tape recorder formats, handling tape, building a collection, engaging in exchanges or trading and duplicating audio recordings, closing with advice as to how to 'increas[e] your enjoyment of the hobby', noting particular reference books, a list of OTR clubs and publications.⁴³⁵ Written as a manual for new collectors, Seeley's brochure explains that they need to acquire two tape devices, preferably of commercial quality (rather than consumer models), which he notes are costly and require technical knowledge to ensure recording quality and limit 'crosstalk' interference. He goes on to explain the main ways to amass a collection, for instance by taping directly off radio, making copies at public libraries, from commercial LPs or from transcription discs, buying from an OTR dealer or sharing within an OTR club with a library.⁴³⁶ When it comes to trading, Seeley encourages new collectors to mimic practices in institutional audio recordkeeping, such as keeping a master copy of each item and generating a catalogue list, with detailed metadata and sound-quality information.⁴³⁷

In the final part of his brochure, Seeley reflects on how additional pleasure can be attained once a collector has 'a few hundred' recordings by prioritizing one's personal listening enjoyment. He suggests that expanding one's historical knowledge can also increase individual pleasure by better understanding the materials, engaging in exchange with fellow hobbyists, or writing for fanzines.⁴³⁸ Furthermore, specializing one's collecting interests is recommended, with examples given of focusing on a particular series or programmes with a particular actor or writer.[439] For some collectors, the pleasure of actually listening to the 'saved' radio recordings one had amassed holds less appeal than that of preparing recordings, expanding one's collection and trading with others. The enjoyment and investment in collecting recordings of past radio extended the circulation of live programmes decades after their original broadcast, and draws attention to how collectors treated radio as a material object, 'understood through possession and absence, acquisition and discovery, as well as regret for programs that remain unobtainable'.[440] Seeley closes the guide by making a somewhat defensive case for the pleasure of listening to radio as a superior experience to that of television or cinema – the dominant mass media of the 1970s. Despite the universalist tone of this account, it primarily addresses the US context, as evidenced in the publications it cites and a US-only list of OTR clubs that all focused exclusively on national radio history. One exception is a Brooklyn-based club devoted to the BBC's highly popular *Goon Show* (1951–60), which was probably spurred on by the formation of the UK-based Goon Show Preservation Society in 1972, with branch representatives also located in Australia, New Zealand, Japan, Canada, Germany and South Africa.[441]

While the UK saw an early (popular) music collecting culture, which will be discussed in Chapter 4, for the collecting of radio recordings there were small associations of which a number had discontinued by the 1990s, such as Savers of Television and Radio (STARS).[442] Another of these groups, the Old-time Radio Show Collectors Association (ORCA), was founded in the mid-1980s and is still in existence today. When new members join, they receive an official membership card (see Figure 18) and the organization's newsletter. The 'Tune Into Yesterday' newsletter, in A4 format, offers its members compilations of historical programme magazines, newspaper articles and archival files about radio, some of which are reprinted with permission from official archives (e.g., the BBC Written Archives Centre in Caversham) or amateur collections (e.g., from the World Radio History website with permission from former broadcaster David Gleason).

The other key service to members is a lending library. Upon becoming a member of ORCA, new members receive several catalogues by post. The first, for the 'cassette lending library', offers a list of over 2,000 cassette tapes maintained by one of its members.

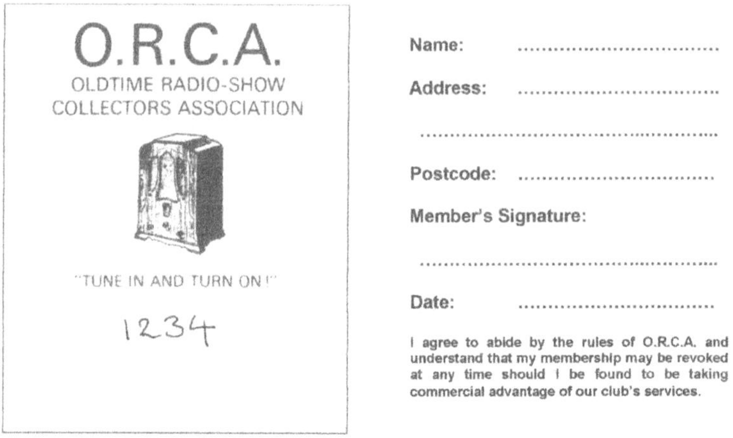

FIGURE 18 *Membership card for the UK-based ORCA (Old-time Radio Show Collectors Association), issued in June 2017, front and back. Courtesy of Graeme Stevenson.*

A second edition, covering another 1,500 items, includes a new column indicating cassette tape vs CD, and a third, and significantly shorter, 'MP3 Audio DVD lending library' catalogue includes just under eighty entries, all with an item number and organized in alphabetical order by the programme title, along with basic descriptive metadata. The front cover used for all three documents (see Figure 19) includes an image of an 'old time' radio set surrounded by a cable which lists the genres considered most relevant from the perspective of ORCA: 'radio drama, comedy, fantasy, mysteries, science fiction, thriller, historical drama, spy tales, radio plays'. Below this image is an additional title, intended to complete the previous sentence: 'not to forget "The Archers"', referring to the aforementioned long-running weekday radio drama on BBC Radio 4 (early 1950s to present), which has a dedicated fan base across multiple online community groups.[443]

The entries are almost exclusively in English, yet to the uninitiated it would not be immediately clear, based on the descriptions, whether programmes had been aired in the UK or United States. Among the few exceptions in the cassette listing is an item titled 'German Propaganda Speeches' and a number of Radio Luxembourg

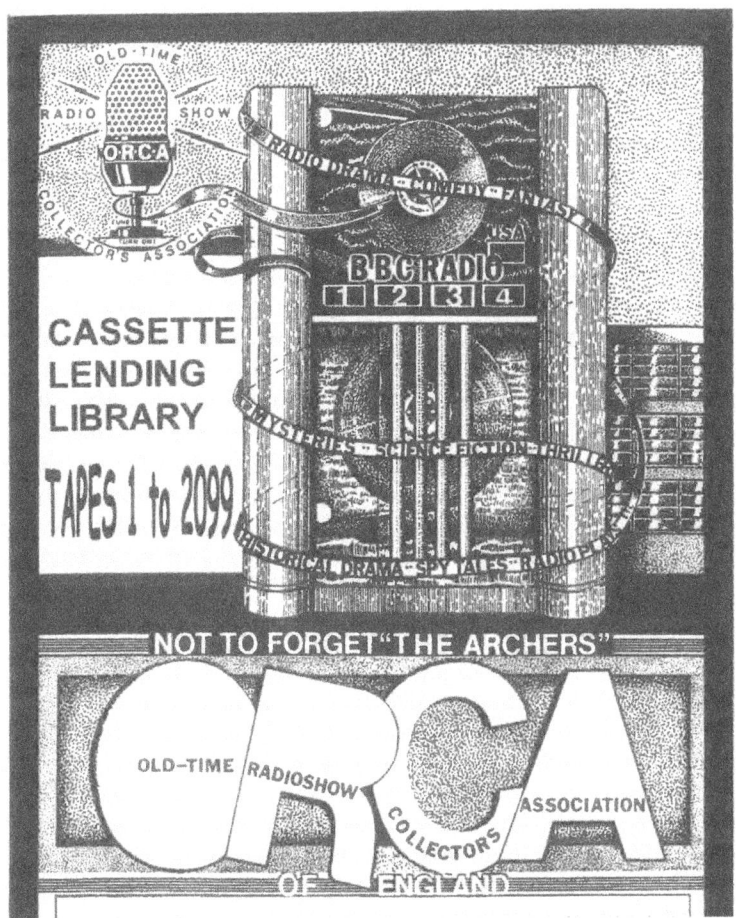

FIGURE 19 ORCA, Cassette Lending Library [Tapes 1 to 2099] catalogue, cover. Courtesy of Graeme Stevenson.

programmes from the 1950s that had been targeted at UK audiences, including the popular melody from the sponsored children's programme *Ovaltiney's Concert Party* (1934–9), a programme pre-recorded in the station's London studio and then aired from Luxembourg.[444] In the case of *The Archers*, the sheer volume of episodes aired between the 1950s and the present mean that it would be near impossible for amateur collector groups to piece together a complete collection. Perhaps precisely because of *The Archers'* ubiquity and cult popularity, the cassette list only has two entries for this programme (early 1970s), while the MP3 list has just one entry within a compilation recording from 1975.

Looking at the three catalogue lists, the cassette list mainly has materials covering the mid-1930s to 1970s, which are generally individual listings of single episodes. The item entries for the MP3 CD and audio DVD list, however, have materials covering up to 2008, with the compilation on DVDs allowing for as many as 500 episodes listed together at the item level, also a reflection of the advanced possibilities for copying as well as compressing, uploading and downloading digital audio using the MP3 format. To give an example of item 59, listed as 'Radio 4 drama: 83 plays 1998–2008', we see that the delivery format provided amateur fans with increased possibilities to stockpile large amounts of episodes, in contrast to earlier efforts to list and underscore the value of separate episodes marked as rare by their mainly individual entries in the previous cassette list. The lending library system initiated by ORCA with cassette tapes still persists up to the present, and operates on a trust system. On the reverse side of the ORCA membership card, a member is required to sign a pledge in which they agree that their 'membership may be revoked at any time should I be found to be taking commercial advantage of our club's services' (see Figure 18). The conditional arrangement in holding large numbers of radio programmes from diverse origins (including private collections, institutional archives and commercial releases) means that the association is dependent on this element of trust to contain the distribution of radio sound recordings to its members only; presumably many of the recordings are already circulating online in an unofficial capacity.[445]

Even well into the era of digital formats, there appear to be ongoing issues with the lending library format, with a newsletter editorial as late as 2017 asking members to 'treat the discs they hire from the library with care' since the librarian had 'some [CDs] returned to him covered in scratches and fingerprints'.[446] It is clear that the digital era has put pressure on the previous model of the old-time radio club lending library, with most members hiring programmes from the CD and MP3 CD/DCD library, although the organization has next to no digital presence in the form of a website or social media accounts.[447] By comparison, the website of the large US-based

Old Time Radio Researchers (OTRR) promotes its library as having over 60,000 radio episodes freely available and a database tool designed so that users can compare their own MP3 collections to a database with over 200,000 listings. The collective preservation efforts of the OTRR organization, furthermore, has led to online resources derived from 'subgroup' activities, including episode listings, scripts, 'certified' series researched by the organization, along with an online encyclopaedia, a collection of images, articles and publications.[448] Such examples are illustrative of the potential for the work of amateur collectors and groups in collectively compiling information about their recordings, for which they frequently have a specialized aim in seeking to 'document entire runs of radio show episodes, air dates, cast information and so forth', as also evidenced in the recent UK-focused audio drama wiki initiative.[449]

Amateur or DIY archiving has remained relevant in the era of digital radio and podcast culture, as many of the episodes of born-digital materials since the 1990s and early 2000s were lost due to a reliance on proprietary platforms and changing infrastructures, even though this has led to (independent) podcast producers becoming disconnected from the technical backend and a 'lack of end-user agency, especially during instances of systems failure'.[450] Even among long-time podcasters, a well-known case is that of prominent former music TV host Adam Curry, who realized in 2014 that he had lost over 800 episodes of his 'Daily Source Code' podcast (2004–13). After launching an appeal to his Twitter followers, Curry was able to retrieve the entire archive from a follower of the podcast, who had been sharing these files with other fans through Bit Torrent Sync, leading to the amateur or 'bootleg' archive of fans supplementing the lost archive of the producer.[451] Along with web initiatives like the Internet Archive, a notable effort in the preservation of and access to past podcasts for fans and researchers is the PodcastRE initiative by a group at the University of Wisconsin, which is aggregating podcast and other audio content, while also facilitating keyword and metadata search in a library search model to make them easier to study. Meanwhile the 'Preserve This Podcast' project has more recently run workshops designed to advise independent podcasters on how to avoid 'catastrophic file loss' through affordable and easy-to-follow preservation procedures.[452]

Whether national, regional, local or community radio initiatives, pertaining to broadcast or born-digital audio content, these examples have pointed to the crucial work of amateur collector and fan-driven activities, particularly in participatory efforts to save the ephemeral content of past radio programmes or podcasts. In some cases, individual radiophilia can be said to be intersecting with other hobby interests in recording technology and music collecting, while in other cases the desire to keep, collect and preserve particular radio or audio content is driven by a specialized interest in a particular announcer/star, programme, station or programme genre/type, such as air checks, station identifiers, jingles or sports programming.[453] Yet while many amateurs or fans described here work without institutional endorsements or professional affiliations, recent research has noted that old-time radio collectors interviewed about their recording activities in the late 1940s to 1960s had a variety of interests and motivations in generating personal collections:

> [A]lmost all of these collectors would go on to work in the radio and television industries as or after they recorded programs off the air. Enlisted as performers, announcers, technicians, directors of photography, engineers, and/or station managers, these individuals sought to understand the industry that had presented them with role models and motivated them to record thousands of broadcast minutes in their creation of personal collections. Their work within the radio and television industries shades another dimension to their recording activities, one that puts into sharp relief the vested interests, desires, and resources these individuals developed for their recordings as 'lost' documents of a significant media era in American history.[454]

Indeed, the categories of professional and amateur (or fan) in the collecting of radio are not always so clear-cut. In more recent decades, we can find crossovers between private collecting hobbies and institutional practices.[455] For instance, there is the case of DokuFunk, a collection initiated by a former international radio employee of the Austrian national broadcaster (ORF). After his retirement, the collection expanded to a documentation centre beyond ORF's purview, though it continued to receive its support, and now constitutes one of the largest collections in the international history of radio.[456] In other cases, the personal collections of radio professionals grew so large and significant that they became the foundation of new institutional structures; this was the case with audio engineer G. Robert Vincent's private collection of 8,000 'historic voices', which formed the basis for the National Voice Library at Michigan State University Library in the 1960s.[457] This theme provides us with a bridge to the next section, which considers institutional contexts for saving radio, but for which the present section has served as a reminder of the various ways in which private collections – often reflecting individual interests, agendas and valuations of radio – sometimes come to form part of institutional radio collections.

This section has covered various amateur or non-institutional efforts to save the sonic traces of radio, which grew from early attempts in the 1930s through to a popular pastime in the era of sound hunting and home recording trends emerging from the late 1940s to the 1970s. In some cases, radio recording was a form of 'hit hunting', for which popular music was gathered by illicit listening and recording across the Iron Curtain in Europe, or by listeners to the UK off-shore pirate stations. We might observe a certain similarity between amateur radio and music record collectors as being 'on the hunt' for 'rare finds' on the basis of format (e.g., cylinders or vinyl) or particular genres, periods or artists.[458] Indeed, the creation of radio recordings may in some cases have served to spur on music enthusiasts to become record collectors, with early collection-building often having its origins in 'copying, usually from the radio or other audio tapes'.[459] And yet there are key differences in terms of general availability. Popular music recordings were widely available if not relatively costly consumer items that could be listened to and acquired in music shops, and later, accessed or borrowed from public libraries. For the first recorded music collections in the decades around 1900, the 'sudden flow of records might have triggered a record collecting fever'[460] due to the significant growth and availability of records to those who could afford them. By contrast, until at least the 1950s, there were virtually no commercial releases of radio programming, and they were therefore not common market commodities that could be bought and sold. This meant that it remained more difficult for audiences to listen to a recording of a programme than play back a commercial music recording, or, for that matter, attend a repeated screening of a film or re-read a book. Since recording and replaying past programmes was not a common practice within many professional broadcasting contexts, we might conclude that the relative ephemerality of radio compared with other types of media served as an important motivating factor for early radiophilia, and, in turn, for amateur efforts to record radio programming, as practised by individuals and, later, by formalized groups devoted to 'old time' radio collecting, trading and archiving.

Nonetheless, it is crucial to note that the above account is heavily skewed towards the radio recording and collecting practices of largely white, middle-class men, with a strong representation in the most visible radio associations in British and North American contexts and focused on English-language materials. In this context, it is helpful to note recent research about Black and Latinx women's music collecting and selecting, analysed as a crucial practice in the emergence of hip hop in New York, which requires scholars to be wary of reproducing 'the alleged connoisseurship of male collectors and their canons'. Thus, developing a female-centric account of women as engaged in 'saving' music can unsettle 'the comfortably masculinist – and overwhelmingly white – images of the "record collector" and "crate digger"'.[461] Working in a similar vein, the Internet Archive is currently gradually digitizing and making accessible the vast television news archive of US civil rights and social activist Marion Stokes in a bid to preserve her rare private broadcast collection, but also foreground her own media archival activism and involvement in local television production.[462] While the research for this book did not uncover new sites of women as private collectors of radio, or as members of collector organizations, it is crucial to acknowledge how recent scholarly accounts of feminist and other community-oriented preservation work have sharpened the existing understanding of radio preservation as a form of social activism.[463] The digital preservation and access provision to community radio archives have been explored as having crucial potential to 're-sound' past histories of feminist radio activism, amidst the multiple challenges of resources, expertise and staff within community radio initiatives.[464] The next section will therefore start with conventional historical sites of institutional collecting of radio, before acknowledging more recent efforts by institutions to work as partners with community stakeholders to facilitate radio preservation, access and outreach.

Archivists, broadcast institutions and the preservation of radio

One day, the boss came in and there were some discs on the floor, and he said 'Oh, clear out all these old discs, and have a tidy up', so [we] got down to work – and this is quite literally true, and I know my memory is not playing me false – there was a pile of discs, getting worn and dusty, and we began to look at them; there was a talk by [George] Bernard Shaw, a talk by H.G. Wells, a talk by [H.H.] Asquith, [Winston] Churchill, [David] Lloyd George, [Cecil] Chesterton. We looked at one another and we said, 'No way can these be destroyed! Something's got to be done.'[465]

In this oral history interview, Marie Slocombe narrates the initial impulse for creating a sound archive at the BBC, shortly after having been hired as a summer employee in the Recorded Programmes Department in 1937. Slocombe and a fellow junior colleague, Timothy Eckersley, were asked to 'tidy up' a stack of disks intended for disposal, before realizing that they documented significant political figures and events. Soon after starting to lobby her superiors to save these recordings, Slocombe was named 'compiler and curator' of the Permanent Library, later the BBC Sound Archive.[466] Reflecting on this event almost fifty years later, in conversation with a former colleague, Slocombe's familiar tone when referring to famous authors, journalists and former prime ministers (by family name) also seemed to reflect the close intimacy achieved in seeking to take care and save the recorded sound legacy of such prominent figures from British public life. As a former colleague later noted, when Slocombe assumed this position, she had to deal with 'a somewhat haphazard collection of recordings, some processed, some still on acetate, stacked here and there'.[467] Slocombe's impassioned response to an institutional context in which existing recordings were being both neglected and discarded served as a strong impulse to 'save' and better organize, but also to significantly expand, what became one of the largest radio archival collections in Europe.

This section will examine the desire to keep, save, or preserve radio, with attention to the passionate endeavour within broadcast institutions to save rare remaining traces of past radio. It will begin with the very earliest archival impulses, from the early 1930s, with the goal of saving radio recordings from neglect or destruction, especially in large publicly-funded radio broadcasters in the European context. I will pinpoint the efforts to preserve radio evident in institutional practices, in which broadcasters made off-air recordings and established radio archives aimed at facilitating programme production and historic preservation. In recognizing that the early period of radio meant that access to recordings was largely limited to insiders, I will first attend to cultural producers working in radio, not least since radiophilia may have been a motivating factor in pursuing employment in radio and playing a role in their professional work, leading to them keeping copies of programmes that they worked on or found significant. Without a doubt, when we think about affective attachments to radio and how they may relate to the desire to record, save or preserve radio, individuals working in institutions might not be the first group of people who come to mind. The activities of sound recording and archiving, moreover, are generally not considered to be occupations that generate passionate attachments to radio, which is reminiscent of the (usually gendered) stereotypes about the profession of librarian.[468] And yet consideration of the role that emotions play in the work of broadcast employees remains a 'missing narrative', which could also help to sharpen our understanding of archivists as 'individuals with their tastes and prejudices, their own talents and flaws and their own views on [broadcasting]'.[469]

In what follows, I will use the radiophilia concept as a way to make sense of the historical impulses to record and preserve radio in broadcast institutions, and I will consider the extent to which radiophilia covers the dynamics in which radio programming has been kept and preserved – as well as neglected, discarded or destroyed – within and beyond institutional settings.

The institutional context underpinning impassioned engagements with recording and archiving radio has diverse origins. In the realm of radio production, the introduction of new audio technologies in the period around 1930 led to opportunities to create new types of programmes and facilitated the new concept of the radio archive. Similar to film libraries, archives and cinematheques established in Europe and North America, the 1930s and 1940s were also key decades for establishing the first institutional frameworks for radio collections and archives.[470] In Berlin, for instance, the Funk-Stunde station's artistic director and radio play pioneer, Hans Flesch, was fascinated by the creative potential of recorded sound technologies and techniques of disc cutting and editing, though such activities initially met resistance due to fears that radio would lose its specific quality as a live medium of transmission.[471] As part of the effort to produce radio-specific aesthetics as an art form, Flesch not only worked on literary radio plays but also non-fictional formats for reporting current affairs.[472] His news compilation programme which aired on New Year's Eve of 1930 included short sound bites from a car race, a foundation stone laying ceremony for a new building in Cologne, and reportage from commemorative events for Germany's deceased foreign minister Gustav Stresemann.[473] In late 1929, Flesch announced his intention to start a radio play archive (Hörspielarchiv) at the Berlin station, initially conceived as a collection of sound recordings that would help to facilitate the production of experimental radio plays.[474]

The importance of creating sound recordings of radio programming was also recognized by the German Broadcasting Corporation (Reichs-Rundfunk-Gesellschaft, or RRG), which officially began such activities in May 1929. With the unveiling of the German Broadcast Corporation's new purpose-built broadcasting house in Berlin in January 1931, the Funk-Stunde audio collection was soon relocated and combined with the general RRG recorded sound archive (RRG-Schallplattenarchiv). In press reporting, the desire to save radio was framed in terms of the collection's ability to support the creation of new programming through reuse, as well as a heritage discourse about saving programmes of (national) cultural and political significance, with a strong emphasis on political figures, significant events or musical performances.[475] Exposed to anti-Semitic attacks, Hans Flesch was forced to resign in mid-1932, with the subsequent National Socialist takeover leading to an expanded political and economic investment in archiving radio on disc (and later tape), culminating in a planned but largely unrealized vision for transferring radio collections to a national sound archive (Reichsschallarchiv).[476]

At the BBC, the introduction of recording technologies and the creative experimentation with them was an important institutional precedent for Slocombe's compelling archival impulse from 1937 onwards. Her collaborator and superior at the Recorded Programmes department, Lynton Fletcher, had a reputation as a keen 'audiophile' and radio technology enthusiast, having also developed a parallel tracking arm device to enable gramophone needles to be exactly placed when wanting to play back an extract from a recorded disc.[477] Fletcher was actively involved in producing actuality programmes in the early 1930s, a number of which used the BBC's recently-acquired Blattnerphone device that recorded onto steel tape, but was rather bulky and less portable than other recording formats and was at least initially primarily used for the Empire Service to play programming at later times for different time zones.[478] An early programme that was explicit in foregrounding recorded radio and its reuse was 'Pieces of Tape' (January 1933), for which Fletcher compiled excerpts of programmes created in 1932 using the Blattnerphone. Spanning a famous British horse race, an international seaplane competition and a relayed and rebroadcast programme from the US, the selection of recordings in this one-off programme was described in *The Radio Times* as follows:

> In a small store-room in Broadcasting House lie some thirty miles of fine steel tape, each mile tightly coiled on a drum ... From all these miles of tape some lengths have been joined together to bring back a few broadcast memories of 1932. They have been chosen, not so much for their artistic value, but because the broadcasts which are reproduced are the sort of programmes which can never repeat themselves. Those who have listened a great deal this last year will recognize many of these strips of tape, while others may capture what Time has already carried past them.[479]

This framing set the compilation of recent events in terms of the development of audience recollections of what they had experienced via radio, and the possibility of better committing these to memory with the aid of recording technology. After this first experiment in selecting and compiling steel tape recordings, Fletcher went on to develop programmes such as *Off the Beaten Track* or *Unusual Recordings*, and edited compilations of contemporary domestic and international events, such as *The Saturday Magazine*, later called *The Radio Gazette*, which highlights the intermedial terminology adopted as the BBC's radio magazine experimented with news-related formats.[480]

While Fletcher generally contributed to topical news programming, during the 1930s numerous historically-themed productions explored the potential of radio to narrate past events and encourage listener reminiscence by means of textual sources or the reuse of historical recordings. In August 1934, the *Historic Occasions* series aired its first episode, 'Twenty Years Ago', intended to be a historical reconstruction of the UK's entry into the First World War in August 1914, using 'diplomatic despatches, telegrams, and extracts from memoirs and diaries' compiled by the military veteran and historian Harold Temperley and adapted for radio by features producer Laurence Gilliam.[481] While this programme was promoted to its audience in a serious manner – with its listing in *The Radio Times* featuring a reproduction of a newspaper front page from 5 August 1914 to emphasize the use of factual evidence – other programming took up the task of recalling the past in a more entertaining manner, in tandem with light music. The concept of the radio scrapbook, discussed in the previous chapter, was drawn on for a new radio series initiated by Leslie Baily in 1932 on a BBC regional service, before becoming a national programme from 1933.[482] *The Radio Times* described *A Scrapbook for 1909* as a 'microphone medley of twenty-five years ago' with spoken-word historical recordings, including suffragette Christabel Pankhurst, Winston Churchill and Ernest Shackleton, interspersed with performances of popular songs from that period (see Figure 20).[483]

For the subsequent episodes on 'historically significant aspects of life' in 1910, 1913, 1914 and 1918, Baily later observed that he had refined the programme's formula in that 'we bring to the microphone' a prominent figure 'who did the things, who saw the things that the "Scrapbook" recalls'.[484] For the 1918 episode, for instance, they found a captain who had been present at the signing of the Armistice in 1918. Citing their intention as 'primarily to entertain', with education as a 'secondary purpose', Baily described the extensive preparations for the programme in combining the BBC's recorded sound collection with contributions by singers, actors, speakers, an orchestra and sound effects, arranging 'the most interesting memories' into 'a well-turned programme'.[485] In contrast to the *Historic Occasions* series, Baily's programmes engaged nostalgia for past musical hits and events through its medley of popular

FIGURE 20 Ogden Oliphant, 'A Scrapbook for 1909', The Radio Times, 16 February 1934, 449. Courtesy of Immediate Media.

music and eyewitness testimony by 'personalities'. The scope was widened further as the programme was renamed *Everybody's Scrapbook* in 1940 to gain a broader audience across the 'Home' and 'Forces' services, and then expanded again for a six-month period between late September 1942 and late March 1943 with domestic broadcasts followed by 'five re-broadcasts at different times of the day and night to reach every part of the Empire'. In this fortnightly series, listeners focused on 'things worth remembering', and content intended to appeal to listeners led to the programme gaining as much popularity in Canada and Australia as it did in Britain. The production of an additional *Songs from the Scrapbooks* summary programme in May 1943 coincided with Empire Day.[486] This nostalgic recollection function of the programme was further highlighted when it offered a *Scrapbook for 1930* in 1940, primarily comprised of BBC radio memories and featured its own stars like Christopher Stone. The end of the war was used as an occasion, throughout 1946, to offer listeners reruns of all previous year-focused programmes from 1909 onwards.[487]

While the BBC Recorded Programmes department contributed recordings to countless other programmes, they also increasingly created programmes designed to facilitate awareness of their work, and the importance of the radio archive for narrating history. Fletcher had previously, in late 1936, initiated a compilation programme, *Room 437*, based on his selection of records taken from Room 437 (the Recorded Programmes Library) at Broadcasting House.[488] In a subsequent programme, *Looking Backwards*, in January 1939, Fletcher played 'a programme of historic BBC records' for the early BBC Television service, thereby remediating the sound archive via the new medium of television.[489] In the context of the Second World War, Fletcher and Slocombe framed and promoted the recorded sound collections in terms of their national and cultural significance, intended to facilitate shared remembering practices. In promotional films like *Museum of Sound* (1943) and several radio programmes, such as *You Have Been Listening to a Recording* (1942), they emphasized that the experience of living through the war needed to be preserved for posterity.[490] In the three-part *History Repeats Itself*, they presented recordings to narrate the recent past with 'great persons'; firstly, prior to the late 1920s, then for the 1930s, and then concluding with '1939 and after'.[491] In a programme listing for this series, Slocombe was described to the public as a gatekeeper who had 'spent some six years in listening' since starting in 1937, during which time she had 'the task of selecting week by week, from the abundance of recordings made, those few which will have true historical significance. These she retains for the ear of the future, while the rest, generally about a thousand of them, are scrapped.'[492] This task may have been manageable in the mid-1930s, when the department produced several hundred recordings, but by 1941 they were managing several thousand per week, necessitating an increase in the number of staff, particularly young women.[493]

The radiophilic impulse led by Fletcher and Slocombe for both the historic preservation of broadcast sound and its reuse in programme production reflects the institutional setting of a public broadcaster, where a strong attachment to a public service mission motivated efforts to participate in recording and archiving radio. As scholars have shown in the context of US commercial radio, copyright restrictions (by advertisers who owned commercial shows) and the market conditions of network syndication posed significant challenges to the formal establishment of recorded sound archives at large networks like CBS and NBC.[494] The high cost and lack of access to disc cutting or pressing equipment meant that the collecting of radio recordings in the US during the 1920s and 1930s was mainly restricted to 'radio executives, producers, performers, and engineers who would sneak discs out or pay radio-clipping companies to record programming'.[495] In the European context, we also find examples of radio producers and others involved in broadcast radio maintaining private recorded sound collections, in part with copies made from institutional archives or radio studios. The British Library, for instance, today holds the H. L. (Lynton) Fletcher Collection, which includes both original field recordings and recordings of radio programmes with which Fletcher was involved, such as *Pieces of Tape*.[496] Such examples are suggestive of the existence of extensive private collections or home recordings among a select group of 'insiders' in institutions or those with access to commercial equipment, before home recording opened up further to the general public between the late 1940s and 1970s.

The radio archives discussed here generally followed the overall trend towards increasing professionalization in the audiovisual archiving field. In the post-1945 era, significant attention was paid to the reconstruction of collections, including under the auspices of UNESCO (United Nations Educational, Scientific and Cultural Organization). Following its formation in 1945, UNESCO became instrumental in encouraging the founding of IAML (International Association of Music Libraries, Archives and Documentation Centres) in 1951, which had working groups on radio archives, the latter branching out, from 1969, into its own organization, IASA (International Association of Sound and Audiovisual Archives).[497] UNESCO also encouraged the foundation of the International Folk Music Council (IFMC) in 1947, with Marie Slocombe actively involved in facilitating the recording of British folk music and dialect, while also selecting her vision of a 'representative cross-section' of national and regional culture, based on its suitability for radio.[498] The close connection between national radio broadcast archives and traditional music and song preservation can be identified as a key activity from the 1950s through to the 1970s, for example in Albania, Ireland, Mongolia, Poland and Switzerland.[499] In other contexts, folk music collecting developed in tandem with radio archiving as part of a mapping of national musical cultures by new broadcasters established during decolonization, exemplified by the Nigerian Broadcasting Service (1951–2), All India Radio (1957) and the Ghana Broadcasting System (1957).[500] In the case of post-revolutionary Mozambique in the 1970s and 1980s, the active recording, collecting and programming of traditional music was a key framework through which the new national broadcaster, Rádio Moçambique, participated in the larger project of 'sonorous' nation-building, including a debate about foregrounding a national or pan-African musical sound.[501]

In Angola, the cultivation of a new sound and national sensibility in the first years of what became Rádio Nacional de Angola (1975–7) reflected certain continuities of personnel and infrastructure from the colonial era, but also changes in programming, with the broadcaster recording revolutionary anthems and sending employees to various regional areas to record musical traditions.[502] At the same time, this new national political agenda led to a 'sonic censorship' of music by popular musicians of the late colonial era, with the evidence of 'deep, intentional scratches in vinyl discs produced in the early 1970s' present decades later in the broadcaster's music library.[503] In establishing a new post-revolutionary context for the love of radio, a national 'Day of Radio' (5 October) was established, and radio's centrality as a mass medium for listeners was affirmed in the context of 'a vibrant oral culture, high illiteracy rate, and low population density spread out across a large territory'.[504] The example of the new Angolan broadcaster seeking a fusion of 'socialist ideals and capitalist practices to create a resilient, state/party media institution' was also found in Vietnam, which reorganized and nationalized its Voice of Vietnam (VOV, launched in 1945) station from 1978. The VOV, as well as establishing a national radio, crafted over time 'a selective archive of recordings that celebrate the CPV [Communist Party of Vietnam] and silence dissenting voices'; also in its buildings, 'the display cabinets in the lobbies of the VOV offices repeat this selective history, foregrounding their close association with the CPV and international support from friendly communist states'.[505] In other words, the commitment of national broadcasters to a particular political agenda is often reflected in the work of the historical radio archive, for which a regime change can, in turn, often lead to new revolutionary or resistance politics being foregrounded in subsequent archival work.[506]

Since the inception of radio archives in the 1930s, the professionals working in them have acquired, collected and organized the sound collections to facilitate radio production, but have also frequently engaged in the careful curation, and sometimes censorship, of spoken word and musical materials in line with fluctuations in national heritage narratives, or party political preferences. There are also examples of radio professionals personally intervening to conceal and save historically-significant sound recordings with the onset of authoritarian rule or military occupation.[507] Elsewhere, stories have been documented of radio archivists who had tried to resell historical radio recordings online, which in one case was identified by the prominent collector David Goldin as a well-known recording he himself had donated to the archive.[508] Meanwhile, the extensive collection of vinyl records and CDs gathered by the Jamaican Broadcasting Corporation music library from 1959 onwards was found, in 2008, to have undergone a loss of 80 per cent of their holdings due to pilfering, leading to an official investigation and call for donations from the public, which led to contributions by former station employees.[509] This terrible loss, as Alejandra Bronfman has outlined, draws attention to the undefined status of commercial music collections in the archive: 'Are the records and CDs historical artefacts? Are they commodities for resale? Are they part of a national heritage, to be preserved and shelved, or ought they to garner a high price and circulate among aficionados?'[510] As such cases indicate, the resale value of commercial music recordings has made them vulnerable to pilfering as well as institutional disposal or deaccessioning, particularly for broadcasters who digitized their collections in tandem with the onset of digital radio production. It is also suggestive of how passionate acts of saving by radio personnel can take a variety of forms, from concealing, removing, rescuing, commercially releasing or helping to restore and rebuild radio collections.

The discourse of the radiophile archivist is somewhat less explicit in the present era of professionalized audio-visual archiving at national broadcasters, perhaps with the exception of passionate appeals to the general public and regulative bodies for financial support for the preservation of 'at risk' collections. In 2015, for instance, the British Library Sound Archive issued a 'Save our Sounds' campaign, along with a call for public donations, while the Australian National Film and Sound Archive (NFSA) issued its 'Deadline 2025' campaign in 2017 to call for donations and investments to address the risk of losing its magnetic tape audio and video collections.[511] Indeed, magnetic tape, which was initially very costly, became the dominant format for radio production and archiving from the 1950s onwards, with reel-to-reel tape largely giving way to digital audio tape (DAT) by the late 1980s.[512] While extensive disc-to-tape copying and duplication took place in many institutions, the ability of tape to be re-recorded over meant that for some radio archives today, disc-based audio collections are better represented in the archive than mid-century materials on tape, though this is also due in part to the poor durability of some tape formats.[513] Such large campaigns sometimes rely on broadly accepted notions of heritage, as indicated by references to Winston Churchill's iconic wartime speeches in the Save our Sounds campaign. However, broad public campaigns also have the potential to motivate individual donations to heritage institutions, such as the case of the 'Gaywaves LGBTI Radio Preservation Program' that allowed the NFSA to digitize and preserve tapes of the first regular gay and lesbian radio programme in Sydney, along with other LGBTI-related community radio recordings across Australia, before clearing rights to make a selection available via Soundcloud.[514]

The domains of archival activism, community partnerships and 'cross sector collaboration' often lead to strong, passionate appeals concerning the saving of radio.[515] Such appeals may be identified in efforts to 'activate' the radio archive and facilitate more exchange and best practices for saving radio in a fully international framework, although as scholarship from the Global South continues to emphasize, it is not a lack of emotional attachment or 'passion' that prevents the implementation of radio preservation strategies, but rather challenges that include 'lack of skills, poor infrastructure and technological obsolescence'.[516] This may apply to contexts where there have been major regime changes or institutional discontinuities, such as radio services moving in and out of exile, as was the case with Haitian radio from the 1970s to the 1990s.[517] International services, whose mission is less straightforward than that of domestic broadcasters, with 'divergent, evolving and overlapping purposes', are vulnerable to significant archival neglect, with some foreign language recordings remaining uncatalogued, or sound and print collections being split from one another, as in the case of the former Radio Netherlands Worldwide, whose archives (sound archive, music library and written archives) were dispersed across a number of archival institutions and music organizations.[518]

In other cases, the work of 'radio preservation' is less about saving sounds than supporting digital history projects that seek to map out radio histories that have been obscured by official national histories, as in the case of the recent La TopoRadio project which highlights the presence of Spanish language radio on both sides of the US–Mexican border and whose interactive map provides information on the history of stations, the location of relevant archives and recent publications documenting their existence.[519] When a radio broadcaster shuts down, or its archive no longer has an institutional home, large university libraries are another framework where collections sometimes 'end up', in some cases with a strong connection, in the case of campus radio, although in other cases due to the research activities of its employees, as in the case of the Irish Pirate Radio Archive at Dublin City University in Ireland.[520] We may also observe radio archival activism in less conventional forms. For example, activist groups may also be engaged in a grassroots effort to monitor radio programmes, as illustrated by the activities of the collective Sortons les radios-poubelles, which seeks to 'save' controversial talk programmes on private radio stations in Québec City, Canada, through documentation and online engagement, constituting acts of ethical 'soundwork' in the absence of monitoring by government bodies.[521] To some degree, this might be seen as an act of archiving by non-fans or anti-fans, whose recording of radio content seeks to draw attention to problematic uses of radio. This builds on a longer tradition of the monitoring of enemy radio, for which those working as monitors were required to listen to hours of content, as well as transcribe, summarize or translate broadcasts, which in turn generated copious archival records, and sometimes recorded sound materials.[522]

Acknowledging this history of diverse forms of affective attachment to radio is instructive for the present account. It underscores the concept of radiophilia as productive for considering the archival impulses of those working within broadcast institutions. Yet it also can help us to understand not only intentional actions or rational decisions but also certain emotional registers such as a love of radio or the fear of losing its ephemeral transmission content which fuelled the work of early radio archival pioneers, and continues to be relevant up to the present day. This attention to the 'emotional lives' of broadcast institutions and their employees has been previously signalled as a significant framework, yet it remains an underdeveloped aspect of radio research on institutional settings and production contexts.[523] Future research would need to further probe other domains of radio, beyond its early decades, in the realms of commercial, local, regional, community, pirate, micro or internet radio.[524] Each of these domains brings with it particular relationships to the radio medium, to regulation and institutions, to technology, infrastructure and production practices, and to communities and audiences, before even turning to questions about how and why programme content was recorded, let alone subject to archiving or preservation practices at the time of transmission or later. These conditions serve to remind us that radiophilia may invoke a love for, or strong attachment to, radio, but that sufficient resources and infrastructures usually need to be in place to fully support the impulse to not only keep and save, but also digitally preserve, radio content.

Conclusion

This chapter opened with an appeal by a broadcast collector, who later became a professional archivist, to stop lamenting the ephemerality of radio and television but to recognize its striking materiality in public life as well as in the archive. Yet, the perceived ephemerality of radio transmissions, as fading after their sounds have been heard, has frequently served as an impulse for audiences and fans of radio to try to capture radio's sounds or other material traces. With this insight in mind, the chapter firstly attended to various aspects of the radiophilic desire to 'save' radio-related objects, starting with the circulation and collection of paper items, such as QSL cards, postcards or tickets, or objects, such as membership badges or pins, and considered the effort to collect and reorganize such materials into scrapbooks made by fans, spanning the amateur radio and broadcast era and including fan clubs and broadcast personnel themselves.

A radiophilic desire to save also extends up to present-day practices seeking to save buildings or infrastructure connected with radio, from drawing attention to abandoned broadcast houses to lobbying for heritage listing and preservation, or working collaboratively to restore a ship used for off-shore pirate broadcasts. In contrast to large-scale public and built environment sites of broadcast heritage, one of the strong attachments in terms of saving by fans has been to keep their own radio receivers, from early crystal radio detectors through to radiograms and transistors. Beyond personal souvenirs, affective acts of saving also take the form of an active collecting of radio receivers and the establishment of radio collector societies to encourage this hobby, from collecting through to tinkering and restoring historical radio receivers. In such practices, a 'community' often forms around in-person events, online forums and trading practices, with the 'love of the objects' sometimes motivated by personal memories of past radio listening or driven by a 'technostalgia' focused on the material form of old radio design.[525]

The act of saving radio, nonetheless, is frequently centred on recording and preserving its sounds. The perceived ephemerality of radio as a live medium has been a key trigger for radio enthusiasts and fans who wanted to record and listen to transmission, whether it be content perceived as historically or politically important, or a favourite programme with particular music, as in the case of my own story of teenage radio listening and recording that opened this book. Affordability, portability and the quality of sound recording equipment were major challenges for those attempting to record radio up to the 1930s and 1940s. However, wire and tape recording became more readily available and portable from the 1950s to the 1970s, facilitating home recording practices, including focused efforts to 'hunt' for radio and musical content. The radiophilic desire to 'save' radio has resulted in the formal organization of dedicated collectors of audio recordings, which is often concentrated on a particular era, presenter, genre or station, such as 'old time radio' collecting communities formed in the 1970s that today have a strong online archival presence, through to online collaborative archiving and rescuing of radio and podcast content. In observing a number of visible and active groups focused on preserving and sharing radio recordings, the analysis has underscored how these examples skew strongly towards communities of mainly white, middle-class men in Britain and North American contexts. A critical sensitivity is required in assessing how such collecting reflects not only particular taste preferences, but also the in-built assumption that the figure of the radio 'collector' is generally male, white and middle class. Such selectivity, in terms of country, language, period, station or genre, not only requires an analytical sensitivity to absences or gaps produced by those who have recorded and later collected and traded historical radio content, but also an awareness of present-day efforts to challenge the selectivity of existing radio collections, whether private or institutional, and establish 'archival disruptions' through community archiving initiatives.[526]

With this insight in mind, the final section on radiophilic acts of 'saving' radio first turned its attention to the early radio archival initiatives in broadcast institutions from the 1930s onwards. It traced the ways in which the attachment to radio and desire to collect and preserve it for posterity took form and was grounded in emotional responses articulated by and among broadcast personnel in institutional settings, which came to be developed in tandem with new production practices but was also given additional rationale and socio-political importance in the context of the Second World War. This section attended to the post-war period of increasing heritage appreciation of recorded sound collections, but also the significant absence or loss of recordings in the magnetic tape era due to re-recording practices and subsequent degradation. It highlighted in particular the significance of the period from the 1950s to the 1970s in the context of decolonization and independence struggles, which led to the establishment of national broadcast institutions and with it, new priorities and uses for radio archival collections, in former colonies in Asia, Africa and the Americas. The final part of this study reflected on the most recent era of 'saving' radio in heritage institutions, as part of efforts towards the digital preservation of collections, but also in the face of calls to unsettle the gatekeeper role of professional archivists to become more involved in collaborative partnerships with community stakeholders to improve not only preservation but also access, contextualization and source donations by users. This final concern serves as a bridge from the current concern with saving to the fourth and final chapter, which focuses on the various ways in which the love of radio has been shared, both past and present.

4

Sharing

[Evening of Sounds] consists of sound requests and callers' narratives recounting personal experiences and memories of contemporary and historical sonic phenomena from urban, agricultural and natural settings . . . This sharing of collective and personal sound memories and narratives sustains a sociocultural history of sound but also feeds back by evoking and constructing new memories for the listeners, changing their experience of everyday sounds in their lives.[527]

Evening of Sounds, a popular series on YLE (Finnish Broadcasting Company) aired between 2012 and 2019, allowed listeners to email or phone with requests for a two-hour, live Sunday evening programme.[528] Among the many types of sounds requested by listeners, media memories were prominent, including typical sounds of Finnish radio, such as 'historical time signals, jingles and the voices of popular radio play characters'.[529] These radio-specific sounds were aired along with listener narratives recalling their own memories of listening to Finnish radio, often during childhood and adolescence. This example of a programme facilitating audience requests to hear particular sounds of the recent and distant past invokes the topic of sharing and its significance within radiophilia. It draws our attention to the possibility of radio facilitating input from listeners, in airing sounds that, in turn, could be familiar or new to other listeners, and in enabling a shared space for a collective listening to these sounds and a discussion of their significance. All of this took place with the support of the YLE Sound Archive, which supplied historical recordings and sourced new field recordings, when necessary, thereby enriching the radio broadcaster's documentation of Finnish soundscapes and listener memories.

While the previous chapter took up amateur and professional practices of radio archiving from the perspective of *saving*, the present and final chapter turns to the theme of *sharing*, and it will have a central concern: how do you share your love of radio? The present chapter will respond to this question by reflecting on how a love of radio is shared with, or put on display for, others. The chapter will start by reflecting on three main aspects of how radio listeners and enthusiasts engaged in sharing their interest in and attachment to radio (and radio listening): namely, particular content, practices and spaces. In each case, I will consider how sharing is enacted by individuals and among collectives, and illustrate examples across the radio century in which this has occurred, either in face-to-face situations or via radio itself as a shared space created in the exchange between radio makers and listening audiences. These three aspects (content, practices and spaces) of radio enthusiasts and listeners engaging in 'sharing' their attachment spans forms of social performance and display, via clothing, accessories or merchandise, through to engaging in shared listening practices, whether informal, self-organized or official events.

The second section will treat the objects and built spaces in which the present and past love of radio have been shared, with a particular interest in the physical arrangements and forms of display that both document and foster the love of radio in the context of radio museums and exhibitions. This range spans highly-visible or organized activities, such as the official or amateur radio museum, through to the efforts made to elicit the recall and sharing of memories by visitors in temporary exhibitions or other smaller or short-term interventions. It will start with museum spaces situated in the built environment, from the first discussions about putting radio (and its history) on display in the 1910s to 1930s through to present day museum spaces and exhibits as spaces for sharing in present and past attachments to radio, often seeking to intervene in the social history and public memory of radio.

The final section will build on the previous section on museum exhibition spaces and consider other sites of curation in radio and how people with a strong attachment to the medium are addressed or engaged. It will treat three sites of curation: firstly, forms of radio-based sharing practices involving audio content, such as curation in broadcasting itself and aired on radio; secondly, it will note non-online forms of curation as demonstrated by compilations of radio sounds, for instance, on vinyl, cassette or CD; and finally, it will survey curation and display practices in online spaces, catering to listening and participation via digital devices, such as smartphones or personal computers. In all such cases, we will encounter instances of sharing and display, but also curatorial presentation, with selections and narratives that may, in turn, overlook other, less conventional types of radio to which listeners may be attached.

Sharing and displaying the love of radio

This section will consider acts of *sharing* in situations involving a shared time and space. One way that media fans have expressed their shared relationship with the object of their interest (whether stars, content or characters) is through the practices of self-fashioning and social performance, in particular via clothing. Perhaps in part due to its audio-oriented content and appeal to the imagination, radio fandom practices have generated significantly less fan production around costume.[530] Across media fandom, we find fashion practices – particularly dressing up as fictional characters – that have evolved from literature (e.g., Sherlock Holmes), television (e.g., the *Star Trek* series) and, more recently, 'cosplay' focused on manga and video games. Such 'embodied and affective practices' allows fans in the present day to 'display their intense attachment to games by producing their own costumes inspired by fictional characters'.[531] In early radio culture, we find examples of the fandom and intense attachment to the experience of radio gaining expression through fancy dress costumes with some relation to radio. For example, in the annual carnival processions in the German city of Düsseldorf in 1928, newsreel footage shows a man dressed as a radio receiver in a costume consisting of a box representing a radio receiver with a tuning dials, while a year later a press photo depicted another man dressed as the Cologne radio station's transmission tower, with the pattern of its metal structure painted on his white jumpsuit, a sign saying 'Caution High Voltage!' and an antenna attached to his head.[532] These examples are illustrative of how the early fascination with radio culture was translated into embodied practices of fancy dress that referenced the material form of radio's reception and transmission.

While such social performance – with its enthusiasm about radio as a new technology – was most likely restricted to the first decade of broadcast radio, it encourages us to think about other uses of clothing or accessories in subsequent decades in which to channel emotive expressions of attachment to radio. For instance, subcultural and fan identification with a particular radio station has often taken the form of badges/buttons, t-shirts, hats and bags, which in some cases could be bought or were acquired via station giveaways. The focus on merchandise giveaways was already established in commercial radio, for instance in the United States during the 1930s and 1940s, with the presence of ordinary people on air being prioritized as 'an analogy [was drawn] between participatory radio, participatory democracy, and a new culture of consumption'.[533] For example, the NBC network programme *Vox Pop* (1932–48) was initially established as a street interview and human interest programme, but then started to expand its quiz elements, for which 'the merchandise giveaways became the most emotionally compelling part of the program, eliciting screams of delight from guests, roars of applause from the live audience, and bags of mail from overwrought listeners'.[534] An average of 1,000 letters per week were received by the programme, and a small selection that has been preserved includes the emotional disputing of 'incorrect' answers in the programme, the sharing of suggested changes to the programme, and responses to the invitation to suggest questions to be posed during the street interviews.[535]

While giveaways were mainly consumer goods linked to station sponsors, such as domestic appliances, vacations or clothing, during the 'post network' era of radio, in subsequent decades, commercial stations started to promote merchandise displaying the station's logo, both through items of clothing that could be worn, but also as stickers, including car bumper stickers, which served as a performative display of emotional attachment and identity formations around particular stations.[536] Merchandise was initially linked to a commercial trend towards narrowcasting and focused 'brand' identities, constituting visible objects that audiences, in turn, tended to use as a means of self-definition, particularly in the 1980s and 1990s, as commercial radio expanded in national markets previously dominated by public broadcasting.[537] This trend could also be found among public and non-profit radio stations across the globe, for which station websites became a crucial mechanism in selling station merchandise by the 2000s, often part of fundraisers for community radio stations (see Figure 21).[538] This post-network context of narrowcasting (or nichecasting) meant that musical genres came to play a more central role in station identities, for example, alternative, jazz, easy listening, rock, bossa nova or electronic dance music. In these circumstances, the wearing of a

FIGURE 21 T-Shirt for the 2SER community radio station, Sydney, Australia, which can be purchased or attained when signing up as a 'Passionate' or 'Lifetime' member. Courtesy of 2SER.

station logo item could be read as a signal to others, who may experience a recognition of fellow fandom, and potentially, of disidentification or derision by non-fans of that station or programme.[539]

Acts of sharing related to radio commonly take place in the form of shared listening practices, which are not only sites of social interaction but also affective practice. Even with crystal radio detectors, which required listeners to wear headphones, early publications were replete with images not only of individuals but small groups of listeners listening to radio, from young children and families to the elderly. Usually such depictions privileged interior, domestic settings, but listening to radio has also often occurred at the thresholds of private and public spaces. Sporting events provided popular live content in early radio and attracted particular attention as opportunities for shared listening, with it being noted in the United States that 'they quickly became some of the most popular broadcasts of the decade. Fans in the 1920s flocked to the shop or home of a friend or neighbor who had radio so they too could hear the World Series [baseball] or a Jack Dempsey fight.'[540] Indeed, in contexts where radio receivers were valuable and scarce, those in possession of them often allowed neighbours to listen in their homes (or on the front porch), or placed the receivers near or on the threshold of the window, so that others could listen.[541] Such practices have been described as particularly commonplace during the 1920s and 1930s, such as in the Philippines, where listening to the (increasingly multilingual) sounds of radio often took place at corner shops, where the reception of radio was overlayed with the sounds of conversation and local gossip, as well as transactions in the shop itself.[542]

While these examples suggest that radio receivers that were relatively 'fixed' in terms of their placement, the introduction of the transistor from the 1950s onwards was crucial in ushering in portable radio receivers, which expanded the terrain of shared listening. In Zambia, for instance, the transistor radio long remained a prized object, reflecting 'the sociality of domestic space'[543] and shared in outdoor spaces during daytime hours, where listening to radio in group settings was interspersed with conversation:

> [T]he consumption of radio includes the culturally-specific ways that people attune themselves to (or attenuate themselves from) the radio machine, its technology, its portability, its commodity

status and the fact that it produces unique sounds which can travel through communities ... In Zambia, people are acutely conscious of radio's physicality and its commodity status, like the ease of its theft, the weakness of its batteries and its potential for display in a social situation ... [R]ather than being consumed by an attentive family, the radio more often plays on within a complex nexus of social relations and activities in which numerous things are happening simultaneously – other media, other sounds, children, visitors, activities like baking buns and pounding maize and so on.[544]

In this context, the radio's status as a portable object has also been observed, as individual receivers 'temporarily became a collective asset within [the owner's] wider kin and friendship networks', sometimes moving across households and figuring significantly in weddings and funeral processions.[545] Radio use in Zambia between the 1960s and 1990s reminds us that the radio set is not a strictly indoors, stationary or invisible item and that attentive listening is not always the norm, but instead is often woven into shared, social activities.

When it comes to shared practices of listening, in West Germany we find that the introduction of the transistor radio in the 1950s and 1960s also led to practices initiated by listeners that exceeded the uses imagined by manufacturers. In early promotional discourses, the transistor was coupled with the idea of the receiver being a 'friend' or 'companion' for travel, reflected in the design of a 'suitcase'-style receiver that could be carried on journeys or in leisure activities.[546] Even though indoor listening to stationary sets remained dominant and also had better sound quality, the advent of the 'pocket' radio gained particular popularity among younger listeners, who were attracted to these cheaper models, whose flexibility allowed the devices to be taken along during visits to friends or to public spaces like parks or squares for shared acts of radio listening. Such acts by young people attracted the ire of adults and the authorities, and in the 1960s and 1970s bans on public listening to radio devices were introduced by transport companies and swimming pools.[547] Teenagers used portable devices to access stations playing popular music (which was initially hard to find on West German public radio), to signal their love of radio (and its popular music content) to others and to circumvent the control of parents over domestic radio consumption in the home.[548] As 'pioneers of a mobile lifestyle', teenagers' radio listening practices included walking through outdoor spaces, which served as a model for mobile listening practices with the Walkman (with headphones) and radio cassette recorders (discussed in the previous chapter in relation to acts of 'saving').[549]

For shared practices of listening, there is one other crucial space when it comes to post-1945 mobile cultures of listening – namely, car radio. While possibilities for car radio reception had been explored since the 1920s, the car became an important site for the consumption of radio stations (and later via in-built stereos with cassettes, CDs and digital file players), particularly with the intensification of commuter traffic from suburban or exurban areas, from 1950s onwards. The development of the transistor radio helped to facilitate shared experiences of radio listening, particularly for the passengers seated in a car together, but also in radio stations dedicated to guiding listeners through their shared experience of commuting to and from work in 'peak hour' periods of traffic. By the 1990s, the notion of the car as a dedicated listening space had been confirmed – 'a site for emotional and spiritual regulation and transportation and a locus for in-betweenness, spatially and temporally'.[550] While car radio may be read as creating a form of 'acoustic shielding',[551] the sociality of radio listening can be found in the direct commentary of radio announcers to listeners about their commute and workday, in the shared acts of recognition of bumper stickers in commuter traffic (as mentioned above), or radio sounds heard emanating from other cars. For certain car-based professions, such as taxi driving, radio listening has been studied as a site in which disputes about station or music choice are prevalent, but it has been noted that a shared music repertoire also has the potential for enacting a 'relational, immersive and empathetic listening' amongst drivers, and between individual drivers and their customers.[552]

Research on the advent of car audio from the 1920s to the 1970s has shown that it shifted in meaning: while initially promoted from the 1920s onwards as 'a companion to the lonely driver, in the 1960s it came to be defined as a sonic assistant helping drivers to cope with their *lack* of solitude on the road: to musically control their temper in situations of traffic jams and badly behaving fellow drivers'.[553]

Radio programming for commuters, in turn, has tended to align itself with this 'mood regulation' by emphasizing the rhythm of the working day (and week) for its listeners, and by engaging them with a variety of interactive and informative content, such as live traffic reports.[554] Following the increased ownership of mobile phones from the 1990s onwards, commercial radio has further foregrounded the space for their listeners to 'call in' to answer questions, make song requests or give traffic tips, thereby facilitating listener acts of sharing or participating, and amplifying the sense for audience members that their commuter listening experience allows not only a shared sonic experience (of radio) but also that of place (commuter traffic). Similar strategies around shared listening have also been in evidence in recent (community) radio and podcast engagement with audiences who were 'listening alone together' during crisis situations such as the recent COVID-19 pandemic.[555]

Certain times of the day can also be said to be more conducive to engaging listeners through their enthusiasm for radio and attachments to particular programmes, as has been shown for the morning, daytime or evening slots allocated to particular genres or types of programming.[556] For instance, in Kuala Lumpur, Malaysia, BFM89.9 is a business and economics station that has gained attention for its indie rock programming during its evening and midnight slots, attracting an urban, middle-class and English-speaking listenership.[557] In Australia, 'talkback' programmes on commercial stations from the late 1960s onwards aimed at a 'housewife audience' for daytime slots, while evenings and weekends slots had a stronger emphasis on sports discussions in an effort to attract male listeners.[558] In recent decades, audience research has shown that interaction between listeners and talkback stations formed an important basis for interpersonal networks for its listeners: some stations have organized social events or facilitated listeners' contact with one another, while for others it served a broader therapeutic role through the discussion of problems, as a 'space for "sharing"' and helping to 'break away from the restrictions on their social identities caused by their disabilities, ill health, mental health problems, and social isolation'.[559] The participatory element of talkback radio experienced by its audiences has evolved from phone calls to a broader use of text-based communication via text messages, emails and station websites. Since the 2010s, social media such as Twitter and Facebook have been actively used to encourage audience interactivity with stations or particular hosts and programmes across public and commercial radio services.[560]

A final type of shared listening practice worth mentioning is gatherings that are officially organized. Organized radio listening might take the form of a live performance for an in-studio audience, which has been an established feature since early radio and replicated more recently with live tapings of podcast programmes in the presence of audience members.[561] The organization of radio listening might also take place in institutional environments, in some cases in a pedagogical context (e.g., a school classroom), and, in others, as a political obligation or in an effort to improve workplace efficiency, such as in factories.[562] An early organized context for listening was the 'radio listening groups' that were prevalent in English-speaking countries between the late 1920s and 1950s:

> Group listening in the early years of broadcasting was in many places the result of a scarcity of radios, but it grew also from a deliberate reform strategy that sought to discipline and instruct the listening audience. Organised radio listening groups were indeed possibly one of the last formal attempts to *teach* people how to interact with mass media ... The idea of a listening group was to have simultaneous listening and then simultaneous post-broadcast discussion, thus bringing national or regional voices into local communities and encouraging active local engagement with them ... Buoyed by such hopes of active citizen listening, the listening group phenomenon spread in the interwar period through Europe (including Scandinavia, Czechoslovakia, the Netherlands, Switzerland, Germany and the Soviet Union), North America, Australasia and parts of Asia. Everywhere it bore the hopes of modernizing reformers who saw in broadcasting some exciting new possibilities and a possible answer to the problem of how to combine the conditions of mass-society modernity with an engaged, informed, locally active democracy.[563]

Group listening therefore was sometimes utilized with the idea of fuelling workplace productivity, while in other cases it was conceived in line with the ideal of democratic participation. We also find more coercive initiatives during the twentieth century, with the installation of loudspeaker systems and organized group listening in an effort to establish the auditory presence of state radio across the private and public spheres. Such practices have been documented, for instance, in National Socialist Germany, Soviet Russia and Maoist China.[564] Similarly, loudspeaker broadcasts were organized by the South African state during the 1940s, using information and entertainment content at particular times, at gold mines and other urban contexts as a means to 'activate the African public's imagination' but also increase the state's 'own technological visibility and sonic presence'.[565]

Beyond these more top-down directed or organized instances of group listening, we also find instances of self-organization by radio listeners. In some countries, like Denmark, self-organized listener associations had a significant presence from the late 1920s onwards, representing the interests of societal groups based on region, class, religion or profession, and engaged in lobbying about broadcast programming policy and organizing events for members.[566] Elsewhere, we find other groups who were eager to create shared conditions for radio (music) listening, often taking place in networks involving a crossover between music, sound recording and radio. One of the first prominent recorded music magazines for ordinary listeners to experience crossover interest with radio was the UK's *The Gramophone*, founded in 1923. Initiated as an explicitly amateur fan publication, in conversation with fellow 'gramophiles', the periodical was initially dedicated solely to reviews of commercial music releases, and then gradually, to radio and later sound film.[567] Its main editor, Christopher Stone, amassed a sizeable gramophone collection and was allowed, from 1927 onwards, to host regular music radio programmes, for which he was credited as the BBC's first 'disc jockey'.[568] In addition to Stone's informal and accessible style, his weekly 'recital of gramophone records' programmes expanded beyond classical or well-known repertoires; he created 'special' programmes mainly skewed towards dance releases from the UK, the US and continental Europe, with his compilation programmes described as spanning '"hot" American tunes, Cuban dance music, African native songs, birds and beasts, and so on'.[569] This description also emphasized Stone's expertise as predicated on needing to 'listen to more records than almost any man in England' in his role as magazine editor and BBC 'gramophone expert'. Such accounts underscored for his audience Stone's dual role as a fellow popular music fan and professional 'tastemaker' in curating sounds from the global music recording industry via the radio.[570]

After a period of several years working for the commercial station Radio Luxembourg, which primarily focused on gramophone concerts but also prioritized new dance music being ignored by the BBC, Stone returned to the BBC as a recognized 'radio personality' in early 1939. There, he hosted several popular recorded music programmes across the war years, culminating in a special programme, *Gramophone Shop*, in 1946, in which Stone visited a well-known music shop and interviewed the customers as they were selecting records for their own collections.[571] This vox pop approach, focusing on the shop as a space of shared music consumption, and prioritizing the voices and opinions of 'ordinary' music fans, inspired a subsequent series in which the regional Midland domestic service ran a series interviewing music consumers across the UK.[572] Beyond this focus on music shops and the fans and collectors who visited them, Stone can be said to have initiated or at least enhanced the concept of the music compilation programme on radio as a designated space of shared listening with fellow music fans, who were identified and addressed as such, working in tandem with *The Gramophone* music fan magazine, who organized group listening during 'gramophone recitals'.

This points us to the fundamental role of both recorded music and radio shops as crucial nodes for the sharing practices fuelling 'crossover' fandoms relating to modern sound culture from the late 1920s onwards. For instance, an early 'aficionado' or music collector culture around 1900 in Barcelona, Spain, was a precedent for the foundation of small record clubs like the *Discòfils* club in the early 1930s, whose listening sessions reflected a strong investment in 'discophilia'.[573] The intersection between radio and music fandom was further developed in Paris, France. A key figure here was Jacques Lévi-Alvarès, who ran the La Boîte à Musique (The Music Box) phonograph and recorded music store, starting in the 1920s, and from 1934 a record label at the same location. During the 1930s, the music store hosted promotional activities such as a radio programme, exhibitions, conferences and events with musicians and authors. These activities took place alongside weekly and eventually daily in-store 'record concerts' as group listening sessions devoted to a specific composer, but in general the store (and the label itself) represented a wide range of classical, folk, jazz and popular music.[574]

A similar development can be found with the activities of recorded music critic and phonograph trader Maurice Dalloz, whose 'disquaire' doubled as a music store and listening salon, thereby attracting music fans and collectors. Following the shop's closure in 1935, and at the suggestion of a dedicated customer, the 'Les Discophiles' club was formed in 1936.[575] Involving both non-professional fans and established experts in the music and radio fields, the club's activities included the production of a magazine and regular meetings and listening sessions until the outbreak of war, with Dalloz himself gaining an appointment as 'disc librarian' at the French Radiodiffusion national broadcaster in the late 1930s. Dalloz held this position for almost two decades, while also presenting radio programmes on 'New Discs' until the late 1950s.[576] A similar pattern can be found with the jazz record store The Music Store, whose co-owner Henri Gédovius had a weekly jazz radio show from 1935 until the outbreak of war, resuming this activity after hostilities ceased. Gédovius remained in employment in radio for the remainder of his career.[577] These examples serve as a reminder of the exchanges occurring between spaces of music, radio and phonographic consumption, and the shared listening practices of enthusiasts from the late 1920s onwards, an intersecting of interests that was further underscored by the existence of a magazine in this period entitled *Phono-radio-musique*.[578] Here we see how dedicated spaces allowed the 'passion for music' and radio fandom to operate together.[579] There is also a certain parallel with the (mainly male) collectors discussed in the previous chapter, whose interest in collecting sound media came to intersect with their field of professional employment.

Similarly in Japan, there was a crossover between music, radio and audio technology fandoms, with a nascent audiophile community during the 1920s and 1930s comprising a 'cross-section of radio (and wireless) fans and music fans (typically classical music and American popular music)'.[580] Prominent owners of acoustic phonographs had already declared their 'love for the object' (*kibutsuai*) in the 1920s, with record collecting emerging in the 1910s among (upper) middle-class music fans, and the expansion of fandoms related to radio, classical/jazz music and phonograph collecting in the pre-war period creating an important base for the emergence of the high-end audio scene after 1950.[581] Similar to the specialized music shops in Europe, the pre-war music cafés (*kissa*) assembled sizeable recorded music collections, creating an accessible, discophile space for shared listening via high-end playback equipment among a predominantly urban male clientele of young students, music collectors and critics. In most cases, the owners or its employees, the 'record girls', acted as music experts, selecting records, taking requests from customers and operating playback equipment.[582] While these cafés created a familiar space for group listening to particular genres, unlike the music stores in Europe, they served as 'public record collector[s]' for smaller genre-oriented communities (e.g., jazz, Western classical music), while also offering a meeting place for the music clubs formed during the early 1930s.[583]

These examples of the establishment of shared spaces for music and radio fans, for group listening at home, outdoors or in other designated spaces, point to the significance of communal sites for sharing the experience of radio and radio listening, a theme that will be further explored in the next section on sharing and display strategies in museums and exhibitions.

Sharing the love of radio in museums and exhibition spaces

In the previous chapter ('Saving'), several examples were noted of historical displays that were put on show at public radio exhibitions, in some cases documenting the most recent histories of radio since the advent of regulated broadcasting, while in other cases narrating the invention of wireless telegraphy from the 1890s onwards, or the development of various devices for radio transmission and reception. In this context, some of the earliest calls for a 'radio museum' emerged from broadcast organizations and their professional staff, usually during their working life, but sometimes after their retirement.

The early 1930s provides an example of an institutionally-conceived radio museum, when two staff members of the German Broadcasting Company, Hans Schlee and Dr Herbert Antoine, were assigned the task of preparing a 'radio museum' for the new purpose-built 'House of Radio' (Haus des Rundfunks) broadcast building in Berlin. Writing in 1931, Schlee described the planned radio museum as one that would document and share with visitors the first years of broadcast radio since 1923, as well as the developments in wireless telegraphy prior to that.[584] Citing the rapid advances within radio in its first years, Schlee suggested that it was essential to help give the public 'a clear picture' of its development, going on to describe how they would engage the public with a 'lively' rather than a 'dead' exhibition format, centring on providing technical equipment for visitors to operate, as well as photography, models, charts and statistics, and a programme of film screenings and lectures accompanied by technical demonstrations.[585] The layout envisaged for the radio museum included a hall of fame for German inventors who contributed to radio technology and for other key figures in the recent history of German radio, with busts and photos of these figures on display, along with notable devices by German inventors such as Heinrich Hertz, credited as the man who discovered electromagnetic waves.[586]

A second, larger part of the exhibition would focus on radio technology, divided into two sub-sections explaining the electrical processes of transmission and reception to the visitor, with technical devices and educational films. The transmission sub-section would show the historical development of recording and amplification, offering visitors the opportunity to see a working replica of the first German radio transmitter and the first radio studio in Berlin, along with displays of microphones, amplification and recording studio equipment and antenna systems. Schlee noted that panoramas and stereoscopic pictures would give an overview of transmitter and recording rooms of German and international radio stations.[587] The reception sub-section would chart the development of radio receivers with headphones through to radio sets. Schlee imagined that each new technical innovation could be communicated with a panel that would be illuminated with backlighting when visitors pressed a button, while the development of receivers by particular companies could be shown in revolving columns, with a special display explaining radio interference and how to deal with it. A final, separate room would be devoted to the latest developments in radio technology, with visitors able to listen to live radio via loudspeakers, or take a look at radio magazines or advertising materials from the radio industry.[588]

Almost as an afterthought, Schlee closed his 1931 outline by noting a third and final section that would be dedicated to broadcast organization and programming. This part would use large illuminated panels to outline how the German broadcast network had expanded, while the development of particular radio genres would be displayed in statistics and pictures, along with insights into the process of programme making and the development of radio programme magazines and amateur and hobbyist radio associations. Additional multimedia elements would include short animation and feature films to communicate the significance of radio for particular occupations and social groups, and a display of German Broadcast Corporation (RRG) posters intended to attract new radio subscribers.[589] This final part suggests some accommodation of radio culture and a limited acknowledgement of the shared domain of radiophilia, in the form of popular radio magazines and amateur associations. However, the predominant theme of the display was a nationally-focused story of great inventors, technological devices and their technical operations. We can find a similar approach in the exhibition marking the thirtieth anniversary of the Dutch wireless radio transmitter company NSF (Nederlandsche Seintoestellen Fabriek) in 1948. Even though this exhibition took place more than fifteen years after the plans devised by Schlee, a newsreel footage sequence indicates the emphasis on technical demonstrations of historical transmitters and receivers, comparing these with modern radio receivers with tuning knobs in the domestic environment, conveying to audiences how their experience of enjoying radio has changed over time.[590]

Schlee offered an optimistic account of the possibilities conceivable at the time for creating a radio museum in the style of a modern, didactic museum.[591] Schlee's vision, which he admitted would require 'great effort and expense', does not appear to have been realized following the unveiling of the building in January 1931, perhaps due to the dire economic situation of that time, nor was it pursued following the ascension to power of the Nazi Party in 1933. A similar call for a National Radio Museum in London based on a 'Radio Museum' display at the annual Radiolympia exhibition in 1937 does not appear to have gained traction after this first initiative, which was projected as a possible corrective to the 'danger of myth and legend taking the place of history' and having the potential to deepen the 'intelligent interest of the public' in radio.[592] Nonetheless, while this blueprint for a radio museum as a space to share the historical narrative and material culture of radio in Germany was not realized, Schlee's colleague Dr Antoine became involved in the post-war creation of a radio museum in West Berlin, serving as its first director upon its opening in 1965. A key difference in this new initiative was that while the tripartite interest in the historical development of radio transmission, reception and programming remained, a larger scope was envisaged for materials from radio enthusiasts, who were invited to contribute pre-1939 equipment for the exhibition.[593] Moreover, the interactive component of the museum was imagined in the form of a data processor computer that could answer questions about the history of radio if visitors entered a code number, and small tape recorders with headphones that listeners could carry individually to receive a guided tour of the museum.[594] Here, as in other science and technology museums of the 1960s, the introduction of the radio-guided tour concept into museum spaces was identified as helping to 'to animate, entertain and educate a group of museum visitors referred to loosely as "the average visitor": a non-technical visitor with a non-specialist interest in science and technology'.[595] The new approaches to exhibition presentation and display made use of spoken narration and sound, 'placing corporeality center stage and shifting the site of sense and meaning-making away from the autonomous object, enclosed behind glass, to the relationship between viewer and viewed'.[596] This dialogical concept was coupled with a more inclusive vision of museum pedagogy, with visitors increasingly including women, families and the working class, for whom the audio tours could provide new knowledge about technologies like radio in an engaging and accessible manner. This potentially opened up space for visitors to engage their own personal experiences of radio, rather than see the history of radio as restricted to narratives centred on famous inventors and technological innovation.

Overall, the impulse to create radio-specific museum spaces appears to be consistent with other national contexts; the desire to put radio history on display in the 1960s was felt strongly among the first generation of radio professionals and amateur enthusiasts, many of whom reached retirement age in that period and wanted to document and share their own experiences with others. This life cycle perspective on the motivation of retired professionals and enthusiasts can partly be explained by the fact that, in Germany, some of the pre-1933 employees and enthusiasts had been fired or thwarted in their activities under National Socialism, and thus perhaps were additionally motivated to retrieve the pre-Nazi history of radio in (West) Germany. A further insight can be provided by the site secured for the museum, which, from 1967, was located at the foot of the Berlin Radio Tower (Berliner Funkturm), which itself received heritage protection shortly before the museum's move to this location. The tower was a major attraction from its creation in the 1920s (and rebuilding following a fire) and a focal point for the activities associated with the annual German radio exhibition until 1939. The location of the museum, in a recognized heritage site and close to the main broadcasting house, reflects a growing sense of the built environment as historically valuable, related to the growth of the modern heritage movement and 'authorised heritage discourse', along with heritage tourism, during the 1960s and 1970s.[597]

A similar development can be observed in the Netherlands, with the idea of a radio museum being first conceived during the German occupation and discussed in 1943, but only coming into full swing when the first radio pioneers of the 1910s, such as Jan Corver, donated personal collections in the mid-1950s to the Dutch national radio board (Nederlands Radio Unie, or NRU).[598] By the time of the official launching of the Netherlands Broadcasting Museum Foundation (Stichting Nederlands Omroepmuseum), in late 1976, a sizeable collection of broadcast devices had been accumulated over thirty years in various buildings and storage spaces in Hilversum. Here, too, the first curator and 'chief collector', Cor van Driel, was a former broadcast employee who carried out this work towards the end of his career, with a subsequent director, former broadcast employee Kees Cabout, carrying out this role as an unpaid 'labour of love' in the early 1980s.[599] The museum, initially housed in former villa space for its first exhibitions from 1984 onwards, was soon overwhelmed by the response of the general public, with 20,000 visitors per year and regular coverage in newspapers and on radio and television.[600] With a move to a larger space in 1993, the museum entered a new 'modern' phase with more interactive components, with visitors invited to enact scenes while standing in a popular sitcom set recreated with cameras and live playback. Radio, by contrast, was assigned a somewhat more 'nostalgic' role in appealing to visitors through the recreation of a 1930s radio dealer shop ('Radiohandel Cabout') inside the museum (see Figure 22). This contained a display window and a shop interior with a counter, cash register and a workshop, along with radio sets, loudspeakers, turntables, radio parts and valve measuring devices, historical price lists and radio construction drawings.[601] The shopfront and interior could serve as a memory trigger, given the prevalence of such specialist radio shops in Dutch shopping streets until the 1950s, after which time many expanded their scope in selling radio and television sets.

FIGURE 22 *Historical recreation of a radio dealer shop inside the museum display at the Nederlands Omroepmusem (Netherlands Broadcast Museum), Hilversum, Netherlands, c. 1993. Courtesy of Netherlands Institute of Sound and Vision.*

The appeal of the 1930s as an important reference point can also be found in the earliest amateur museums that emerged from the 1960s and 1970s onwards, and in some cases led to the opening up of private homes as shared spaces dedicated to the love of (old) radio. One of the most prominent of such museums is the Dulwich Wireless Museum, recently renamed the British Vintage Wireless and Television Museum. Its founder, Gerry (Gerald) Wells (1929–2014), developed what he described as an 'obsession' with radio during his childhood in the 1930s and 1940s.[602] While his intense 'overriding passion' to tinker with radio and other electrical items led to school expulsion, he eventually started a radio and TV repair business in 1957 and eventually inherited his family home in South London, where he claimed the back shed as his workshop.[603] In 1974, after his business failed, Wells decided to start to build up his vintage wireless museum starting from his own personal collection, after which time 'it took off' and became 'a place of pilgrimage for enthusiasts'.[604] By 1986, when he was featured in a book devoted to 'passionate' collecting habits in the UK, Wells described how he had filled the rooms of his childhood home, a red brick Victorian family dwelling, and mapped the scale of British radio history onto the interior spaces of the house. While the earliest British wireless sets (1917–30) were put on display in a former bedroom,[605] Wells organized the 1930s receivers according to manufacturers in the 'Daventry Room' (named after the first BBC longwave station), while the Bakelite receivers were located in the 'Droitwich Room' (named after a transmitter).[606] The dining room was filled with pre-war television sets, while Wells's own bedroom had a historic console for record playback and radio transmission, from which he installed a radio transmitter that allowed for him to be 'in touch with the whole complex'.[607]

It is in this sense that the museum project reproduces the idea of an extended radio network of 1930s Britain, with the home reconceived as a 'broadcast house', imaginatively covering studio production to the transmission towers through to reception via domestic radio sets. Despite this expansive understanding, the museum concept was constrained by Wells's own aesthetic judgements about the best manufacturers in terms of design and component parts. When asked to comment on his favourite radio sets, Wells suggested that the best British ones were made in 1936, 'when we reached our peak'. Nonetheless, the museum fulfils the collector's idea of pursuing a 'complete' collection of early radio receivers and valves, which are categorized according to manufacturer and year. But the majority of the activities pursued by Wells revolved around sharing the love of (early) radio: leading tours, helping others with receiver repair and hosting weekend workshops. In his desire to share a vision of the mid-1930s as the high point in British wireless design, Wells created a room within the museum that was intended to have the appearance of a wireless shop in 1936. As he explained to a visiting reporter in 2010, the authentic features included a shop counter, a telephone, a valve test on the counter and a 1936 copy of *The Radio Times*. The inference here is that the shop would best convey how the receivers and valves were presented and sold to customers, and thereby give a sense of the context of radio in everyday life.[608] In reflecting on his own experience of radio in the 1930s, Wells explained that the radio set was a 'focal point' in the living room, 'like a member of the family', and his efforts to open his own childhood home to others in order to experience pre-war radio can be understood as a desire to share with those who had the same experience and try to convey a sense of that period to those who did not live through it.

Among amateur museums around the world, it is not unusual to find a private residence, hall or commercial space repurposed for the needs of an amateur collection or local radio museum. Refashioning of a pre-existing space can be seen, for instance, in the example of the Japan Radio Museum (日本ラジオ博物館). While its title suggests a national museum space, it is mainly the work of a single enthusiast who first opened the space in 2012 (see Figure 23). Director Tadanobu Okabe set out to document the history of

FIGURE 23 *The exterior of the Japan Radio Museum, Matsumoto, Japan. Courtesy of Tadanobu Okabe.*

Japanese radio from its inception in 1925 to the present, and the museum tries to present the history of technology from vacuum tube receivers to transistors, but also including other domestic consumer items such as televisions, washing machines and Walkman devices. In terms of organization, it tries to showcase Japanese designed devices, though it uses 1945 to separate the first two decades of Japanese radio from the post-war period, which is bracketed as ending in the 1960s with the decline of valve or tube radio sets (see Figure 24).[609] On the museum's blog, Okabe indicates that he grew after the end of the Second World War and in the wake of Japan's surrender and military occupation, which may provide some insight into his childhood connection to radio and his decision to use 1945 as the main dividing point of the collection.[610] Looking worldwide, this strong focus on collections of radio receivers appears to be one of the most common threads for amateur museums, as visualized on the world map at Radiomuseum.org. A listing on the site provides a total of almost 5,000 technical museums (that are still open) with almost 600 of these focused on radio, covering individual and smaller amateur initiatives through to

FIGURE 24 *Tadanobu Okabe, director of the Japan Radio Museum, standing beside a display of historical wireless sets in the museum. Courtesy of Tadanobu Okabe.*

national media or technology museums.⁶¹¹ In other cases, we find radio museums hosted by regional or civic museums, as is the case of the Zhongshan Radio Museum (中山收音机博物馆), which has been hosted since 2005 in an annex of the Zhongshan City Museum, not far from Macau and Hong Kong: the only museum of its kind in China and one that is largely derived from a large donation by a private collector.⁶¹² Similarly in Izmir, Turkey, the Konak municipal government has supported the creation of the Radio and Democracy Museum (Radyo ve Demokrasi Muzesi), which presents its historical collection of 150 historical radio receivers within the narrative frame of radio policies pursued following the founding of Turkey in 1923.⁶¹³

While amateur museums sometimes demonstrate grander ambitions in their titles, such as the Japan Radio Museum, it is in fact a modest operation compared to the scale and ambition of the NHK Broadcast Museum in Tokyo. First opened in 1956, the museum historically maintained a strong technological focus, with the collections currently holding 20,000 pieces of broadcasting equipment. However, in recent renovations, there has not only been an effort to connect the exhibits – organized chronologically – to social, economic and political history, but also to emphasize this national media museum as an 'experience', as suggested by the name of an interactive studio in the four-level museum space.⁶¹⁴ A recent video documenting the museum shows how the national public broadcaster NHK seeks to engage the public with the history of radio and television, with motion activated audio segments communicated to visitors from sound showers offering additional narration on the displays of objects, along with texts, graphics, photos and silent video screens. Additional interactive elements include touchscreens allowing visitors to scroll through for additional contextual information, mock studios with a closed-circuit display for presenting a live news programme or operating cameras, and sound effects objects employed in radio drama that visitors can use to reproduce the sounds of footsteps, waves or a door opening.⁶¹⁵ In a similar manner, the Beeld en Geluid Experience (Sound and Vision Experience) exhibition space in the Netherlands, opened in 2006, used the notion of an immersive 'experience' and playful, interactive museum elements as a means of engaging a general public with Dutch broadcast history, with temporary exhibitions intended to attract repeat visits to the newly-built

Netherlands Institute of Sound and Vision building at the edge of the 'Media Park' complex for public broadcasters.[616]

What the above examples show is how the 'script' of radio exhibition spaces for their audiences was created not only via the display of objects and techniques for communication, but that they frequently traded on the built environment and location of the museum, with a number located at key sites of early radio broadcast history, prompting radio enthusiasts to enact 'pilgrimages' to particular sites or built objects.[617] In the context of former colonial territories, we find that the Taiwan National Radio Museum is located in a building first completed in 1940 under Japanese rule as the Minxiong Broadcast Station, whose main purpose was psychological warfare via international shortwave transmissions during the Second World War (see Figure 25). The history of the building and its contents means that the museum is not just offering a narrative of national radio, but also stresses the international context of its original creation (under colonial rule), along with the building's history as the centre of Radio Taiwan International radio operations for propaganda transmissions aimed at mainland China following the Chinese Civil War in 1949.[618] The museum, opened in 1998, has maintained the transmitter used under Japanese rule as

FIGURE 25 *Exterior of the Taiwan National Radio Museum, housed in the former Minxiong Broadcast Station, built in 1940. Courtesy of Po-Yi Chen/Shu-Ching Yang.*

FIGURE 26 *Transmission technology on display, with a screen for visitor information, Taiwan National Radio Museum. Courtesy of Po-Yi Chen/ Shu-Ching Yang.*

part of its permanent display (see Figure 26), as well as hosting temporary exhibitions, some focusing on intercepted broadcasts detected by monitors at the site between the 1970s and the 1990s.[619]

In general, these examples demonstrate an ever-increasing incorporation of interactive and immersive media elements, and a growing sensitivity to social history, in the pedagogical strategies adopted for radio-specific museums and more recently in the broadcast or media museums unveiled in the years around 2000. It may be in the format of the temporary exhibition that we find a more specific effort to cater to specific forms of radiophilia as attached to particular genres (such as sport or radio drama), stars or radio stations. For the domain of radio art, for instance, the exhibition 'Radiophonic Spaces' toured during 2018–19 offering visitors the experience of an interactive 'walk-in archive' of German-language and international radio art.[620] Upon entering the gallery space, the visitor received a set of headphones attached to a handheld device, and then had the opportunity to walk through the space where suspended transmitters (and a Wi-Fi tracking system) triggered audio clips, thereby inviting the visitor to follow key narratives about a century of radio art. In the gallery space, several fixed 'media stations' allowed visitors to search for further information about the collection of over 200 works and their creators, and view a network visualization linking related works.[621] While this example focused on the artistic content of radio and treated its materiality mainly in the form of the radio signal (and its potential interference), in more recent approaches to media archaeology we find new visions of to how historical radio devices and other media technologies should be presented: not only as functioning objects, but also according to the logic of their technical workings rather than historical chronology or medium specificity.[622]

Even though sound and, more specifically, radio have been considered difficult cultural objects to exhibit in conventional museum spaces, there are possibilities not just to embed radio in social and cultural histories within the museum,[623] but also interlink strong emotive attachments to radio with popular and local histories of music. For example, the temporary exhibition 'Shout Out! UK Pirate Radio in the 1980s', held at the ICA art centre in London in 2015, took as its focus the tower block pirate radio movement in the UK, which grew to around sixty stations in London and over 600 stations across the UK, before being subject to official bans and raids by police.[624] The approach of the exhibition was to uncover this vibrant radio culture and its connection to local music scenes that were underrepresented on public and commercial stations in the UK at the time. With objects largely sourced from a pirate radio archival initiative, the exhibition narrative sought to highlight how pirate radio became an increasingly important space for Black DJs, for programming jazz, soul, funk, reggae, garage and hip hop and as a pathbreaker for the emerging UK rave scene.[625] As such, the strong emotional attachment of listeners to the stations, their DJs and programming is conveyed by a display of posters, films, memorabilia, news reports, photos and oral histories.[626]

The stress on the radio stations as embedded in local music (sub)cultures and identities has been similarly explored in a 2016 exhibition, 'Alternative Radio', in Christchurch, New Zealand. Held at a local institution, the Canterbury Museum, the exhibition marked the fortieth anniversary of the Christchurch student radio station RDU.[627] RDU, which emerged in 1976 from a radio club associated with the University of Canterbury Student Association, was one of the first student radio stations in New Zealand, largely run in a volunteer capacity and associated with punk and other alternative music scenes emerging at the time.[628] In the exhibition space there was an effort not only to appeal to the core fan base of the RDU community and its listeners, but also develop a museum narrative that would appeal to a broader audience, which revolved around the themes of 'broadcasting', 'music', 'events', and 'people'. A historical timeline was used to guide visitors through the station's history (see Figure 27), which was connected to developments in local music scenes in Christchurch and the history of the city, which underwent a major earthquake in 2011, leading to the station being without a permanent station space until 2015.[629]

The exhibition team not only used objects from the station's own archival collection, but borrowed objects from individual fan collections, which together included posters, photos, documents, t-shirts and other memorabilia, allowing personal 'sound souvenirs' and memories of the station to be incorporated into the narrative of the station's history, and thereby emphasizing the shared experiences and participation of listeners as part of the culture of the station.[630] The exhibition narrative sought to bring together the broadcast process, the production culture of the station and its volunteers and

FIGURE 27 *Rachel Morton (RDU station) shows the radio journalist Yadana Saw the historical timeline within the space of the 'Alternative Radio' exhibition, Canterbury Museum, Christchurch, New Zealand. Photo by Rebekah Parsons-King. Courtesy of Radio New Zealand.*

its embedding in local and national music scenes. As researcher Zita Joyce has argued, a radio station:

> ... is not simply a vehicle for recorded music, but part of a broader cultural scene. It is a node in a network of staff, volunteers, musicians, promoters, technical crew, venue workers, poster designers, printers, billstickers, advertisers, sponsors, and the active listening audience itself. The live gigs and broadcasts made this explicit, and emphasised that RDU's role in this creative network is not an object of heritage, but a core part of the station's ongoing practice and identity.[631]

Indeed, a range of objects was used to give visual and material form to radio, demonstrating the work of the radio station and its connection to the local music scene, with the sounds in the space including a pre-selected soundtrack and a number of live radio shows and music performances (some of which were broadcast live to air).[632] A series of public performances helped museum visitors not only to experience the history of the station, but also to affirm personal and shared attachments to the radio station, the local music scene and the city itself.

This section has mainly focused on indoor and built spaces, such as the exhibition and museum, which have been harnessed to demonstrate and engage others in shared attachments to radio, whether that be in a national or local framework. I close this section with an offshore radio station in Israel – itself without a fixed institutional home or part of a national broadcast narrative – that has been memorialized in public space, on the initiative of the Tel Aviv municipality in 2007. The marble plaque, located near where the 'Voice of Peace' station's ship used to dock between 1973 and 1993, has a text in Hebrew and English that reads '5 km off this shore Abie Nathan's peace ship was anchored, broadcasting messages of peace, love and understanding' (see Figure 28). Since its initial placement, the original plaque and sound device have been embedded in a wooden framework, so that station fans or incidental pedestrians on the beach promenade can stop to listen to the recordings activated by the button. The recordings include clips from the station's history, with the Voice of Peace station's signature tune, spoken by station founder and owner Nathan himself: 'You're listening to the Voice of Peace, broadcasting from somewhere in the Mediterranean.'[633] While

FIGURE 28 *A memorial plaque for offshore radio station The Voice of Peace in Tel Aviv, Israel, and the accompanying device through which historical clips of the station can be played. Photo by Avishai Teicher.*

offshore radio history does not have a presence in institutional museum narratives,[634] this plaque and sound installation demonstrates the potential to engage former fans and the general public in an outdoor space. It is also significant that not only a commemorative text but also the intimate broadcast sounds of this commercial, English-language radio station – now more than thirty years old – are brought into the public domain. The use of a touch button to activate the recordings, moreover, potentially creates an accessible pilgrimage site for fans of the former station and deploys the 'power of touch' to prompt a shared context for the memory of the station at Tel Aviv's shoreline.[635] Other personal memories and recordings of the Voice of Peace can be found in online spaces dedicated to offshore radio in general, and this station in particular, contributing an alternative script to the authorized heritage narratives of national radio in this national context. The next section picks up this thread and will focus on publishing and online practices of sharing and displaying the history of radio and its recorded sounds.

Curated sharing: radio, publishing and online spaces

The most prominent form of curation of radio has been through radio broadcasting itself. Hence, the present section will consider radio itself as a space for the organization and curation of shared listening experiences and remembering practices, and will highlight how the passion communicated by DJs and programme presenters for the music they want to share (and their interactions with listeners) demonstrate how they serve as ambassadors for radiophilia within the broadcast system. It will then consider various forms of publication that have served as a means of distribution and circulation that allow listeners to listen and share their attachment to radio. Finally, this section will attend to the circulation of radio content through informal circuits such as YouTube and other curated spaces for radio as part of officially-endorsed projects. It will also note community-based online interventions that frequently generate alternative visions of radio's past, its contents and the experience of audiences, thereby creating new modes of engagement and potential for sharing via web comments, listening or interactive content.

Radio programmes' shared space and time for collective listening experiences – as a site of radiophilic attachment to radio – is perhaps best exemplified by programmes that attract significant (national) audiences, such as a coronation, election results or a major sports event. For example, the *Evening of Sounds* series, discussed at the start of this chapter, facilitates the sharing of a variety of memories, including experiences relating to other national contexts, although the sounds were 'remembered and placed within a national narrative, regardless of their transnational origin'.[636] In other words, while the call-in format of the programme allowed a diversity of recalled experiences to be contributed by listeners, the programme's episodes – as shared listening events – were constructed around a selection of these contributions and framed within a narrative of Finnish national sound heritage. The sense of shared listening through radio events sustained over a number of days is illustrated by a programme dedicated to the 'Top 2000' songs, which has aired on Dutch public radio since 1999, starting at midnight each Christmas Eve and ending at midnight on New Year's Eve. The popularity of the 'Top 2000' event is indicated by the size of its audience; for example, in 2004 more than one million listeners contributed votes for their favourite songs via the website, 6.5 million listened to the radio programme and 5 million watched the accompanying television programme, making it 'unprecedented in the history of mediated events in the Netherlands'.[637] The trend towards multiplatform 'live event-spaces' has further intensified, as reflected in the 3FM radio 'Serious Request' charity fundraising event in the Netherlands and numerous other countries, in which audience experiences are constituted through attending a public event, tuning in via radio and television, and participating in social media engagement and sharing.[638]

More than half the Dutch population listened to the 'Top 2000' programme at its peak, with the songs and narratives shared by voters, often in a group setting during the end-of-year holidays, enveloped by a sense of suspense as to which songs would be included in the evolving list. The event facilitated articulations of personal memory within a public framework of music remembering, as a 'space for consensus building a national heritage of pop songs, while simultaneously serving as a podium for collective nostalgia and communal reminiscences'.[639] That radio is the main vehicle for this passionate sharing of musical memories is perhaps not so surprising, since it also reflects national public broadcasters' view of music as 'inexpensive and highly accessible content that straddles the line between the global brand extension of public media institutions and ideas about the fundamental role of public media in their support of national culture'.[640] While multiple generations participate in the 'Top 2000' events, the skewing towards popular music from the 1970s, and the comments by voters, suggest a high presence of childhood and teenage memories for those who are middle-aged or retired, which is consistent with recent research indicating the importance of passion and nostalgia for generational experiences of media technologies and content, as well as 'peak music experiences'.[641] Overall, the top selections generally favoured 'classic' or mainstream rock music, with international artists such as Queen, the Eagles, Led Zeppelin or Deep Purple interspersed with Dutch songs that have a larger range in genre and period.[642] This is consistent with other research critiquing such radio programmes as centring on a masculinist 'hegemonic rock ideal', one that presents this musical taste as 'timeless' and highlights how a limited musical canon is reaffirmed and contributes to the structural underrepresentation of women in projections of national music heritage via radio.[643]

Recent uses of radio as a space for real-time sharing and remembering have their origins in the early period of radio, which itself built on the existing popular cultures of memory and affect connected with recorded music.[644] As noted in the previous chapter, broadcasters from the 1920s built up sizeable commercial music libraries, and from around 1930 their own collections of studio sound effects recordings and off-air recordings of music, spoken word and special event programming. Having the dual purpose of historical preservation and the production of archives for reuse in programmes, enhanced – in most contexts – radio's status as a medium for accessing commercial musical recordings, as well as live musical performances and recorded radio content.[645] In the previous chapter, particular attention was devoted to recordings of speech-based and special event programmes presented as compilations to listeners in the early 1930s, as part of the development of topical or actuality programming, with a strong relation to materials 'kept' or 'saved' in the archive.

We find a similar example of popular presenters in radio working as architects of public memory practices, from the early 1930s onwards. A good example is the BBC's first 'disc jockey', Christopher Stone. He not only took on the role in programming and sharing recent and new music releases in his regular programmes, but from the early 1930s through to the early 1950s, compiled musical programmes that were explicitly focused on narrating history through past recordings, invoking listener nostalgia through shared experiences of (radio) music. For instance, at the BBC in 1933, Stone hosted a twelve-part series entitled *Tunes we all know* and, following his switch to Radio Luxembourg, a programme entitled *Memories*, among others.[646] Prior to his departure from the BBC in 1934, Stone compiled a programme of new and old recordings for Empire Day in May 1939, and upon his return to the BBC, his increasingly developed programming focused on an historical repertoire, such as *Time for a Tune*, described as 'a regular series of gramophone-record presentations ... not with new records but with records of tunes that are established as popular favourites'.[647] Stone was positioned as a popular and influential personality, a 'cultural intermediary' whose selections of new releases had the potential to influence recorded music sales but whose selections of 'popular favourites' made him part of the shared remembering practices on radio.

Following the outbreak of war, Stone served as a compere for episodes of *Saturday at Nine-Thirty*, devoted to 'Edwardian memories' or 'favourite songs and orchestral music popular forty years ago'.[648] Stone further developed memory-oriented programming during the first years of the war, as in *Songs my mother taught me*, *Anniversaries* and *Have you any memories?*[649] He also revived an earlier programme, recycling the format for BBC audiences, in collaboration with fellow collector and BBC employee Gordon McConnel:

> The first of these programmes was produced ten years ago at Savoy Hill. The old songs are collected by Gordon McConnel from his library of early Victorian and Georgian albums, whilst the modern contrasts or equivalents are recordings of present-day popular singers chosen by Christopher Stone. In this programme, for instance, the early-Victorian ditty 'Don't come teasing me, sir' will be contrasted with Bing Crosby's interpretation of 'You're a sweet little headache', and so on.[650]

Later in the war, such uses of sentimentality were criticized due to concerns that it was detrimental to morale among civilians and forces.[651] Nonetheless, the notion of sharing a musical song repertoire with listeners, as fellow music fans, continued to be underscored in the post-war programmes that Stone presented, such as *Starlight* (in which wartime stars like Vera Lynn performed live), *Dance Parade – 25 Years*, *Today and Yesterday*, *Those were the Days*, *Fifty Years of Song* and *These Radio Times*.[652] As these titles suggest, musical repertoire, radio and 'the past' were presented to audiences as intertwined. Even though the earliest musical repertoire pre-dated the advent of radio, the function of radio can be imagined as facilitating personal memories of musical experiences now reframed as opportunities for acts of communal remembering via Stone's programmes.

Stone, in this sense, spearheaded the role of the disc jockey on radio as a tastemaker for shared musical experiences of both past and present repertoires, serving to 'remediate' institutional and private music collections within a shared practice of listening along with the audience. However, as commercial radio developed in the early post-war period in the US, the format of the disc jockey music programme, along with the block news format, have been read as 'an intermediate step toward a unified station sound and away from discrete, short programmes'.[653] The independence of the disc jockey in selecting tracks changed as production teams became larger, with greater planning of music choice according to a 'Top 40' of high rotation, giving way to music directors 'with [a] mandate to decide what music to play during the day [and who] managed the playlists of radio stations'.[654]

In the digital era, music continues to be 'an integral component of public service media', although programming practices are also undergoing transformation in the context of 'networked digital media', amidst the growth of public media engagement with podcasts and other digital delivery strategies.[655] Nonetheless, the radio host's agency in selecting music content has remained a constant in other contexts, from non-commercial public and cultural radio through to campus and community radio, which have been understood as having a more heterogeneous palette of programme types and musical content in their schedules.[656] Indeed, the proliferation of pirate, campus, community and independent media in the post-war era has been associated not only with alternative, niche or 'unpredictable' programming, but credited with creating the infrastructures for music subcultures and 'counterpublics', in many cases formed in relation to minority languages, religion, race, ethnicity, gender, class, sexuality and/or political affiliation.[657] Such instances of music programming to specific listener groups are crucial domains in which the address to specific communities of listeners also forms the backbone to the experience with radio, whereby intimacy and passionate connection can be sustained across new delivery formats, from pre-programmed content to smartphone-based teleconference radio for indigenous and diasporic communities.[658]

We see the development of this idea of curating important moments of radio's past becoming solidified in the post-1945 era, with a growing market for spoken word records.[659] In this same period, radio transcriptions – consisting of pre-recorded programmes and segments – became a mainstay in US commercial radio, both within the major networks and in companies that had operated since the 1930s, such as the Frederick W. Ziv Company and the World Broadcasting System (WBS). While later reuse had not been the original intention with these 16-inch discs, with fifteen minutes of playtime, their 'very existence . . .

began to fuel the nostalgia' for 'old time' content by the 1960s.⁶⁶⁰ The growth of the spoken word records market from around 1950 led to broadcasters and music publishers collaborating on archive compilations, with a particular stress on the Second World War, as evidenced by multi-disc shellac and LP releases using BBC historical materials, such as *The Sounds of Time: A Dramatisation of the Years 1934–1949* (1949) and *I Can Hear It Now: Winston Churchill* (1955), or the later Dutch release *Nederland 1940/1945* (1965). Such records usually had high sales and multiple reissues, and were also promoted in the press and at radio exhibitions (see Figure 29) as a way for radio

FIGURE 29 *Poster board promoting the Philips LP commercial release 'I Can Hear It Now: Winston Churchill', 1957 Radio Show, Earls Court, London, UK, printed in the* Evening Standard, *11 September 1957. Courtesy of Getty Images.*

fans to re-experience important events and speeches from the Second World War. In New York, David Goldin, a teenage radio fan and transcription disc collector who subsequently became an engineer for NBC and CBS in the 1960s, started a side business in 1967 distributing copies of historical radio recordings via the Radio Yesteryear mail order service (later through Radiola Records), with the first major project being 'Themes Like Old Times' (1969), a highly-popular compilation of ninety radio show themes that tapped into the nostalgic desire to listen to past theme songs.[661]

In Europe, publication of radio recordings was already of pre-war life, via the format of 'sound books' (*tönende Bücher*). The pioneer of this format, Ludwig Koch, at the Lindström record company in Berlin, initiated a series of sound books combining sound, image and text around 1930. Koch went on to collaborate with the German Broadcasting Corporation (RRG), publishing the popular book *Vom 30. Januar zum 21. März* (1933), documenting the first weeks of the Nazi Party in power, with Adolf Hitler giving permission for archived radio speeches to be released with the book on two accompanying records.[662] A final project conceived by Koch, prior to going in to exile, *Olympia Tonbuch 1936* (1936), was promoted after the Berlin Olympics as a selection of 'original RRG recordings' that would provide a 'lasting memory' via radio recordings in conjunction with colour images and text in the book.[663] Indeed, in keeping with the 'record/book analogy', the embedding of sound recordings in illustrated publications gave the recordings an additional cultural prestige.[664] This is one of the few instances of a radio recording crossover with a book publication. Beyond the archival LP and CD releases of historical recordings from the 1950s to the 1990s, such as the German Radio Archive's *Voices of the Twentieth Century* CD series (begun in 1995), by the 2000s, the onset of digital audio delivery challenged some of these earlier publication strategies. The BBC, for instance, had already launched the BBC Radio Collection in 1988, dominated by releases of popular comedy, detective stories and novel adaptations, which were sold on cassette tape, then CD, along with their book publications in bookshops.[665] With the arrival and rapid dissemination of the iPod from 2001 onwards, the publication market for archival radio on CD was diminishing rapidly.[666]

In this context, the BBC eventually came to launch iPlayerRadio in 2012 (renamed BBC Sounds in 2018), where radio, music and podcast content can be accessed via a single portal. While offered as a 'single point of interaction' between audiences and the BBC's radio content, the active commissioning and curation of innovative online-only content for young audiences via BBC Sounds represents a vision for digital audio delivery in which podcast is not simply treated as a 'remediated form of radio' or subjected to the discourse of 'radioness'.[667] The curation work of podcasting has less in common with the acquisition of the 'material' form of an LP, cassette or CD, but instead, in a manner similar to digital music platforms, operates through forms of recommendation, with its 'infrastructures of discovery' originating in recommendations in newsletters and on blogs, and increasingly, via podcast ratings and rankings.[668]

The formal licensing and publication on physical formats is one of the key ways in which a substantial amount of historical (and recently-made) radio content was made accessible to audiences, the so-called 'remediation' processes, understood as the reuse of one medium in another, or in the new media borrowing from or imitating features of existing media.[669] In the case of historical radio recordings, the popularity of certain archival content can be understood in part due to their reuse not only in radio, but also in television and film productions, such as documentaries or compilation films. In particular, the recycling of particular spoken word or musical content (e.g., sound bites, idents or jingles) not only enacts a sharing of the archive, but operates as iterations that produce selective, canonized understandings of the radio past.[670] In the television era, moreover, the presence of radio on the film and TV screen was proof of radio's ongoing relevance, or heralded an ode to radio in popular culture and memory, as articulated through novels, songs, film and television programmes.[671] The introduction of MTV in the early 1980s has also been understood as 'remediating' features of FM radio in a bid to apply the popular style of commercial radio DJs, music and jingles to authenticate this new television format with youth audiences.[672]

The practice of remediating radio also continues as a form of 'publication' and sharing in migrant media production, as in the case of participatory radio in the form of teleconferencing, for instance by Hmong communities in the United States, whose producers and audiences often enthusiastically post this content on YouTube as a form of sharing and informal archiving, thereby also altering the definition of what 'radio' is.[673] The contemporary notion of radio as a screen medium has been underscored by many radio stations setting up in-studio webcams, so that their listeners can follow the radio transmission on a livestream via the station webpage or other streaming media.[674] Similarly, in podcasting there is a current debate about not only livestreaming podcast recording but a trend towards video podcasts, partly fuelled by the possibilities of creating and sharing audiovisual clips via YouTube, Instagram and TikTok.[675]

The final domain of sharing by and with audiences that will be treated here is curated spaces that emerge as part of official projects as well as by community interventions, frequently generating alternative visions of radio's past, its contents and audiences. The onset of internet radio, facilitating 'sound on screens', has not only generated new dimensions to radio production and transmission, but also created new modes of engagement and potential for sharing through web-based portals or curated web content, as well as experiments in 3D virtual representations and augmented reality.[676] In the domain of public history, for instance, we not only find more conventional anniversaries and dates being celebrated, such as the present centenary celebrations of radio, but also explorations of how (audio)visual and textual data might be organized into a permanent exhibition and online timeline of events, objects, technology, history and culture, as in the case of the bilingual 'Centenary of Radio in Canada' project (2020).[677] The timeline visualization format can also be used as a form of intervention in narratives of national (radio) history, as evidenced by the 'Resistance Radio' (2019) online exhibition as part of the Interference Archive in New York, which created numerous timelines around themes such as Black Liberation, worker's radio, radio and squatting and prison radio, along with a list of DIY radio resources and research materials.[678]

In online presentations of past radio we can observe efforts to include audience and fan content and provide space for feedback or contributions, as evidenced in the Irish Pirate Radio Archive, which has a strong commitment to making recordings digitally available via their site and publicizing this via social media.[679] Other web initiatives have a similarly strong oral history component, such as the work of the Birmingham Black Radio Museum: a community museum and archive which takes a participatory approach to documentation, but which also uses its archive to promote and share materials from the histories of Black radio, including both production and audience perspectives.⁶⁸⁰ Access remains a key concern for curation projects dealing with radio history, yet a number of recent projects have explored the dimension of play and interactivity in audience engagement. One such project is the 'Radio Garden' initiative (www.radio.garden), which has brought not just pleasure and delight to its users, as they navigate a web interface of the globe which allows access to radio streaming content from all over the world, but also 'social and educational benefits' and the possibility to 'escape from the bubble of nationality'.⁶⁸¹ The launch of the Radio Garden site on World Radio Day, launched by UNESCO in 2012, also draws significant public attention to radio, providing an opportunity for members of the public to tweet, like and share the project while engaged in playful acts of radiophilia when 'tuning in' to live radio from across the globe.

Conclusion

This chapter opened with the example of the Finnish radio programme *Evening of Sounds*, and its engagement with radio listeners who responded enthusiastically to the invitation to submit requests to hear sounds of the past and present, and then tuned in to hear the programme's playing back of such sounds, reading out of listener reminiscences and framing of these within Finnish sound history. This popular programme's success in creating a framework for soliciting listener input and then engaging in shared listening via radio can be seen as a reflection of radio's basic mission: 'to broadcast sound content which is emotionally and intellectually meaningful to listeners'.⁶⁸² Precisely this sharing in the significance, mutual interest and affection for radio, along with the experience of 'shared' listening via radio in real time – reflecting the 'for anyone as someone' structures of radio⁶⁸³ – has been a key concern in this chapter.

The chapter has addressed the question of how a love of radio can be shared or put on display for others, considering such practices and strategies across a number of spaces and medial forms. The first section delved into the ways in which clothing, accessories and merchandise have been a crucial site through which enthusiasts for particular stations, programmes or genres put their attachment on display for others and in the urban environment, is evident in the ongoing presence of stickers and car bumper stickers in public life. Acts of sharing through joint listening were also studied in terms of the various sites through which listeners have informally gathered for group listening in the home, in outdoor and mobile spaces, such as in the car, along with contexts, such as in Zambia, in which the radio device has a portability as a social object taking up various public uses and that can dynamically move between its owner and friend and in kinship networks. The consideration of radio as part of a self-organized or official structure also highlighted the public presence of radio in the coercive structures of the colonial state and by repressive regimes, as well as underscoring radio not as simply a strictly indoor medium in the family living room, but as an infrastructure involved in the 'technologizing' of public urban space.[684] Moreover, this section drew attention to the development of crossovers between radio, music and audiophile fandom, evidenced by semi-public spaces of consumption, such as music shops and cafes, the formation of music listening clubs and the involvement of key figures in creating music-focused radio broadcasts.

Building on this awareness of radio's public life and spaces of shared listening, the second section zoomed in on the radio museum and exhibition as a key space in elaborating the public history and memory of radio. The analysis spotlighted the perceived need to establish radio museums and exhibits from the earliest amateur period up to the present, and considered the 'scripts' for documenting past attachments to radio, sustaining and encouraging its survival, in the shared co-presence enabled by the museum space. It was noted how national radio museums developed narratives of past radio within the history of the nation state and nation-building, while sometimes also documenting the Cold War-era radio geopolitics, as in Taiwan.[685] The analysis drew attention to the role of sensory appeal and interactive elements in more recent radio museums and temporary exhibits, as part of the effort to produce an affective shared encounter with radio's past and present, and in foregrounding the role of radio audiences and fans and the material cultures of radio that they have helped generate and preserve.

Following this attention to the organization of objects, the engagement of audiences and crafting of narratives in the exhibition space, the final section reflected on how the sharing of radio is constituted through acts of curation, distribution and access, turning first to radio itself as a key site for the curation of 'favourite', 'best', or 'timeless' music within the shared recollection of past radio and musical experience, facilitated in real-time programmes which foster individual and collective remembering practices, often with a national framework helping guide these sharing acts of group listening. The curation and distribution of radio for audiences was considered in terms of the various forms of publication sought by some, usually more well-resourced, broadcasters on vinyl, cassette or CD, generally with a focus on a particular period, programme or performer. These activities have served as a key means by which the sounds of radio are distributed, circulated and shared among listeners and fans, and by which they also enter the informal circuits of collectors and online sharing via platforms such as YouTube. This analysis of the digital presence and presentation of radio sounds for its audiences concluded with a consideration of how radio is curated and displayed in online spaces and how shared experience is facilitated and crafted for users. It then dealt with the potential for alternative narratives of attachments to radio created by community-based digital history and heritage initiatives.

Conclusion

Where love and desire are concerned, there are no adequate examples, and all of our objects must bear the burden of exemplifying and failing what drives our attachment to them.

LAUREN BERLANT[686]

Where there is consumption there is pleasure, and where there is pleasure there is agency. Freedom, on the other hand, is a rather more elusive commodity.

ARJUN APPADURAI[687]

In opening this study, I recalled how I developed a strong attachment to radio as a teenager during a particular phase in my personal biography, and in a specific time and place. My avid consumption and taping of radio, in those circumstances, constituted a thrilling, affective practice. It enacted a sense of being transported beyond my immediate circumstances and gaining independence. I felt boosted by the music selection and presenter delivery, and invited to share in the co-presence of the presenters and their listening audience. Now, at the end of this book, and with the life cycle perspective in mind, I turn to my present-day consumption habits and attachments. I still depend on radio, but no longer on a single device for private reception, nor tune in with a rapt engagement or to tape record its content. My primary radio consumption each morning is via an analogue clock radio, which is permanently tuned to an upbeat commercial station selected for its unlikeable presentation style as a way to quickly get up on workdays. Beyond this terrestrial radio consumption – in a fixed location, with an assigned function and via a cheap analogue receiver – I also listen to internet radio, music streaming and podcast audio, across multiple devices, spanning a phone, a laptop and a stereo system with an in-built audio streaming device. In this user experience, I now assume more autonomy, if not agency, in the choice of content and delivery when switching between devices. Compared with the past, there is a noticeable increase in listening to interview-, documentary- and narrative-based formats that might not only be indicative of the shifts associated with the 'podcast revolution', but also reflective of my age and professional interests.[688]

In writing this book, I've often thought about the work of cultural theorists Lauren Berlant and Arjun Appadurai, in a conversation staged in a similar fashion to the epigraph to this chapter. Both scholars' writings are heavily invested in the cultural politics of affect and emotion, even if their arguments work towards somewhat different ends.[689] Berlant's later work probes the 'cruel optimism' that shapes the lived worlds of embodied subjects in our neoliberal late capitalist present, asking what it means to desire an unattainable 'good life', in which such attachments can leave subjects vulnerable to ever more precarious situations.[690] Earlier writing by Berlant interrogates the paradoxes of desire and love: love tends to be conventional and constricted by the 'working of romance across personal life and commodity culture, the places where subjects learn to inhabit fantasy in the ordinary course of their actual lives'.[691] Desire is usually generated towards an object or person, but it is also a disturbance: 'the impulse that most destabilizes people'; as such, it prompts an encounter not only with the self but with the 'normative world', determined by the strictures of heteronormative ideologies about romance, intimacy, gender and sexuality.[692]

Appadurai's work grapples with the cultural consequences of globalization, the material flows, circulations and imaginations it has enabled, but also the problems, risk and uncertainty a global capitalist condition has heralded, with the 'the deeply disjunctive relationships among human movement, technological flow, and financial transfers'.[693] A central interest in his work is the imagination as a site of social practice, in which he highlights the generative capacity of media for producing a 'community of sentiment' in collectives that start to 'imagine and feel things together', across manifest differences, facilitating a dense interweaving of 'diverse local experiences of taste, pleasure and politics'.[694] While taking consumption into account as a key component of capitalist relations, Appadurai underscores the potential of the pleasure of consumption to create space for agency, as media content is appropriated by its audiences and 'moved into local repertoires of irony, anger, humor and resistance'.[695] As such, media provide a space that allows for imagining and experiencing collectivity at different scales (local, national, transnational): collective formations that can serve as a 'fuel for action'.[696]

Each author offers a different and valuable perspective on radiophilia. Writing about the ideologies of love, Berlant suggests that they are 'marketed by the entertainment industries of western mass culture' and remains critical of the narrow manner by which love 'became a way of imagining particular utopias of gender and sex'.[697] In other words, to think with Berlant about radiophilia is to warn against the naïve celebration of radio as a 'free space' for the formation of love, affection or attachment. This is a caution for future scholarship studying 'radio love' to remain aware of how, historically, radio has 'put fixed social identities into play in highly public ways', with voices, performances and identities deemed as transgressive, subject to forms of policing, derision or exclusion from the airwaves.[698] Berlant also insists on the positionality of the scholar, who in choosing examples for an analysis of desire/love must necessarily recognize their partiality in selecting a corpus; and yet despite 'the problem of getting exemplification right', suggests that subjecting a corpus of examples to analysis still has a generative potential for one's readers to 'see [these patterns] elsewhere or to not see them, and to invent other explanations'.[699] By contrast, Appadurai's attention to the imagination shows how it not only has the potential to reinforce the status quo, but also transform or subvert it, which invites an acknowledgement of the imaginative capacity of a love of radio, of its potential for facilitating collectivities and affective ties across diverse bodies and lived experiences. Guided by an interest in global flows, migration and diaspora, Appadurai's analysis of media is accompanied by a recognition of transnational media flows and media consumption across national borders, which is a crucial insight for future research into radiophilia. And yet, despite writing meaningfully about the intertwining of radio, sport and nationhood in India, Appadurai's general theorization is almost exclusively about visual images and viewers of film, television and video, thereby conflating image and imagination in the concept of 'mediascape'.

The respective insights of Berlant and Appadurai reflect a dynamic that the future study of radiophilia should continue to keep in check. On the one hand, that radio inhabits enormous potential as a space for the imagination, fantasy and worldmaking, and that listeners may experience pleasure, joy or comfort and engage in a variety of embodied expressions, practices and collective formations as they start to 'imagine and feel things together', as per Appadurai. On the other hand, it remains crucial to understand both radio and its audiences' experiences and uses of it as shaped by the cultural repertoires, preoccupations and politics of a particular time and setting, or what Berlant refers to as 'the normative world'.

This book opened with the question of how to trace the diverse possibilities for conceptualizing *radiophilia* over its long century, from early wireless and radio broadcasting through to digital radio and audio in the present. It has acknowledged that what we call 'radio' is not stable across this timeframe, as its technologies and production, distribution and reception practices have been in a dynamic relation, even if some aspects of radio content, form and genre remained relatively stable over time. In developing a framework to make sense of the 'love of radio' across the twentieth and into the twenty-first centuries, I posed four main questions. What is the love of radio, and how do you enact or express this loving? How do you know the thing you love? How do you save the thing you love? And how do you share your love of radio? As such, the study identified four central themes – loving, knowing, saving and sharing – which structured the book's investigation into affective attachments to radio.

Along with these questions, the larger aim of the book has been to survey a century of radio, including its major transformations and renewal in the digital age. Charting the changes and continuities in the love of the new and renewed medium of radio has served as a central theme. I've stressed the plurality, dynamism and heterogeneity of radiophilia, while remaining mindful of the situatedness of specific individual biography, or the influence of historical or socio-political and cultural factors. In particular, the chapters have pinpointed how the love of radio has gone through phases since its introduction as a 'new' medium, while the renewals of radio have gone hand in hand with changing listening practices, social formations and technological developments. The cultural image of the 'obsessed' radio listener in early radio, has been replicated in the 'technopathologies' activated with each new technological development in radio reception, whether for the transistor radio, the Walkman or podcast's 'binge' listeners.

In addition to questions about historical change and continuity, this study has highlighted how radio's temporal structures have generally settled into ordinary and reliable rhythms and integrated into listeners' everyday habits, spanning a spectrum from rapt attention through to an intermittent or distracted consumption while performing other tasks. Overall, it has shown that attachments to radio have been shaped by this everyday quality as well as by memorable occasions, from national celebrations or sporting events through to collective experiences of crisis, conflict and war. In attending to specific spaces of radiophilia, the study has devoted attention to both individual and communal practices across a century of radio. On the one hand, attention to specific sites focused on phases within the individual life cycle and personal situation highlighted the attachment to radio of children and teenagers, families, older people and those who are physically, geographically or socially isolated. On the other hand, it observed collective practices initiated during early wireless and broadcast radio, starting with the formation of radio clubs and amateur radio associations, followed by listening in domestic spaces by families, neighbours and friends. The book also traced the subsequent expansion of affective practices around radio into other private, public and outdoor spaces, from the bedroom and the 'mobile privatized' space of the car through to public squares, workplaces, schools and political and social ceremonies. Other spaces shown by the study to have shaped or fuelled radiophilia include the museum, the public exhibition, record shops, music cafés and the cinema, as well as sites related to radio production, such as the radio studio, broadcast building and radio tower.

In terms of particular practices, the chapters have highlighted the historical continuities, across various contexts, of diverse forms of listener participation and interaction, from the writing of letters, postcards and QSL cards through to phoning in, sending text messages and other forms of web-based participation in radio and digital formats. The book has acknowledged how adjacent hobbies and interests – whether news, music, sport, literature, drama and comedy-variety, religion, politics or other media such as film – served to fuel radiophilia. Such 'crossover' fandoms remain significant in forging emotional communities in the post-network era of nichecasting, internet radio and digital audio formats, such as podcasting. Other affective engagements with radio, with a strong interpersonal dimension, were pinpointed in the chapters, underscoring the significance of pedagogy, learning and knowing (Chapter 2), efforts to save the ephemeral traces of radio through collecting, recording or other forms of archiving (Chapter 3) and participation in acts of display through clothing, accessories or merchandise or in shared listening practices, such as informal, self-organized groups or those that are officially mandated (Chapter 4). Acts of sharing in particular have had a particular *longue durée* from early radio culture through to more recent transformations of radio as digital audio, for which sharing has emerged as a key mechanism within the 'affective fabrics' of digital media culture and a broader process of the 'mediatisation of memory'.[700] Finally, this study has shown how certain practices and objects associated with the love of radio have been durable and gained visibility or social approval, whereas other, often less institutionalized aspects have left scant remains in public discourse or in the material form of objects, documentation or archival collections.

Having revisited the findings of the chapters, it is worth considering what this study offers the fields it draws on, and the potential for future further research that will expand the research agenda proposed here. In the field of sound studies, which has gained recognition and institutionalization since the early 2000s, there has been a strong focus on auditory culture and the related histories of sound technology and mediated listening. In line with this field, the present study has staked its interest in the affects, emotions and feelings generated by acts of embodied radio listening and related practices. It thereby acknowledges 'the role played by auditory cultures in shaping affective responses to sound', but does not cast (sonic) affect as 'beyond signification and representation'.[701] Having sought to underscore the presence of multiple ontologies of radio, it also recognizes the urgency of calls to 'remap sound studies' given its inherent slant towards Western epistemologies of sound, a predominance of case studies from North America and Western Europe and the overrepresentation of English-language contexts in the existing scholarship.[702] This study therefore takes seriously Steven Feld's concerns about there being a disproportionate emphasis in sound studies on technologies, genres and objects, while also seeing this focus – as in the present study – as not necessarily excluding the possibility of opening up radio to questions of agency, relationality and plural ontologies.[703]

This book is also intended to encourage the historical sound research field to devote more attention to radio, which, as a medium of 'transmission', has been under-researched in favour of histories of recording technologies.[704] Radio studies has been infused with a 'sound studies' sensibility in recent decades, enriching this field and its analysis of radio sound, listening experience and sound cultures, subsequently giving way to a fruitful crossover between podcast studies and digital sound studies.[705] One of the contributions of this book to radio studies has been to urge more focus on the visual and material cultures of radio; to consider the 'look and feel' of radio as one of its key attractions; and to consider the multisensory dimensions to the engagement with radio, in tandem with photography, newspapers and magazines, as well as personal computers, smartphones and sound recording devices. And to a certain degree, the present study has rectified a reluctance in both sound and radio studies to engage with questions of fandom, whereby a concern with love, enjoyment and pleasure tends to be sidelined or relegated to the domains of popular music studies or fan studies.

In response to fan studies, this analysis of radiophilia has sought to carve out more space for studying media fandoms beyond a predominant interest in film, television and games (and, to a lesser degree, in music). This offers productive ground on which media fandom research can refine its existing theorizations of affect and embodied engagement, thereby redressing a preoccupation with the visual and textual and the consequential status of radio as 'almost entirely and structurally absent from debates about fan identity'.[706] Radio fandom also provides a historical basis for the burgeoning scholarship on podcast and digital audio fan practices, facilitating observation of longer genealogies for the 'affective publics' formed around and through modern media.[708] Moreover, an historical perspective on radio fan practices, across the twentieth and into the twenty-first century, challenges a tendency in media fan research to focus on 'historic' fandoms as mainly restricted to print media, or skewing towards sci-fi television fandoms for the period since the 1960s and 1970s. By considering multiple and sometimes overlapping fandoms from around 1900 onwards, this book has given more prominence to the early media fandoms of girls and young women than fan history timelines typically offer, and has considered the connections between radio and music fandoms, as well as other related practices such as home sound recording, amateur film and photography. Radiophilia has thus been presented as a site of rich potential for thinking about transmedial stardom and global fandom, as well as cutting across diverse sensory abilities and age, generation, linguistic or faith-based communities.

These observations have led this study to consider media history from the vantage point of feminist media studies and global media studies. While the book has sought to give more analytical space to gender, and to women's media consumption spanning childhood to older age, I have also taken care not to overstate the centrality of domestic settings and to include a critical awareness of radio as a public technology, in which portable radio receivers are used for social purposes, such as in funeral ceremonies, or are shared with friends and family. Rather than ignore the narration of media history according to masculinist master narratives, I've sought to engage these accounts and explain their influence, underlining, for instance, how radio exhibition practices contributed to the canonization of male 'inventor genius' figures of radio history.[708] The creation of male-dominated communities around radio – from radio hobby and amateur radio clubs through to historical societies and collector communities – has been highlighted, whereby certain collectives of radio enthusiasts and fans have gained particular visibility. At the same time, the chapters have insisted on looking beyond such cases to attend to other attachments to radio, ways of knowing or related forms of social action. In including examples of radio in anti-colonial struggle, this book has emphasized radio as a key social infrastructure and affective practice during conflict and the subsequent national radio systems of newly-independent nations. At the same time, I've pointed to research findings that highlight how key legacies of colonial-era radio remained in tact, from staff and technical infrastructure through to colonial language politics, noting that only more recent liberalization policies have led to space being made for local languages to establish a presence in independent, commercial radio or community media outlets.[709] In hyper-local or micro media practices, and other forms of digital innovation in community broadcasting, offering much scope to further challenge the predominance of national frameworks in radio research, and for the consideration of listening audiences and their love of radio.[710]

Finally, a significant initial theoretical inspiration for this study has been recent debates in the history of the emotions field, which have suggested that 'affective practice' is a productive concept to account for the workings of emotion, affect and feeling within individual embodiment and social formations, both past and present. Building on this, the concept of 'affective *heritage* practice' has been proposed as a meaningful way to consider affect, emotion and embodiment within memory dynamics and heritage sites.[711] In turn, the focus of the present study's attention to radio in memory practices and heritage spaces has provided an impulse for future research to further incorporate sound, listening and media histories into the study of memory and heritage. The 'material turn' in media studies has often prioritized the role of cinema and television in the museum, but there is further potential to consider how radio is adopted for atmosphere creation in museum spaces, the uses of radio material culture in exhibitions and the diverse attachments developed by heritage professionals in their efforts to save and preserve radio and narrate its significance to museum and online publics.

NOTES

1 From the late 1980s until the present, the Australian public broadcaster ABC has aired music videos on television from Friday evenings until Saturday morning, and from Saturday evenings until Sunday mornings, featuring both chart music ('ARIA Top Fifty') and alternative curation ('Rage').

2 This practice took place in a home environment in which recording had become quite commonplace, with my family owning a VHS tape recorder along with successive models of VHS cassette and digital 'handycam' video camera devices. While off-air television recording took place in the family living room, my recordings of radio were a more solitary act in which recording and playback took place on private devices. For household media in the Australian context, see Jenny Kennedy et al., *Digital Domesticity: Media, Materiality, and Home Life* (New York: Oxford University Press, 2020), 225.

3 Apart from one instructive account on 'radiophile' vintage radio receiver collecting and trading practices, discussed in Chapter 3, the only other published work on 'radiophilia' uses this term in the context of medical research: Rebecca M. Ellis and Anna Haywood, 'Virtual_radiophile (163): eBay and the Changing Collecting Practices of the U.K. Vintage Radio Community', in *Everyday eBay: Culture, Collecting, and Desire*, ed. Ken Hillis and Michael Petit (New York and London: Routledge, 2006), 45–61; Hamid Abdollahi and Malakeh Malekzadeh, 'Radiophilia: A Common Case of Excessive Radiation Exposure in Healthcare', *OMICS Journal of Radiology* 5, no. 3 (2016): 1-3.

4 Paddy Scannell, *Radio, Television and Modern Life: A Phenomenological Approach* (Oxford: Blackwell, 1996); Jo Tacchi, 'Radio and Affective Rhythm in the Everyday', *Radio Journal: International Studies in Broadcast & Audio Media* 7, no. 2 (2009): 171–83; Ilana Emmett, 'Feeling at Home: Sound, Affect and Domesticity on Radio Soap Operas', *Radio Journal: International Studies in Broadcast & Audio Media* 19, no. 1 (2021): 23–39.

5 For radio's key sonic components (voice, music and sound effects) and types of programming (music, drama, news, sports etc.), see, e.g.,

Rudolf Arnheim, *Radio* (London: Faber & Faber, 1936); Andrew Crisell, *Understanding Radio*, 2nd edn (London: Routledge, 1994); Martin Shingler and Cindy Wieringa, *On Air: Methods and Meanings of Radio* (London: Arnold, 1998). On the 'magical' ether of wireless, see Jeffrey Sconce, *Haunted Media: Electronic Presence from Telegraphy to Television* (Durham, NC: Duke University Press, 2000), 59–91.

6 Jason Loviglio, *Radio's Intimate Public: Network Broadcasting and Mass-Mediated Democracy* (Minneapolis: University of Minnesota Press, 2005), xviii; also Michele Hilmes, *Radio Voices: American Broadcasting, 1922–1952* (Minneapolis: University of Minnesota Press, 1997), Susan Merrill Squier, ed., *Communities of the Air: Radio Century, Radio Culture* (Durham, NC: Duke University Press, 2003); Elena Razlogova, *The Listener's Voice: Early Radio and the American Public* (Philadelphia: University of Pennsylvania Press, 2011); Kate Lacey, *Listening Publics: The Politics of Audiences in the Media Age* (Cambridge: Polity, 2013); Jennifer Lynn Stoever, *The Sonic Color Line: Race and the Cultural Politics of Listening* (New York: New York University Press, 2016).

7 For this aversion to radio, especially its 'noise', see Karin Bijsterveld, 'A Wall of Sound: The Gramophone, the Radio, and the Noise of Neighbors', in *Mechanical Sound: Technology, Culture, and Public Problems of Noise in the Twentieth Century* (Cambridge, MA: MIT Press, 2008), 159–91. For 'lovers' vs 'haters', see Ien Ang, *Watching Dallas: Soap Operas and the Melodramatic Imagination* (London: Methuen 1985), 89–111. For non-users and (digital) disengagement, see Sally Wyatt, 'Non-Users also Matter: The Construction of Users and Non-Users of the Internet', in *How Users Matter: The Co-construction of Users and Technology*, ed. Nelly Oudshoorn and Trevor Pinch (Cambridge, MA: MIT Press), 67–80; Adi Kuntsman and Esperanza Miyake, 'The Paradox and Continuum of Digital Disengagement: Denaturalising Digital Sociality and Technological Connectivity', *Media, Culture & Society* 41, no. 6 (2019): 901–13. For a long-running state-enforced radio programme generally disliked by audiences despite efforts to make it more appealing, see Leonardo Cardoso, '*A Voz do Brasil*: Radio, Salience, and Resilience', *Global South* 15, no.2 (2022): 58–77.

8 Tiziano Bonini, Belén Monclús and Salvatore Scifo, 'Radio as a Social Media', *Radio Journal: International Studies in Broadcast & Audio Media* 18, no. 1 (2020): 5–12; Guy Starkey, 'Radio: The Resilient Medium in Today's Increasingly Diverse Multiplatform Media Environment', *Convergence: The International Journal of Research into New Media Technologies* 23, no. 6 (2017): 660–70; Mia Lindgren and Gail Phillips, 'Radio Reinvented: The Enduring Appeal of Audio

in the Digital Age', *Australian Journalism Review* 36, no. 2 (2014): 5–9; Ariana Moscote Freire, 'Remediating Radio: Audio Streaming, Music Recommendation and the Discourse of Radioness', *Radio Journal: International Studies in Broadcast & Audio Media* 5, no. 2–3 (2008): 97–112.

9 For iHeartRadio's expansion globally, see Rufus McEwan, 'Digital Radio Platforms in the New Zealand Context: Implementing The Wireless and iHeartRadio', *Radio Journal: International Studies in Broadcast & Audio Media* 15, no. 2 (2017): 259–77.

10 Andrew J. Bottomley, *Sound Streams: A Cultural History of Radio–Internet Convergence* (Ann Arbor: University of Michigan Press, 2020), 19, 94, 124, 200–27; Dario Llinares, Neil Fox and Richard Berry, 'Introduction: Podcasting and Podcasts – Parameters of a New Aural Culture', in *Podcasting: New Aural Cultures and Digital Media*, ed. Dario Llinares, Neil Fox and Richard Berry (Cham: Palgrave Macmillan, 2018), 2; Matt Sienkiewicz and Deborah L. Jaramillo, 'Podcasting, the Intimate Self, and the Public Sphere', *Popular Communication* 17, no. 4 (2019): 268–72. For an early example of a medicalized framing, see Carie Windham, 'Confessions of a Podcast Junkie', *Educause Review* 42, no. 3 (2007): 51–2.

11 Michele Hilmes, 'The New Materiality of Radio: Sound on Screens', in *Radio's New Wave: Global Sound in the Digital Era*, ed. Michele Hilmes and Jason Loviglio (New York: Routledge, 2013), 43–61.

12 For the different 'affective capitals' of two Italian radio stations, see Tiziano Bonini, Alessandro Caliandro and Alessandra Massarelli, 'Understanding the Value of Networked Publics in Radio: Employing Digital Methods and Social Network Analysis to Understand the Twitter Publics of Two Italian National Radio Stations', *Information, Communication & Society* 19, no. 1 (2016): 40–58; Zizi Papacharissi, *Affective Publics: Sentiment, Technology and Politics* (Oxford: Oxford University Press, 2015).

13 The present study does not elaborate on the distinctions or 'boundaries' between radio and podcasting, yet it is necessary to emphasize that contemporary radio consists of multiple 'competing sounds', along with podcasts and music streaming, vying for listener attention in everyday life. See Ellis Jones and Jeremy Morris, 'Competing Sounds? Podcasting and Popular Music', *Radio Journal: International Studies in Broadcast & Audio Media* 20, no.1 (2022): 3–15; Richard Berry, 'What is a Podcast? Mapping the Technical, Cultural, and Sonic Boundaries between Radio and Podcasting', in *The Routledge Companion to Radio and Podcast Studies*, ed. Mia Lindgren and Jason Loviglio (Abingdon and New York: Routledge, 2022), 399–407.

14 Carolyn Birdsall and Anthony Enns, eds, *Sonic Mediations: Body, Sound, Technology* (Newcastle upon Tyne: Cambridge Scholars, 2008); Steve Goodman, *Sonic Warfare: Sound, Affect, and the Ecology of Fear* (Cambridge, MA: MIT Press, 2009). For sound technologies and memory practices, see Karin Bijsterveld and José van Dijck, eds, *Sound Souvenirs: Audio Technologies, Memory and Cultural Practices* (Amsterdam: Amsterdam University Press, 2009); Elodie A. Roy, *Media, Materiality and Memory: Grounding the Groove* (Abingdon and New York: Routledge, 2016). For mediated communication in terms of philosophical concepts of love (e.g., eros, agape, philia), see John Durham Peters, *Speaking into the Air: A History of the Idea of Communication* (Chicago: University of Chicago Press, 1999); Paddy Scannell, *Love and Communication* (Cambridge: Polity, 2021).

15 For example, Tacchi, 'Radio and Affective Rhythm'; David Hendy, 'Listening in the Dark: Night-time Radio and a "Deep History" of Media', *Media History* 16, no. 2 (2010): 215–32; Siobhán McHugh, 'The Affective Power of Sound: Oral History on Radio', *Oral History Review* 39, no. 2 (2012): 187–206; Lisa Yuk Ming Leung, 'Online Radio Listening as "Affective Publics"? (Closeted) Participation in the Post-Umbrella Movement Everyday', *Cultural Studies* 32, no. 4 (2018): 511–29.

16 Antoine Hennion, *The Passion for Music: A Sociology of Mediation*, trans. Margaret Rigaud and Peter Collier (Farnham: Ashgate, 2015).

17 Mark Katz, 'Beware of Gramomania: The Pleasures and Pathologies of Record Collecting', in *The Record: Contemporary Art and Vinyl*, ed. Trevor Schoonmaker (Durham, NC: Duke University Press, 2010), 62–5; John Davis, 'Going Analog: Vinylphiles and the Consumption of the "Obsolete" Vinyl Record', in *Residual Media*, ed. Charles R. Acland (Minneapolis: University of Minnesota Press, 2007), 222–38.

18 Marc Perlman, 'Golden Ears and Meter Readers: The Contest for Epistemic Authority in Audiophilia', *Social Studies of Science* 34, no. 5 (2004): 783–807.

19 Perlman, 'Golden Ears and Meter Readers', 788.

20 Matt Hills, *Fan Cultures* (London: Routledge, 2002), xvii, 11.

21 Cornel Sandvoss, Jonathan Gray and C. Lee Harrington, 'Introduction: Why Still Study Fans?', in *Fandom: Identities and Communities in a Mediated World*, ed. Jonathan Gray, Cornel Sandvoss and C. Lee Harrington (New York: New York University Press, 2017), 10.

22 Lincoln Geraghty, *Cult Collectors: Nostalgia, Fandom and Collecting Popular Culture* (New York: Routledge, 2014), 180.

23 Matt Hills, 'Fandom from Cradle to Grave?', *Journal of Fandom Studies* 7, no. 2 (2019): 87–92.

24 A recent exception is research on fans of the US radio presenter and music star Rudy Vallée in the 1920s: Allison McCracken, *Real Men don't Sing: Crooning in American Culture* (Durham, NC, and London: Duke University Press, 2015), 126–58; also Matt Hills, 'From BBC Radio Personality to Online Audience Personae: The Relevance of Fan Studies to Terry Wogan and the TOGs', *Radio Journal: International Studies in Broadcast & Audio Media* 7, no.1 (2009), 67–88; Henrik Linden and Sara Linden, *Fans and Fan Cultures* (London: Palgrave Macmillan, 2017), 179; Allison McCracken, 'A History of Fandom in Broadcasting', in *A Companion to the History of American Broadcasting*, ed. Aniko Bodroghkozy (New York: Blackwell, 2018), 413–41.

25 Daniel Cavicchi, 'Fandom Before "Fan": Shaping the History of Enthusiastic Audiences', *Reception: Texts, Readers, Audiences, History* 6, no. 1 (2014): 52–72. On early interactions between music-loving publics and recorded music, see Emily Thompson, 'Machines, Music, and the Quest for Fidelity: Marketing the Edison Phonograph in America, 1877–1925', *Musical Quarterly* 79, no. 1 (1995): 131–71.

26 Diana W. Anselmo, 'Bound by Paper: Girl Fans, Movie Scrapbooks, and Hollywood Reception during World War I', *Film History* 31, no. 3 (2019): 141–72.

27 Kathryn Fuller-Seeley, 'Archaeologies of Fandom: Using Historical Methods to Explore Fan Cultures of the Past', in *The Routledge Companion to Media Fandom*, ed. Melissa A. Click and Suzanne Scott (New York: Routledge, 2017), 27–35; Hye-Kyung Lee, 'Transnational Cultural Fandom', in *The Ashgate Research Companion to Fan Cultures*, ed. Linda Duits, Koos Zwaan and Stijn Reijnders (Farnham: Ashgate Publishing, 2014), 195–208; Anne Kustritz, 'Transnationalism, Localization, and Translation in European Fandom: Fan studies as Global Media and Audience Studies', *Transformative Works and Cultures* 19 (2015), https://doi.org/10.3983/twc.2015.0682.

28 For example, María Angélica Thumala Olave, 'Book Love: A Cultural Sociological Interpretation of the Attachment to Books', *Poetics* 81 (2020): 1–11; John Caughie, 'Telephilia and Distraction: Terms of Engagement', *Journal of British Cinema and Television* 3, no. 1 (2006): 5–18.

29 Zhang Zhen, *An Amorous History of the Silver Screen: Shanghai Cinema 1896–1937* (Chicago: University of Chicago Press, 2005); Marijke de Valck and Malte Hagener, eds, *Cinephilia: Movies, Love,*

and Memory (Amsterdam: Amsterdam University Press, 2005); Belén Vidal, 'Cinephilia Goes Global: Loving Cinema in the Post-Cinematic Age', in *The Routledge Companion to World Cinema*, ed. Rob Stone et al. (New York: Routledge, 2017), 404–14; Abhija Ghosh, 'Memories of Action: Tracing Film Society Cinephilia in India', *BioScope: South Asian Screen Studies* 9, no. 2 (2019): 137–64.

30 On the centrality of fear and anxiety in cinephilia, see Sarah Keller, *Anxious Cinephilia: Pleasure and Peril at the Movies* (New York: Columbia University Press 2020). On how the fear/love dynamic operates in relation to sexuality and normativity, see Lauren Berlant, *Desire/Love* (New York: Punctum Books, (2000–2) 2012).

31 Keller, *Anxious Cinephilia*, 22–3.

32 Carolyn Birdsall and Elinor Carmi, 'Feminist Avenues for *listening in*: Amplifying Silenced Histories of Media and Communication', *Women's History Review* 31, no. 4 (2022): 542–60.

33 Raka Shome, 'When Postcolonial Studies Interrupts Media Studies', *Communication, Culture & Critique* 12, no. 3 (2019): 305. On whiteness in audience and fan research see Vicki Mayer, 'Research beyond the Pale: Whiteness in Audience Studies and Media Ethnography', *Communication Theory* 15, no. 2 (2005): 148–67; Mel Stanfill, 'The Unbearable Whiteness of Fandom and Fan Studies', in *A Companion to Media Fandom and Fan Studies*, ed. Paul Booth (Hoboken, NJ: John Wiley & Sons, 2018), 305–17.

34 Andy O'Dwyer, 'Digitising Context: The Case of *The Radio Times*', *VIEW: Journal of European Television History and Culture* 1, no. 1 (2012): 53–6. On the skewing of radio histories towards the Global North, to English-language scholarship and British and US case studies, see Kate Lacey, 'Up in the Air? The Matter of Radio Studies', *Radio Journal: International Studies in Broadcast & Audio Media* 16, no. 2 (2018): 114; Teresa Piñeiro Otero and Daniel Martín Pena, 'Radio Studies: An Overview from the Ibero-American Academia', *Comunicar: Media Education Research Journal* 26, no. 57 (2018): 101–11.

35 Noah Arceneaux, 'American Radio History: Created and Maintained by David Gleason, www. Americanradiohistory.com', *American Journalism* 32, no. 3 (2015), 379–80.

36 Carolyn Marvin, *When Old Technologies were New: Thinking about Electric Communication in the Late Nineteenth Century* (New York: Oxford University Press, 1988); Sheila Jasanoff and Sang-Hyun Kim, eds, *Dreamscapes of Modernity: Sociotechnical Imaginaries and the Fabrication of Power* (Chicago: University of Chicago Press, 2015).

37 Jasanoff and Kim, *Dreamscapes of Modernity*.

38 bell hooks, *All about Love: New Visions* (New York: William Morrow, 2018), 4. The recognition of love as a powerful action constitutes a significant thread in hooks' work on strategies of resistance against white supremacy and other forms of oppression, particularly in the US context. For her previous work in developing an intersectional, feminist approach to love, see bell hooks, *Salvation: Black People and Love* (New York: William Morrow, 2001); bell hooks, 'Loving Blackness as Political Resistance', in *Black Looks: Race and Representation* (Boston: South End Press, 1992), 9–20.

39 hooks, *All about Love*, 4, 10, 13.

40 Barbara Frederickson, 'Love: Positivity Resonance as a Fresh, Evidence-Based Perspective on an Age-Old Topic', in *Handbook of Emotions*, 4th edn, ed. Lisa Feldman Barrett, Michael Lewis and Jeannette M. Haviland-Jones (New York and London: Guilford Press, 2016), 855.

41 Frederickson, 'Love', 852.

42 Timothy C. Campbell, *Wireless Writing in the Age of Marconi* (Minneapolis: University of Minnesota Press, 2006), 69–70; F. T. Marinetti, 'Destruction of Syntax – Wireless Imagination – Words in Freedom', in *Lacerba*, 11 May and 15 June 1913, in *Stung by Salt and War: Creative Texts of the Italian Avant-Gardist F. T. Marinetti*, ed. Richard J. Pioli (New York: Peter Lang, 1987), 45–53.

43 Susan J. Douglas, *Inventing American Broadcasting* (Baltimore, MD: Johns Hopkins University, 1987), 191.

44 Sconce, *Haunted Media*, 65–6; Maria Rikitianskaia, Gabriele Balbi and Katharina Lobinger, 'The Mediatization of the Air: Wireless Telegraphy and the Origins of a Transnational Space of Communication, 1900–1910s', *Journal of Communication* 68, no. 4 (2018): 758–79.

45 Susan J. Douglas, *Listening In: Radio and the American Imagination* (Minneapolis: University of Minnesota Press, 2013), 73–5; Hilmes, *Radio Voices*, 130–50; Carolyn Birdsall and Senta Siewert, 'Of Sound Mind: Mental Distress and Sound in Twentieth-Century Media Culture', *TMG: Journal for Media History* 16, no. 1 (2013): 27–45.

46 On amateur radio fans appropriating such pathologies with pride, with self-descriptions of being afflicted with 'radioitis' or 'wirelessitis', see Susanne Johnston and Tim Beddow, eds, *Collecting: The Passionate Pastime* (Harmondsworth, etc.: Viking, 1986), 133.

47 Eve Rosenhaft, 'Lesewut, Kinosucht, Radiotismus: Zur (geschlechter-) politischen Relevanz neuer Massenmedien in den 1920er Jahren', in *Amerikanisierung: Traum und Alptraum im Deutschland des 20.*

Jahrhunderts, ed. Alf Lüdtke, Inge Marssolek and Adelheid von Saldern (Stuttgart: Steiner, 1996), 119–43; Bill Kirkpatrick, 'Radio Fever? The Health Roots of Early Radio', in Lindgren and Loviglio, *The Routledge Companion to Radio and Podcast Studies*, 167–78.

48 D. Travers Scott, *Pathology and Technology: Killer Apps and Sick Users* (New York: Peter Lang, 2018), 26–7.

49 Kennedy, *Digital Domesticity*, 17.

50 Michele Hilmes, *Only Connect: A Cultural History of Broadcasting in the United States* (Boston: Cengage, 2013), 23–7. For the significance of jazz and dance music in UK radio programming from its early years onwards, see Tim Wall, *Jazz on BBC Radio, 1922–1972* (Sheffield: Equinox, forthcoming).

51 Jina Kim, *Urban Modernities in Colonial Korea and Taiwan* (Leiden and Boston: Brill, 2019), 76; Stephen Lovell, *Russia in the Microphone Age: A History of Soviet Radio, 1919–1970* (Oxford: Oxford University Press, 2015), 27, 34–5, 48–51, 146.

52 Lawrence Grossberg, 'Is There a Fan in the House? The Affective Sensibility of Fandom', in *The Adoring Audience: Fan Culture and Popular Media*, ed. Lisa A. Lewis (London: Routledge, 1992), 57–63.

53 On the concept of the 'radiogenic', see Lacey, *Listening Publics*, 92–110.

54 Seán Street, *The Memory of Sound: Preserving the Sonic Past* (New York: Routledge, 2014), 114.

55 On sport in early broadcasting in the US, see Ronald A. Smith, *Play-By-Play: Radio, Television, and Big-Time College Sport* (Baltimore, MD: Johns Hopkins University Press, 2001). For 'radio calisthenics' programming across Japan and its empire, see Sumei Wang, 'Radio and Urban Rhythms in 1930s Colonial Taiwan', *Historical Journal of Film, Radio and Television* 38, no. 1 (2018): 147–62. For religion and radio, see Russell P. Skelchy, 'The Afterlife of Colonial Radio in Christian Missionary Broadcasting of the Philippines', *South East Asia Research* 28, no. 3 (2020): 344–62.

56 Paul Young, *The Cinema Dreams its Rivals: Media Fantasy Films from Radio to the Internet* (Minneapolis: University of Minnesota Press, 2006); Martin Cooper, *Radio's Legacy in Popular Culture: The Sounds of British Broadcasting over the Decades* (New York: Bloomsbury, 2022); Alasdair Pinkerton, *Radio: Making Waves in Sound* (London: Reaktion Books, 2019), 176–208. For a radio programme at the intersection of radio and comics during the 1960s, see Richard Legay and Jessica Burton, 'From the Comics Strip to the Airwaves: The Short-lived Experiment of *Le Feu de camp du dimanche matin* on Europe n° 1', *Media History* (2022): 1–14.

57 Richard Butsch, 'Crystal Sets and Scarf-pin Radios: Gender, Technology and the Construction of American Radio Listening in the 1920s', *Media, Culture & Society* 20, no. 4 (1998): 557–72. On 'train-radio' as facilitating a sense of being connected across vast distances, see Jody Berland, *North of Empire: Essays on the Cultural Technologies of Space* (Durham, NC: Duke University Press, 2009), 105–7.

58 Noah Arceneaux, 'The Wireless in the Window: Department Stores and Radio Retailing in the 1920s', *Journalism & Mass Communication Quarterly* 83, no. 3 (2006): 581–95; Debra R. Cohen, Michael Coyle and Jane Lewty, eds, *Broadcasting Modernism* (Gainesville: University Press of Florida, 2009).

59 On domestic intimacy and the power dynamics of the home around broadcast media, see David Morley, *Family Television: Cultural Power and Domestic Leisure* (London: Routledge, Chapman and Hall, 1986); Ann Gray, *Video Playtime: The Gendering of a Leisure Technology* (London: Routledge, 1992); Douglas, Listening In, 124–60; Hilmes, *Radio Voices*, 130–50; José Ricardo Carvalheiro, 'Radio, Reception and Memory: Portuguese Female Audiences and Housewife Politics from the 1930s to the 1950s', *Rádio-Leituras* 5, no. 1 (2014): 141–63.

60 For the key qualities associated with broadcasting, see Lynn Spigel, *Make Room for TV: Television and the Family Ideal in Postwar America* (Chicago: University of Chicago Press, 1992).

61 Benedict Anderson, *Imagined Communities: Reflections on the Origin and Spread of Nationalism*, rev. edn (London: Verso, 2006); Michele Hilmes, 'Radio and the Imagined Community', in *The Sound Studies Reader*, ed. Jonathan Sterne (Abingdon and New York: Routledge, 2012), 351–62; Squier, *Communities of the Air*. For how people live and have lived in emotional communities, with their own particular norms and emotional styles, see Barbara H. Rosenwein, *Emotional Communities in the Early Middle Ages* (Ithaca, NY: Cornell University Press, 2006).

62 Scannell, *Radio, Television and Modern Life*, 23, 74, 152–3.

63 Hilmes, *Radio Voices*; Liz Gunner, *Radio Soundings: South Africa and the Black Modern* (Cambridge: Cambridge University Press, 2019); Stephen Lovell, 'Broadcasting Bolshevik: The Radio Voice of Soviet Culture, 1920s–1950s', *Journal of Contemporary History* 48, no. 1 (2013): 78–97.

64 For debates about 'correct' or 'standard' pronunciation in radio, including official guidelines and dictionaries, see Viktoria Tkaczyk, 'Archival Traces of Applied Research: Language Planning and

Psychotechnics in Interwar Germany', *Technology and Culture* 60, no. 2 (2019): S64–S95; Christopher A. Chávez, 'Whose is the Voice of the American Public? Latinx Speech and the Standard Language Ideology of Public Radio', *Communication and Critical/Cultural Studies* 16, no. 4 (2019): 308–25; Anne Karpf, 'Fear and Loathing of Women on the Radio', *Guardian*, 1 February 2013; Christine Ehrick, *Radio and the Gendered Soundscape: Women and Broadcasting in Argentina and Uruguay, 1930–1950* (New York: Cambridge University Press, 2015).

65 McCracken, *Real Men don't Sing*, 126.

66 Thokozani Mhlambi, 'African Pioneer: KE Masinga and the Zulu "Radio Voice" in the 1940s', *Journal of Radio & Audio Media* 26, no. 2 (2019): 210–30.

67 For example, Natália Oliveira Ferreira and Mark Turin, 'Rádios Indígenas: Brazil's Indigenous Language Broadcasting Landscape', *Journal of Radio & Audio Media* (2021): 1–25. On local languages in a liberalized, commercial radio landscape, see Sarah Akrofi-Quarcoo and Audrey Gadzekpo, 'Indigenizing Radio in Ghana', *Radio Journal: International Studies in Broadcast & Audio Media* 18, no. 1 (2020): 95–112.

68 Radio culture under US colonial rule in 1930s Philippines was modelled on the commercial US networks, and radio personalities 'had become bigger celebrities than the movie stars', with fan clubs rapidly forming around popular stars: Elizabeth L. Enriquez, *Appropriation of Colonial Broadcasting: A History of Early Radio in the Philippines* (Quezon City: University of the Philippines Press, 2009), 105. For the changing culture of radio DJ performance, see David Crider, *Performing Personality: On-Air Radio Identities in a Changing Media Landscape* (Lanham, MD: Lexington, 2016).

69 Emma Robertson, '"I get a real kick out of Big Ben": BBC Versions of Britishness on the Empire and General Overseas Service, 1932–1948', *Historical Journal of Film, Radio and Television* 28, no. 4 (2008): 459–73.

70 Street, *The Memory of Sound*, 3, 25–6.

71 Neil Verma, *Theater of the Mind: Imagination, Aesthetics, and American Radio Drama* (Chicago: University of Chicago Press, 2012); Emmett, 'Feeling at Home'.

72 Street, *The Memory of Sound*, 31, 40.

73 On early agricultural market reports and educational programming, see Steve Craig, '"The Farmer's Friend": Radio Comes to Rural America, 1920–1927', *Journal of Radio Studies* 8, no. 2 (2001):

330–46; David Goodman and Joy Elizabeth Hayes, *New Deal Radio: The Educational Radio Project* (New Brunswick, NJ: Rutgers University Press, 2022). On contemporary examples of expert advice and information in radio, see Wanning Sun and Wei Lei, 'In Search of Intimacy in China: The Emergence of Advice Media for the Privatized Self', *Communication, Culture & Critique* 10, no. 1 (2017): 20–38; Jona Fras, 'Tuning in to God: Authorising Religious Talk in Jordanian Islamic Advice Programmes', *Contemporary Levant* 5, no. 2 (2020): 126–43.

74 Anahid Kassabian, *Ubiquitous Listening: Affect, Attention, and Distributed Subjectivity* (Berkeley: University of California Press, 2013), xii, xxiv, 4–5.

75 Tia DeNora, *Music in Everyday Life* (Cambridge: Cambridge University Press, 2004), 61.

76 For example, Loviglio, *Radio's Intimate Public*; Shaun Moores, '"The Box on the Dresser": Memories of Early Radio and Everyday Life', *Media, Culture & Society* 10, no. 1 (1988): 23–40.

77 Tacchi, 'Radio and Affective Rhythm', 171.

78 Brian Larkin, *Signal and Noise: Media, Infrastructure, and Urban Culture in Nigeria* (Durham, NC: Duke University Press, 2008), 50.

79 Christian Breunig, 'Mobile Medien im digitalen Zeitalter: Neue Entwicklungen, Angebote, Geschäftsmodelle und Nutzung', *Media Perspektiven* (2006): 5, in Heike Weber, 'Taking Your Favorite Sound Along: Portable Audio Technologies for Mobile Music Listening', in Bijsterveld and van Dijck, *Sound Souvenirs*, 69.

80 Jo Tacchi, 'Radio Texture: Between Self and Others', in *Material Cultures: Why Some Things Matter*, ed. Daniel Miller (Chicago: University of Chicago Press, 1998), 25–46.

81 Scannell, *Radio, Television and Modern Life*, 155.

82 Maria Rikitianskaia and Gabriele Balbi, 'What Time Is It? History and Typology of Time Signals from the Telegraph to the Digital', *International Journal of Communication* 15 (2021).

83 Maggie Andrews, 'Homes Both Sides of the Microphone: The Wireless and Domestic Space in Inter-War Britain', *Women's History Review* 21, no. 4 (2012): 605–21. For the creation of a 'radio room' within modernist domestic interiors around 1927–8, see https://collection.cooperhewitt.org/exhibitions/874305559/large-print?pt=18.

84 For example, the 'Aunty Beeb' nickname for the BBC. For 'aunt' and 'uncle' figures in Australian radio, see Bridget Griffen-Foley, *Australian Radio Listeners and Television Viewers: Historical Perspectives* (Cham: Palgrave Macmillan, 2020), 7–28.

85 Sanna Inthorn, 'Listening While Doing Things: Radio, Gender and Older Women', *Radio Journal: International Studies in Broadcast & Audio Media* 18, no. 2 (2020): 221.

86 For example, Tim Wall and Nick Webber, 'Changing Cultural Coordinates: The Transistor Radio and Space / Time / Identity', in *Oxford Handbook of Mobile Music*, vol 1., ed. Sumanth Gopinath and Jason Stanyek (New York: Oxford University Press, 2014), 118–31. On how the Walkman allowed listeners to seek forms of private and intimate spaces of 'sanctuary', see Michael Bull, *Sounding out the City: Personal Stereos and the Management of Everyday Life* (Oxford and New York: Berg, 2000).

87 Bill Kirkpatrick, '"A Blessed Boon": Radio, Disability, Governmentality, and the Discourse of the "Shut-in," 1920–1930', *Critical Studies in Media Communication* 29, no. 3 (2012): 172; Rebecca P. Scales, 'Radio Broadcasting, Disabled Veterans, and the Politics of National Recovery in Interwar France', *French Historical Studies* 31, no. 4 (2008): 643–78.

88 This argument could also be extended to a pleasurable anxiety in radio consumption, such as for the 1940s thriller drama, which exploited 'the horror of the disembodied voice'. Allison McCracken, 'Scary Women and Scarred Men: *Suspense*, Gender Trouble, and Postwar Change', in *Radio Reader: Essays in the Cultural History of Radio*, ed. Michele Hilmes and Jason Loviglio (New York: Routledge, 2002), 184.

89 Carolyn Birdsall, *Nazi Soundscapes: Sound, Technology and Urban Space in Germany, 1933–1945* (Amsterdam: Amsterdam University Press, 2012), 135; Michael Guida, *Listening to British Nature: Wartime, Radio, and Modern Life, 1914–1945* (Oxford: Oxford University Press, 2021). For radio sets as intimate and valuable objects for Jewish survivors after 1945 and during their migration journeys, see Michael Windover, 'Listening for Design: Agency and History in a Philips Aachen-Super D 52', in *Design and Agency: Critical Perspectives on Identities, Histories, and Practices*, ed. John Potvin and Marie-Ève Marchand (London and New York: Bloomsbury, 2020), 97–109.

90 On 'after dark' listening to offshore radio in the UK, sometimes taking place under the bed covers, see Kimberley Peters, *Sound, Space and Society: Rebel Radio* (London: Palgrave, 2017), 60. On foreign radio listening in China, see Hang Wu, 'Broadcasting Infrastructures and Electromagnetic Fatality: Listening to Enemy Radio in Socialist China', in *Sound Communities in the Asia Pacific: Music, Media, and Technology*, ed. Lonán Ó Briain and Min Yen Ong (New York: Bloomsbury, 2021), 171–19; Shmuel Breslew, in *Archiwum Ringelbluma*, vol. 22, ed. Maria Ferenc Piotrowska and Franciszek

Zakrzewski (Warsaw: Żydowski Instytut Historyczny, 2016), 6, quoted in Maria Ferenc Piotrowska, '"Listening Became Indispensable for Life . . .": Strategies and Goals of Radio Monitoring in the Warsaw Ghetto', *Media History* 25, no. 4 (2019): 430.

91 Tom Rice, 'Sounds Inside: Prison, Prisoners and Acoustical Agency', *Sound Studies* 2, no. 1 (2016): 6–20; Eleanor R. Benson, 'Love is in the Airwaves: Contesting Mass Incarceration with Prisoners' Radio', *Tapestries: Interwoven Voices of Local and Global Identities* 7, no. 1 (2018); Tiziano Bonini, 'Crazy Radio: The Domestication of Mental Illness over the Airwaves', *Radio Journal: International Studies in Broadcast & Audio Media* 3, no. 3 (2005): 145–53; Tiziano Bonini and Marta Perrotta, 'On and Off the Air: Radio-Listening Experiences in the San Vittore Prison', *Media, Culture & Society* 29, no. 2 (2007): 179–93; Sophia Geng, 'Music and Sound in Weihsien Internment Camp in Japanese-Occupied China', in *Sonic Histories of Occupation: Experiencing Sound and Empire in a Global Context*, ed. Russell P. Skelchy and Jeremy E. Taylor (London and New York: Bloomsbury, 2021), 73–93.

92 Kristin M. Peterson, '"The Bad Things are just too Close Right Now": Podcasts Cultivate Spaces to Sit with the Messiness of Grief', *Mortality* (2022): 1–15; Mia Lindgren, 'Intimacy and Emotions in Podcast Journalism: A Study of Award-Winning Australian and British Podcasts', *Journalism Practice* (2021): 1–16; Alyn Euritt, *Podcasting as an Intimate Medium* (Abingdon: Routledge, 2022).

93 Joli Jensen, 'Fandom as Pathology: The Consequences of a Characterisation', in Lewis, *The Adoring Audience*, 9–29. Obsession and insatiable desire have been identified as powerful fantasies of love in the past and present: Barbara H. Rosenwein, *Love: A History in Five Fantasies* (Cambridge: Polity, 2022).

94 Grossberg, 'Is There a Fan in the House?', 56.

95 In this same year, Henry Jenkins refuted the notion of the indifferent or passive spectator of television, and discussed how fans have fluctuations of attention and could narrate their own transition from having a 'casual interest' in a television show and developing a 'strong emotional investment in the series and its characters'. Henry Jenkins, *Textual Poachers: Television Fans and Participatory Culture* (New York and London: Routledge, 1992), 57–8.

96 Hills, *Fan Cultures*, x.

97 Hills, *Fan Cultures*, 80. Grossberg suggests that these maps guide individuals 'how to navigate our way into and through various moods, and how to live within emotional and ideological histories'. Grossberg, 'Is There a Fan in the House?', 57, 59.

98 Hills, *Fan Cultures*, 78, 80.
99 Hills, *Fan Cultures*, 65.
100 Mark Duffett, *Understanding Fandom: An Introduction to the Study of Media Fan Culture* (New York: Bloomsbury, 2013), 171.
101 Nicolle Lamerichs, *Productive Fandom: Intermediality and Affective Reception in Fan Cultures* (Amsterdam: Amsterdam University Press, 2018), 280.
102 Lamerichs, *Productive Fandom*, 208, 236.
103 Hills, 'Fandom from Cradle to Grave?'.
104 Mads Krogh and Morten Michelsen, 'Introduction: Complexities of Genre, of Mediation, and of Community', in *Music Radio: Building Communities, Mediating Genres*, ed. Morten Michelsen et al. (New York: Bloomsbury, 2019), 15–6.
105 Ute Frevert, 'The History of Emotions', in *Handbook of Emotions*, 4th edn, ed. Lisa Feldman Barrett, Michael Lewis and Jeannette M. Haviland-Jones (New York and London: Guilford Press, 2016), 56, 62.
106 Katie Barclay, *The History of Emotions: A Student Guide to Methods and Sources* (New York: Bloomsbury, 2020), 2.
107 Monique Scheer, 'Are Emotions a Kind of Practice (And is That What Makes Them Have a History)? A Bourdieuian Approach to Understanding Emotion', *History and Theory* 51, no. 2 (2012): 199.
108 Scheer, 'Are Emotions a Kind of Practice (And is That What Makes Them Have a History)?, 200.
109 Pierre Bourdieu, *Distinction: A Social Critique of the Judgement of Taste* (London: Routledge and Kegan Paul, 1984); Pierre Bourdieu, *The Logic of Practices* (Cambridge: Polity, 1990).
110 Scheer, 'Are Emotions a Kind of Practice (And is That What Makes Them Have a History)?', 205.
111 On the coercive dimensions to habitus in relation to radio listening and sensory disciplining, see Carolyn Birdsall, 'Earwitnessing: Sound Memories of the Nazi Period', in Bijsterveld and van Dijck, *Sound Souvenirs*, 169–81.
112 Scheer, 'Are Emotions a Kind of Practice (And is That What Makes Them Have a History)?', 218.
113 Scheer, 'Are Emotions a Kind of Practice (And is That What Makes Them Have a History)?', 218.
114 Margaret Wetherell, *Affect and Emotion: A New Social Science Understanding* (Los Angeles and London: Sage, 2012), 11.

115 Wetherell, *Affect and Emotion*, 4
116 Wetherell, *Affect and Emotion*, 23.
117 Wetherell, *Affect and Emotion*, 159.
118 Daniel Fisher, 'Radio', in *Keywords in Sound*, ed. David Novak and Matt Sakakeeny (Durham, NC: Duke University Press, 2015), 151–64.
119 For example, Constance Classen, *Worlds of Sense: Exploring the Senses in History and across Cultures* (London and New York: Routledge, 1993).
120 For example, Laura U. Marks, *Touch: Sensuous Theory and Multisensory Media* (Minneapolis: University of Minnesota Press, 2002).
121 Andreas Fickers, 'Visibly Audible: The Radio Dial as Mediating Interface', in *The Oxford Handbook of Sound Studies*, ed. Trevor Pinch and Karin Bijsterveld (Oxford and New York: Oxford University Press, 2012), 411–39.
122 David Parisi, *Archaeologies of Touch: Interfacing with Haptics from Electricity to Computing* (Minneapolis: University of Minnesota Press, 2018), 287.
123 Bill Kirkpatrick, 'Disability, Cultural Accessibility, and the Radio Archive', *New Review of Film and Television Studies* 16, no. 4 (2018): 474;
124 Artemis Yagou, 'Is Everyday Technology Serious or Fun? Reflections on Emotional Styles in Product Design', *Icon* (2011): 40–56.
125 Shawn VanCour and Kyle Barnett, 'Eat What You Hear: Gustasonic Discourses and the Material Culture of Commercial Sound Recording', *Journal of Material Culture* 22, no. 1 (2017): 93–109.
126 Phillip D. Vannini, Dennis Waskul and Simon Gottschalk, *The Senses in Self, Society and Culture: A Sociology of the Senses* (London: Routledge, 2012), 8–10.
127 For example, Mark M. Smith, *Sensing the Past: Seeing, Hearing, Smelling, Tasting, and Touching in History* (Berkeley and Los Angeles: University of California Press, 2007).
128 Shundana Yusaf, 'Wireless Sites: Architecture in the Space of British Radio, 1927–1945', *Traditional Dwellings and Settlements Review* (2008): 69–80; Elizabeth Darling, 'From Cockpit to Domestic Interior: the Great War and the Architecture of Wells Coates', *Journal of Architecture* 19, no. 6 (2014): 903–22; Tom Wilkinson, 'Art History on the Radio: Walter Benjamin and Wilhelm Pinder, 1930/1940', *Oxford Art Journal* 39, no. 1 (2016): 49–66.

129 Adrian Forty, *Objects of Desire: Design and Society since 1750* (London: Thames and Hudson, 1986), 11–12.

130 W. J. T. Mitchell, 'There are No Visual Media', *Journal of Visual Culture* 4, no. 2 (2005): 257, 262. For the 'remediation' of the content of one medium into another, see Jay David Bolter and Richard Grusin, *Remediation: Understanding New Media* (Cambridge, MA: MIT Press, 1999).

131 Debra Spitulnik, 'Mediated Modernities: Encounters with the Electronic in Zambia', *Visual Anthropology Review* 14, no. 2 (1998/1999): 63–84. On modern listening techniques developed in the context of modern medicine and sound telegraphy up to the 1900s, see Jonathan Sterne, *The Audible Past: Cultural Origins of Sound Reproduction* (Durham, NC, Duke University Press, 2003), 3.

132 Irina Rajewsky, 'Intermediality, Intertextuality, and Remediation', *Intermédialités* 6 (2005): 43–64.

133 Birgit Van Puymbroeck, 'Periodical Studies, Intermediality, and Cinema: Film in The Listener', in *Mapping Movie Magazines: Digitization, Periodicals and Cinema History*, ed. Lies Van de Vijver and Daniël Biltereyst (Cham: Palgrave Macmillan, 2020), 57–76; Paul Rixon, 'Radio and Popular Journalism in Britain: Early Radio Critics and Radio Criticism', *Radio Journal: International Studies in Broadcast & Audio Media* 13, no. 1–2 (2015): 23–36.

134 For example, Louisa Stein, *Millennial Fandom: Television Audiences in the Transmedia Age* (Iowa City: University of Iowa Press, 2015); Henry Jenkins, Sam Ford and Joshua Green, eds, *Spreadable Media: Creating Value and Meaning in a Networked Culture* (New York: New York University Press, 2018).

135 Cavicchi, 'Fandom before "Fan"'.

136 Georgina Born, 'Introduction – Music, Sound and Space: Transformations of Public and Private Experience', in *Music, Space and Sound: Transformations of Public and Private Experience*, ed. Georgina Born (Cambridge: Cambridge University Press, 2013), 3.

137 David Morley and Roger Silverstone, 'Domestic Communication: Technologies and Meanings', *Media, Culture, and Society* 12, no. 1 (1990): 31–55.

138 For the emphasis on love and materiality, and recent developments in Feminist Love Studies, see Anna Malinowska and Michael Gratzke, 'Introduction: Love Matters', in *The Materiality of Love: Essays on Affection and Cultural Practice*, ed. Anna Malinowska and Michael Gratzke (New York and London: Routledge, 2018), 1–9; Sara Ahmed, 'Happy Objects', in *The Affect Theory Reader*, ed. Melissa

Gregg and Gregory J. Seigworth (Durham, NC: Duke University Press, 2010), 29–52.

139 For example, Artemis Yagou, 'Shaping Technology for Everyday Use: The Case of Radio Set Design', *Design Journal* 5, no. 1 (2002): 2–13. On the history of the radiogram, see David Morton, *Off the Record: The Technology and Culture of Sound Recording in America* (New Brunswick, NJ: Rutgers University Press, 2000), 26–8.

140 Fickers, 'Visibly Audible'.

141 Anna Moran and Sorcha O'Brien, 'Editors' Foreword', in *Love Objects: Emotion, Design and Material Culture*, ed. Anna Moran and Sorcha O'Brien (London, etc.: Bloomsbury, 2014), xv.

142 Spitulnik, 'Mediated Modernities'; Larkin, *Signal and Noise*, 48–72.

143 Gavin Steingo and Jim Sykes, 'Introduction: Remapping Sound Studies in the Global South', in *Remapping Sound Studies*, ed. Gavin Steingo and Jim Sykes (Durham, NC: Duke University Press, 2019), 1–36.

144 Michael Windover, 'Art Deco and the Fashioning of Radio Spaces', in *The Routledge Companion to Art Deco*, ed. Bridget Elliott and Michael Windover (Basingstoke: Routledge, 2019), 139–58.

145 Arjun Appadurai, 'Introduction: Commodities and the Politics of Value', in *The Social Life of Things: Commodities in Cultural Perspective*, ed. Arjun Appadurai (Cambridge and New York: Cambridge University Press, 1986), 3–63; Igor Kopytoff, 'The Cultural Biography of Things: Commoditization as Process', in Appadurai, *The Social Life of Things*, 64–91.

146 Janet Hoskins, 'Agency, Biography and Objects', in *Handbook of Material Culture*, ed. Christopher Y. Tilley et al. (London and Thousand Oaks, CA: Sage, 2006), 74–84.

147 Hoskins, 'Agency, Biography and Objects', 82.

148 For example, Susan M. Pearce, *On Collecting: An Investigation into Collecting in the European Tradition* (London and New York: Routledge, 1995), 290–5, 393–6; Karen F. Gracy, 'Moving Image Preservation and Cultural Capital', *Library Trends* 56, no. 1 (2007): 183–97.

149 Birdsall and Carmi, 'Feminist Avenues for *listening in*'; Gascia Ouzounian, 'Contemporary Radio Art and Spatial Politics: The Critical Radio Utopias of Anna Friz', *Radio Journal: International Studies in Broadcast & Audio Media* 5, no. 2–3 (2008): 129–42.

150 For example, Caroline Mitchell, 'Re-Sounding Feminist Radio: A Journey through Women's Community Radio Archives', *Feminist*

Media Histories 1, no. 4 (2015): 126–43; Windover, 'Listening for Design'.

151 Shawn VanCour, 'The Informal Economy of the Amateur Archive: Collectors as Cultural Intermediaries', *Flow* (2015), https://www.flowjournal.org/2015/05/the-informal-economy-of-the-amateur-archive/.

152 Maurice Halbwachs, *On Collective Memory*, ed. Edward A. Coser (Chicago: University of Chicago Press, 1992).

153 Bijsterveld and van Dijck, *Sound Souvenirs*.

154 For example, Tim van der Heijden, 'Technostalgia of the Present: From Technologies of Memory to a Memory of Technologies', *NECSUS: European Journal of Media Studies* 4, no. 2 (2015), https://necsus-ejms.org/portfolio/autumn-2015_vintage/.

155 For example, Sarah Baker, ed., *Preserving Popular Music Heritage: Do-it-yourself, Do-it-together* (New York and London: Routledge, 2015); Jez Collins, 'Citizen Archiving and Virtual Sites of Musical Memory in Online Communities', in *The Routledge Companion to Popular Music History and Heritage*, ed. Sarah Baker et al. (Abingdon and New York: Routledge, 2018), 247–57; Lauren Istvandity, Sarah Baker and Zelmarie Cantillon, eds., *Remembering Popular Musics Past: Memory–Heritage–History* (London and New York: Anthem Press, 2019).

156 Margaret Wetherell, Laurajane Smith and Gary Campbell, 'Introduction: Affective Heritage Practices', in *Emotion, Affective Practices, and the Past in the Present*, ed. Laurajane Smith, Margaret Wetherell and Gary Campbell (London: Routledge, 2018), 1–21.

157 Laura LaPlaca, '"Something into Nothing": On the Materiality of the Broadcast Archive', *Antenna*, 27 July 2015, https://blog.commarts.wisc.edu/2015/07/27/something-into-nothing-on-the-materiality-of-the-broadcast-archive/.

158 Douglas, *Listening In*, 329.

159 Hills, *Fan Cultures*, 72.

160 'Hams' is used to describe those who build two-way radios, whereas 'bcl' was an abbreviation for 'broadcast listener' – those who liked to tune in to frequencies from others, but not engage in conversation.

161 Jasanoff and Kim, *Dreamscapes of Modernity*; Sheila Jasanoff, 'Ordering Knowledge, Ordering Society', in *States of Knowledge: The Co-production of Science and the Social Order*, ed. Sheila Jasanoff (New York: Routledge, 2004), 13–45.

162 On the longer history of the distinction between the amateur and the professional (also in relation to competitive sport), see Vera Keller, 'The "Lover" and Early Modern Fandom', *Transformative Works and Cultures* 7 (2011).

163 Eddie Bohan, *A Century of Irish Radio, 1900–2000* (self published, 2019), 74–9.

164 Michael Friedewald, 'The Beginnings of Radio Communication in Germany, 1897–1918', *Journal of Radio Studies* 7, no. 2 (2000): 441–63; Rebecca P. Scales, *Radio and the Politics of Sound in Interwar France, 1921–1939* (Cambridge: Cambridge University Press, 2016), 12.

165 For radio and colonial modernity, see Enriquez, *Appropriation of Colonial Broadcasting*; Andrew F. Jones, *Yellow Music: Media Culture and Colonial Modernity in the Chinese Jazz Age* (Durham, NC: Duke University Press, 2001); Erich DeWald, 'Taking to the Waves: Vietnamese Society Around the Radio in the 1930s', *Modern Asian Studies* 46, no. 1 (2012): 143–65; Rudolf Mràzek, *Engineers of Happy Land: Technology and Nationalism in a Colony* (Princeton, NJ: Princeton University Press, 2002); Nelson Ribeiro, 'A Polycentric Broadcasting Model: Radio and the Promotion of Portuguese Colonialism', *Journal of Radio & Audio Media* 29, no.1 (2022): 13–17; Melissa Moorman, *Powerful Frequencies: Radio State Power, and the Cold War in Angola, 1931–2002* (Athens: Ohio University Press, 2019), 19–48.

166 Simon Potter, 'Out of the Ether: The Wireless World and New Histories of International Radio Broadcasting', in *The Wireless World: Global Histories of International Radio Broadcasting*, ed. Simon Potter et al. (Oxford: Oxford University Press, 2022), 19–20.

167 For early amateur societies and the relationship between radio and nationalism in Argentina, see Robert Howard Claxton, *From Parsifal to Perón: Early Radio in Argentina, 1920–1944* (Gainesville: University Press of Florida, 2007), 1–25, 90–114; Lovell, *Russia in the Microphone Age*, 26–7, 43–69.

168 Gabriele Balbi and Simone Natale, 'The Double Birth of Wireless: Italian Radio Amateurs and the Interpretative Flexibility of New Media', *Journal of Radio & Audio Media* 22, no. 1 (2015): 27–8.

169 Maria Rikitianskaia, 'A Transnational Approach to Radio Amateurism in the 1910s', in *Transnationalizing Radio Research: New Approaches to an Old Medium*, ed. Golo Föllmer and Alexander Badenoch (Bielefeld: Transcript, 2018), 139.

170 'The First Amateur Radio Club in America', *Radio Broadcast* 2, no. 2 (December 1922): 222–7.
171 Elmer E. Bucher, *The Wireless Experimenter's Manual, Incorporating How to Conduct a Radio Club* (New York: Wireless Press, 1920), 1.
172 Bucher, *The Wireless Experimenter's Manual*, 12–8.
173 Bruce Campbell, *The Radio Hobby, Private Associations, and the Challenge of Modernity in Germany* (London: Palgrave Macmillan, 2019), 58.
174 Campbell, *The Radio Hobby*, 312.
175 On the theory of 'domestication' of new media like radio into the home environment, see Roger Silverstone and Eric Hirsch, 'Introduction', in *Consuming Technologies: Media and Information in Domestic Spaces*, ed. Roger Silverstone and Eric Hirsch (London: Routledge, 1992), 1–10.
176 Aitor Anduaga, *Wireless and Empire: Geopolitics, Radio Industry, and Ionosphere in the British Empire, 1918–1939* (Oxford: Oxford University Press, 2009), 107; Gordon Bussey, *Wireless, the Crucial Decade: History of the British Wireless Industry, 1924–34* (London: Peter Peregrinus, 1990), 91–119.
177 For a 1930 reference to amateurs as 'fans', in contrast to a growing audience of 'ordinary' radio listeners for whom radio was not a technical hobby, see P. Wilson, 'The Olympiads', *The Gramophone* 89 (October 1930): 246.
178 Douglas, *Listening In*, 24–5, 38, 57–8, 61, 73–82.
179 Campbell, *The Radio Hobby*, 8.
180 In Germany, licenses for amateur radio operators were issued by postal services and the German Amateur Transmission and Monitoring Service. Campbell, *The Radio Hobby*, 216–17.
181 Kristen Haring, *Ham Radio's Technical Culture* (Cambridge, MA, and London: MIT Press, 2007), ix, x–xi.
182 See, for instance, the amended version of the 1928 code of conduct listed at ARRL (National Association for Amateur Radio), https://www.arrl.org/amateur-code.
183 Douglas, *Listening In*, 333.
184 Sidney Gernsback, *Radio Encyclopedia* (New York: Gernsback, 1927), 128–9.
185 Haring, *Ham Radio's Technical Culture*, 30–1.
186 For the active participation of amateurs in the Caribbean, and their participation in requesting and providing QSL cards, see Alejandra

Bronfman, *Isles of Noise: Sonic Media in the Caribbean* (Chapel Hill: University of North Carolina Press, 2016), 70, 152–3.

187 Vincent Kuitenbrouwer, '"The Brightness You Bring into Our Otherwise Very Dull Existence": Responses to Dutch Global Radio Broadcasts from the British Empire in the 1920s and 1930s', in *The MacKenzie Moment and Imperial History: Essays in Honour of John M. Mackenzie*, ed. Stephanie L. Barczewski and Martin Farr (Cham: Palgrave Macmillan, 2019), 361–81.

188 An example of overlaps between amateur hobbies is inventor Hiram Perry Maxim, who had been co-founder of the American Radio League in 1914 and later used this organization as a model when founding the Amateur Cinema League in 1926. Haring, *Ham Radio's Technical Culture*, 5–6.

189 'Het Amateur Congres te Parijs (14–19 April)', *Radio-Expres* 19 (8 May 1925): 338–40.

190 Michel de Certeau, *The Practice of Everyday Life* (Berkeley: University of California Press, 1984), 34, cited in Campbell, *The Radio Hobby*, 236.

191 Yuzo Takahashi, 'A Network of Tinkerers: The Advent of the Radio and Television Receiver Industry in Japan', *Technology and Culture* 41, no. 3 (2000): 460–4.

192 The JARL, still in existence today, had its first annual convention in 1931, and amateur activities were covered extensively by the monthly magazine *Musen to Jikken* (Radio Experimenters).

193 There were multiple political-economic reasons for this, including the wartime endorsement of simple receivers by the state, which also made long-distance listening more difficult: Takahashi, 'A Network of Tinkerers', 470–1. By contrast, a study of the British *Wireless World* magazine (started in 1913) has found that superheterodyne models comprised 17 per cent of the models cited in the magazine in 1932, and 62 per cent in 1934, which gives an indication of how DIY self-building of radio receivers went into decline with the rise of the superheterodynes, which required high-level skills and professional tools to adjust its circuits. Keith Geddes and Gordon Bussey, *The Setmakers: A History of the Radio and Television Industry* (London: BREMA, 1991), 107.

194 For the significance of Akihabara Electric Town for the active participation of users and fans, see Jakob Nobuoka, 'User Innovation and Creative Consumption in Japanese Culture Industries: The Case of Akihabara, Tokyo', *Geografiska Annaler: Series B, Human Geography* 92, no. 3 (2010): 205–18.

195 Takahashi, 'A Network of Tinkerers', 470–1.

196 Amateurs also took a leading role in developing affordable television receivers following the inception of television broadcasts from 1953 onwards, having already set up an amateur television research group in 1950, which carried out experiments and contests for self-made receivers. Takahashi, 'A Network of Tinkerers', 471–3, 475–9.

197 Douglas, *Listening In*, 332. In Soviet Russia, where radio clubs had a stronger representation of workers, the members remained overwhelmingly young and male, with 0.5 per cent of members estimated to be women in 1925. Lovell, *Russia in the Microphone Age*, 50.

198 Haring, *Ham Radio's Technical Culture*, xii.

199 Haring, *Ham Radio's Technical Culture*, 47.

200 Campbell, *The Radio Hobby*, 136–41; Haring, *Ham Radio's Technical Culture*, 47–8.

201 Douglas, *Listening In*, 290. For the persistence of DXing as a male-dominated technical culture up to the present, see Michael Nevradakis, 'Disembodied Voices and Dislocated Signals: The World of Modern-Day DXing', *Journal of Radio and Audio Media* 20, no. 1 (2013): 68–86.

202 Birdsall and Carmi, 'Feminist Avenues for *listening in*'.

203 Haring, *Ham Radio's Technical Culture*, 36–7.

204 Tara Rodgers, 'Tinkering with Cultural Memory: Gender and the Politics of Synthesizer Historiography', *Feminist Media Histories* 1, no. 4 (2015): 24; Jeannine Baker, Kate Murphy and Kristin Skoog, eds, 'Transnational Broadcasting', special issue, *Feminist Media Histories* 5, no. 3 (2019).

205 For example, a photo dated 1954 from *QST* magazine depicts teenagers Sonia and Karen Carlsen who had gained their amateur radio license, yet this achievement is covered in relation to their status as daughters of Kurt Carlsen, a highly-regarded sea captain and amateur radio operator. However, mixed up in the metadata for this image is an announcement noting that a number of women amateur radio enthusiasts had protested against the terms YL (young lady) and XYL (ex-young lady), and wanted their licenses to be recognized, suggesting instead the abbreviations MYL (married woman with license), SYL (single woman without license) and XYL (married woman without license). See Alamy, https://bit.ly/3M9Ta61. For a Black family in the US who all became licensed amateurs in the 1950s, see Alamy, https://bit.ly/3mgIoQQ.

206 See Ryan Ellet, *Encylopedia of Black Radio in the United States, 1921–1955* (Jefferson and London: McFarland, 2012), 4, 11, 36, 41, 42, 50, 67, 95, 129, 137, 141, 168.
207 For the YLRL, see Eleanor Wilson, 'Congratulations YLRL!', *QST* 43, no. 1 (January 1959): 62; 'How many Yls?', *QST* 43, no. 1 (January 1959): 64–5.
208 For example, Christina Dunbar-Hester, 'Geeks, Meta-geeks, and Gender Trouble: Activism, Identity, and Low-Power FM Radio', *Social Studies of Science* 38, no. 2 (2008): 201–32; Last Moyo, 'Participation, Citizenship, and Pirate Radio as Empowerment: The Case of Radio Dialogue in Zimbabwe', *International Journal of Communication* 6 (2012), https://ijoc.org/index.php/ijoc/article/view/1229; Amanda Wasielewski, 'Cracking the Ether', in *From City Space to Cyberspace: Art, Squatting, and Internet Culture in the Netherlands* (Amsterdam: Amsterdam University Press, 2021), 127–67.
209 Anduaga, *Wireless and Empire*, xxiii.
210 For the competition between Telefunken and Marconi, see Roland Wittje, *The Age of Electroacoustics: Transforming Science and Sound* (Cambridge, MA: MIT Press, 2016), 14.
211 Wittje, *The Age of Electroacoustics*, 11–12; Daqing Yang, *Technology of Empire: Telecommunications and Japanese Expansion in Asia, 1883–1945* (Cambridge, MA: Harvard University Press, 2010).
212 Dwayne R. Winseck and Robert M. Pike, *Communication and Empire: Media, Markets, and Globalization, 1860–1930* (Durham, NC: Duke University Press, 2007).
213 Tom Western, 'Securing the Aural Border: Fieldwork and Interference in Post-war BBC Audio Nationalism', *Sound Studies* 1, no. 1 (2015): 77–97; Timothy D. Taylor, 'Music and the Rise of Radio in 1920s America: Technological Imperialism, Socialization, and the Transformation of Intimacy', *Historical Journal of Film, Radio and Television* 22, no. 4 (2002): 428.
214 On 'imagined community' in relation to radio, see Hilmes, *Radio Voices*, xiii, 6, 11–33. On exclusionary notions of 'the listener' and radio's imagined community on the basis of race and ethnicity, see Stoever, *The Sonic Color Line*; Birdsall, *Nazi Soundscapes*.
215 Young, *The Cinema Dreams its Rivals*, 51.
216 For further discussion of this film, see Carolyn Birdsall, 'Sound Aesthetics and the Global Imagination in German Media Culture around 1930', in *Sounds of Modern History: Auditory Cultures in*

19th- and 20th-Century Europe, ed. Daniel Morat (New York: Berghahn, 2014), 262–3.

217 Arceneaux, 'The Wireless in the Window'. On the radio-phonograph combination player (or 'radiogram') and its role in helping to revive record sales in the second half of the 1920s, which had been affected by the introduction of (network) radio in the mid-1920s, see Morton, *Off the Record*, 26–8.

218 Douglas Kahn, *Noise, Water, Meat: A History of Sound in the Arts* (Cambridge, MA: MIT Press, 1999), 71, 98, 123–56.

219 In German-speaking contexts the concept of 'radio film' (*Radio-Kino*) was prevalent. On Soviet experiments in sound film aesthetics, see Dmitri Zakharine, 'Auditory Channels: Crowing Roosters and Wailing Sirens', in *Media and Communication in the Soviet Union (1917–1953)*, ed. Kirill Postoutenko, Alexey Tikhomirov and Dmitri Zakharine (Cham: Palgrave Macmillan, 2022), 95–120.

220 Walter F. Fitze, 'Fünf Jahre Arbeit: 1924–1928', in *Norag: Das fünfte Jahr* (Hamburg: Rufu Verlang, 1929), 11.

221 For the exchange between the film, music and electroacoustic industries in the sound transition years, and patent applications by the Tobis conglomerate, see Wolfgang Mühl-Benninghaus, *Das Ringen um den Tonfilm: Strategien der Elektro- und der Filmindustrie in den 20er und 30er Jahren* (Düsseldorf: Droste Verlag, 1999), 81–205.

222 For Ruttmann's experimental work, including 'Weekend', see Daniel Gilfillan, *Pieces of Sound: German Experimental Radio* (Minneapolis and London: University of Minnesota Press, 2009), 1–6, 77.

223 The script is reprinted in the censorship report no. 19946, Berlin Film-Prüfstelle, 30 August 1928, Bundesarchiv Filmarchiv, Berlin. On the role of Edmund Meisel as the composer, see Fiona Ford, 'The Film Music of Edmund Meisel (1894–1930)', dissertation, University of Nottingham, 2011, 219–23.

224 The AVRO (Algemeene Vereeniging 'Radio Omroep' or General Association for 'Radio Broadcasting') considered itself as having a broad 'liberal' outlook. The socialist-oriented station was the VARA (Vereeniging van Arbeiders Radio Amateurs, or Association of Worker Radio Amateurs), established in late 1925. In addition, three religious broadcasters were established in the period 1924–6: KRO (Katholieke Radio Omroep, or Catholic Radio Broadcaster), the NCRV (Nederlandse Christelijke Radio Vereniging, or Dutch Christian Radio Association) and the VPRO (Vrijzinnig Protestantse Radio Omroep or Liberal Protestant Radio Broadcaster). See Bert

Hogenkamp, Sonja de Leeuw and Huub Wijfjes, eds, *Een eeuw van beeld en geluid: Cultuurgeschiedenis van radio en televisie in Nederland* (Hilversum: Nederlands Instituut voor Beeld en Geluid, 2012).

225 Edward Borsboom and Bert Hogenkamp, *Radio in beeld: Nederlandse omroepfilms, 1931–1955* (Amsterdam: Stichting Film en Wetenschap, 1995), 18–23.

226 For examples of non-fiction shorts, such as 'Museum of Sound' (1943) and 'Rundfunk im Kriege' (1943), see Carolyn Birdsall, 'Divisions of Labour: Radio Archiving as Gendered Work in Wartime Britain and Germany', *International Yearbook of Women's History* 37 (2017): 107–33. For a comparison of feature-length German and British wartime films, see Jo Fox, '"The Mediator": Images of Radio in Wartime Feature Film in Britain and Germany', in *War and the Media*, ed. Mark Connelly and David Welch (New York: I.B. Tauris, 2005), 92–111. For Italian fascist-era films about radio, see Marta Perrotta, 'Radioscreens: Radio and Cinema in Italy, Radio on Italian Cinema', *Radio Journal: International Studies in Broadcast & Audio Media* 6, no. 2–3 (2008): 152.

227 Borsboom and Hogenkamp, *Radio in Beeld*, 33–41.

228 David E. Nye, *Electrifying America: Social Meanings of a New Technology, 1880–1940* (Cambridge and London: MIT Press, 1990), 156.

229 Kenneth G. Beauchamp, *Exhibiting Electricity* (London: Institution of Electrical Engineers, 1997), xi.

230 Tony Bennett, 'Thinking (with) Museums: From Exhibitionary Complex to Governmental Assemblage', in *The International Handbooks of Museum Studies*, vol. 1, ed. Sharon Macdonald and Helen Rees Leahy (Chichester: Wiley/Blackwell: 2013), 3–20.

231 For the first BBC broadcast of King George V opening the British Empire Exhibition in 1924, see Asa Briggs, *The History of Broadcasting in the United Kingdom*, vol. 1: *The Birth of Broadcasting* (London: Oxford University Press, 1961), 290. For 'The Truth of the Colonies' exhibition and its use of radio and recorded music, see David Bate, 'Surrealism, Colonialism and Photography', in *Empire and Culture: The French Experience, 1830–1940*, ed. Martin Evans (Basingstoke and New York: Palgrave Macmillan, 2004), 65. On radio's potential in the anti-colonial struggle and decolonization, see Franz Fanon, 'This is the Voice of Algeria', in *A Dying Colonialism*, trans. Haakon Chevalier (New York: Grove Press, 1965), 69–97; Rebecca P. Scales, 'Subversive Sound: Transnational Radio, Arabic Recordings, and the Dangers of Listening in French

Colonial Algeria, 1934–1939', *Comparative Studies in Society and History* 52, no. 2 (2010): 384–417; Sorcha Amy MacGregor Thomson, 'Worldmaking in the Palestinian Radio Stations (1965–1982): Revolutionary Love and Anticolonial Afterlives', *Global South* 15, no. 2 (2022): 99–116.

232 J[ohannes] Corver, *Hoe het begin van de radio is geweest: Uitgegeven ter gelegenheid van de 25ste jaargang van Radio Bulletin* (Bussum: U.M. de Muiderkring, 1956), 21–2.

233 Corver, *Hoe het begin van de radio is geweest*, 22.

234 For the first All-British Wireless Exhibition in London in 1922 through to the Radiolympia (from 1926 onwards), see, for instance, Bussey, *Wireless*, 3–11.

235 As Bruce Campbell notes, the innovative ideas coming out of amateur clubs was part of the reason that some receiver manufacturing companies sponsored amateur radio clubs for their staff members: Campbell, *The Radio Hobby*, 58.

236 Jasanoff, 'Ordering Knowledge, Ordering Society'.

237 See the site plan for the 1930 Berlin radio exhibition at https://soundandscience.de/node/1864.

238 For the presentation of television at pre-war exhibitions, see Anne-Katrin Weber, *Television before TV: New Media and Exhibition Culture in Europe and the USA, 1928–1939* (Amsterdam: Amsterdam University Press, 2022).

239 'Int. Radio-Tentoonstelling Amsterdam', *Radio-Expres* 19 (8 May 1925): 340.

240 For this review, which was predominantly positive about the 1930 Radiolympia radio exhibition in London, see Wilson, 'The Olympiads'.

241 Hannah Forsyth, 'Small is Big: The AWA tower and Wireless Monumentality', *Continuum* 17, no. 4 (2003): 419–31. For an extensive set of postcards collected for stations globally, see http://www.ontheshortwaves.com/Postcards/Postcards.html.

242 Pierre Descaves, *Quand la radio s'appelait Tour Eiffel* (Paris: La table rond, 1963), 69–70, quoted in Rebecca P. Scales, *Radio*, 26.

243 By 1938, the station's medium and shortwave transmissions were described as a 'modernistic studio standing on a low mound in the outskirts of Dairen, [which] calls forth nightly to its countless number of international radio fans throughout the world'. 'Manchuria's Electrical Communications', *Far Eastern Review* (September 1938): 342, quoted in Edward Denison and Guangyu

Ren, *Ultra-modernism: Architecture and Modernity in Manchuria* (Hong Kong: Hong Kong University Press, 2016), 95, 97.

244 Nick Couldry, *Media Rituals: A Critical Approach* (London and New York: Routledge, 2003), 55–74. For examples of reviews of the radio exhibitions in Berlin, Paris, Brussels and London in *Wireless World*, see Bussey, *Wireless*, 49–52, 74.

245 An official programme was provided for media industry professionals, alongside conferences, seminars, workshops and meetings of organizations and networks, while the overall event comprised multiple forms of knowledge dissemination to the general public as facilitated by journalistic coverage, promotional discourse and interpersonal encounters at the event itself. Eva Susanne Bressler, *Von der Experimentierbühne zum Propagandainstrument: Die Geschichte der Funkausstellung von 1924 bis 1939* (Cologne: Böhlau, 2009), 19–23, 55, 142, 156.

246 Bressler, *Von der Experimentierbühne zum Propagandainstrument*, 322–6, 328–30, 336–43.

247 This interactive participation was expanded during the National Socialist era with the establishment of a 'people's radio station' (*Volkssender*) at the exhibition. Bressler, *Von der Experimentierbühne zum Propagandainstrument*, 76–7.

248 For an example of newsreel footage from the opening of Radiolympia in 1947, see 'Radiolympia Exhibition Opens', British Pathé, 6 October 1947, https://www.britishpathe.com/asset/79352/.

249 For the promotion of the event with images and names of the BBC 'disc jockeys' who would be playing music programmes during the exhibition, see the cover of *The Radio Times*, 21 August 1959, https://genome.ch.bbc.co.uk/f524db820cbe4a35913afad11a709284. For the radio show as an opportunity for radio fans to get close to their favourite stars and try to get an autograph, see the BBC Archives newsreel 'Earls Court Radio Show', 1951, https://www.facebook.com/BBCArchive/videos/1951-newsreel-earls-court-radio-show/318973315986259/.

250 Newsreel footage of this event can be viewed in the archives of British Pathé: *Transistor Exhibition in London*, 1959, https://www.britishpathe.com/asset/245979/.

251 For photos of exhibition displays in the photo albums created by the Marconi Company, see MS. Photogr. B. 71 and MS. Photogr. B. 72 in the Marconi Archives, Bodleian Libraries, Oxford, UK.

252 Beginning in 1955, the annual Japan Audio Fair was a significant site for the promotion of new radio and audio models, including the Sony Walkman. For the international dimension to Sony's promotion of this device, see Shu Ueyama, 'The Selling of the "Walkman"' [1982], in *Doing Cultural Studies: The Story of the Sony Walkman*, ed. Paul Du Gay et al., 2nd edn (Milton Keynes: Open University, 2013), 131–2.

253 For the involvement of universities and their researchers in public broadcasting in early US broadcasting, see Hugh Richard Slotten, *Radio's Hidden Voice: The Origins of Public Broadcasting in the United States* (Urbana and Chicago: University of Illinois Press, 2009).

254 For the 'science on radio' model, see Carolyn Birdsall, 'Radio Documents: Broadcasting, Sound Archiving, and the Rise of Radio Studies in Interwar Germany', *Technology and Culture* 60, no. 2 (2019): S96–S128. On 'radio teaching' at universities in post-war England, see Alfredo Thiermann, 'Learning to Learn: Review of "The University is Now on Air: Broadcasting Modern Architecture"', *ARQ* 102 (2019), http://dx.doi.org/10.4067/S0717-69962019000200003.

255 For examples of radio yearbooks in the European context, note Germany (where there were regional and national yearbooks), the UK (for which the BBC produced an annual yearbook known as the *BBC Handbook* (or *BBC Year-Book*) between 1928 and 1987), or the US (for which the *Broadcasting Yearbook* was published between 1935 and 2010). Some of these publications can be viewed at www.worldradiohistory.com.

256 For a photo-illustrated book, produced for German-speaking readers, about key radio presenters across Europe and North America, see Hans S. von Heister, *Das Buch der Ansager: Die ständigen Rundfunk-Ansager der europäischen Sender und der großen amerikanischen Rundfunk-Gesellschaften in Wort und Bild* (Berlin: Rothgiesser & Diesing, 1932).

257 Oliver Lodge, 'Harmsworth's Wireless Encyclopedia', in *Harmsworth's Wireless Encyclopedia: The Only ABC guide to a Fascinating Science-Hobby*, vol. 1 (London: Harmsworth, 1923–4), i. In addition to Lodge, a number of prominent figures had been enlisted to offer short contributions to the first volume, including prominent inventors and researchers, along with engineers from the BBC and Marconi Company. For the individual volumes of the encyclopaedia, see https://worldradiohistory.com/Harmsworth's-Wireless-Encyclopedia.htm.

258 John Alexander Hammerton, 'To Our Readers', in *Harmsworth's Wireless Encyclopedia*, n.p.

259 Gernsback, *Radio Encyclopedia*; Michel Adam, *Encyclopédie de la radio: Dictionnaire encyclopédique de la radioélectricité* (Paris: É. Chiron, 1928). For the dominance of the international radio industry in France over the domestic one, see Bussey, *Wireless*, 51–2.

260 In particular, van Zuylen pays particular note to developments closer to home, with the photo inserts featuring not only the Dutch broadcasters' various buildings but also those of Radio Luxembourg (Luxembourg) and the National Radio Institute in Brussels (Belgium), reflecting the assumption that its readers were tuning in to broadcasts from their immediate region.

261 J. J. L. van Zuylen, *Encyclopaedie voor radio-luisteraars* (Baarn: Schuyt, 1939), 5.

262 For the 'Big Ben' entry, see van Zuylen, *Encyclopaedie voor radio-luisteraars*, 36.

263 J. J. L. van Zuylen, *Radio-encyclopaedie* (Amsterdam: Breughel, 1949), 3. The demand for this publication is suggested by the production of a third edition several years later, which was further expanded in scope, as indicated by the reference to Belgium and to television in the main title. J. J. L. van Zuylen, *Radio- en televisie-encylopedie voor Nederland en België* (Amsterdam: Breughel, 1956).

264 Jutta Haider and Olof Sundin, 'Beyond the Legacy of the Enlightenment? Online Encyclopaedias as Digital Heterotopias', *First Monday* 15, no. 1 (2009).

265 Vanessa A. Rasoamampianin, 'Reviewing Encyclopaedia Authority', *Culture Unbound* 6 (2014): 547–68.

266 Van Zuylen, *Encyclopaedie*, 140, 202–3.

267 Tiszay Andor and Géza Falk, eds, *Rádióhallgatók Lexikona: Az irodalom, zene, színház, film, rádió, rádiótechnika, gramofon és sport enciklopédiája*, 2 vols (Budapest: Vajda-Wichmann, 1944).

268 A number of entries suggest support for the regime of Miklós Horthy (1920 to March 1944), whereas other entries are dedicated to figures with a stronger left-wing association, such as avant-garde author Lajos Kassák. See Andor and Falk, *Rádióhallgatók Lexikona* , vol. 2, 336. Thanks to Eszter Polónyi for her help with the translation and interpretation of this publication.

269 This inclusion also suggests that the publication project had probably been started earlier but delayed due to the war. For such contributions, see, for instance, the entries on 'radio audio control panel' by the BBC radio pioneer Val Gielgud (London) and on 'radio

actor training' by Theo Fleischmann (Brussels), who was also well known for his contribution to radio drama aesthetics. Andor and Falk, *Rádióhallgatók Lexikona*, vol. 2, 233–5.

270 *Rádió újság* (Radio-News), published from 1924 by the Hungarian Electrotechnical Association (Magyar Elektrotechnikai Egyesület), and *Rádióélet* (Radio-Life), published from 1929 onwards, were both discontinued in 1944, whereas *Magyar rádió újság* (Hungarian Radio News), an illustrated technical publication, had a short run from May to December 1944. See the MTVA Archívum website (https://archivum.mtva.hu/news_archive/?category=rel) and the Hungarian Media History website (https://mediatortenet.wordpress.com/).

271 As Kompare notes, there is a significant range from the more factual bibliographic approach through to 'passionately evaluative top-ten lists found all over blogs and YouTube, [and] to lengthy published exegeses'. Derek Kompare, 'Fan Curators and the Gateways into Fandom', in *The Routledge Companion to Media Fandom*, ed. Melissa A. Click and Suzanne Scott (New York: Routledge, 2018), 107–13.

272 For further discussion of 'old time radio' fans' information-gathering and knowledge dissemination activities, see Chapter 3. Publications include John Dunning, *Tune in Yesterday: Ultimate Encyclopedia of Old Time Radio, 1926–1976* (Englewood Cliffs, NJ: Prentice-Hall, 1976); Vincent Terrace, *The Encyclopedia of Radio Programmes: The Golden Years, 1930–1960* (South Brunswick, NJ: AS Barnes, 1980); John Dunning, *On the Air: The Encyclopedia of Old-Time Radio* (New York: Oxford University Press, 1998); Luther F. Sies, *Encyclopedia of American Radio, 1920–1960* (Jefferson, NC: McFarland, 2000); Leora M. Sies and Luther F. Sies, *The Encyclopedia of Women in Radio, 1920–1960* (Jefferson, NC: McFarland, 2003); Robert C. Reinehr and Jon David Schwartz, *Historical Dictionary of Old-Time Radio* (Lanham, MD: Scarecrow Press, 2007); Robert C. Reinehr and Jon David Schwartz, *The A to Z of Old Time Radio* (Lanham, MD: Scarecrow Press, 2010).

273 For the US context, see, for instance, Donald G. Godfrey and Frederic A. Leigh, eds, *Historical Dictionary of American Radio* (Westport, CT: Greenwood Press, 1998); Christopher H. Sterling and Michael C. Keith, *The Museum of Broadcast Communications' Encyclopedia of Radio*, 3 vols (New York and London: Fitzroy Dearborn, 2004); Christopher H. Sterling, Cary O'Dell and Michael C. Keith, *The Concise Encyclopedia of American Radio* (New York: Routledge, 2010); Ellet, *Encyclopedia of Black Radio in the United States*. For other national contexts, see Jean-Noël Jeanneney and

Agnès Chauveau, *L'écho du siècle: Dictionnaire historique de la radio et de la télévision en France* (Paris: Hachette Littératures, 2001); Peppino Ortoleva and Barbara Scaramucci, *Enciclopedia della radio* (Milan: Garzanti, 2003); P. C. Sinha, *Encyclopaedia of Broadcasting, Television and Radio* (New Delhi: Anmol, 2005); Séan Street, *Historical Dictionary of British Radio*, 2nd edn (Lanham, MD: Rowman & Littlefield, 2015).

274 For one of the first readers published for radio studies, see Michele Hilmes and Jason Loviglio, eds, *Radio Reader: Essays in the Cultural History of Radio* (New York: Routledge, 2002). The two most recognized academic journals for radio studies are *Journal of Radio & Audio Media* (since 1992) and *The Radio Journal: International Studies in Broadcast Media* (since 2003). For an overview of the radio research field, see, for instance, Hugh Chignell, *Key Concepts in Radio Studies* (Los Angeles: Sage, 2009).

275 Young, *The Cinema Dreams its Rivals*.

276 While this concept does not entirely square with Lisa Gitelman's concept of the 'knowledge work' underpinning paper and print/copy job formats, my use of the term is intended to gesture to her insights about the role of print culture (and journalistic genres) as a key infrastructure in generating, facilitating and circulating knowledge about modern media, such as photography, cinema, the telephone, the gramophone and radio. Lisa Gitelman, *Paper Knowledge: Toward a Media History of Documents* (Durham, NC: Duke University Press, 2014).

277 Anderson, *Imagined Communities*.

278 Lacey, *Listening Publics*.

279 Richard Abel, *Menus for Movieland: Newspapers and the Emergence of American Film Culture, 1913–1916.* (Berkeley: University of California Press, 2015); Barry King, *Taking Fame to Market: On the Pre-history and Post-history of Hollywood Stardom* (New York: Palgrave Macmillan, 2014). For an extensive collection of US film and radio fan magazines, see The Media History Digital Library, https://mediahistoryproject.org/fanmagazines/.

280 Marsha Orgeron, '"You Are Invited to Participate": Interactive Fandom in the Age of the Movie Magazine', *Journal of Film and Video* 61, no. 3 (2009): 4.

281 At the same time, a gender-coded mode of intimate address was sustained through advice columns designed to connect a community of readers for which films were a vehicle for negotiating personal identities and everyday lives. Such magazine content was

accompanied by notions of self-improvement, often taking the form of beauty and fashion advice that was frequently modelled on emulating popular film stars. Orgeron, '"You Are Invited to Participate"', 10–3.

282 Charlene Simmons, 'Dear Radio Broadcaster: Fan Mail as a Form of Perceived Interactivity', *Journal of Broadcasting & Electronic Media* 53, no. 3 (2009): 448, 451–2.

283 'Our Listeners', *The Indian Listener* 1, no. 1 (22 December 1935): 19, https://worldradiohistory.com/INTERNATIONAL/Indian-Listener/30s/The-Indian-Listener-1935-22-12-1935.pdf. This programme magazine, which ran under this title until 1958, took over from the *Indian Radio Times*, which had been published since 1927. For this period of AIR programming, while subject to censorship prior to independence in 1947, see Indira Baptista Gupta, 'From the BBC's Shadows? Fledgling AIR Finding Its Feet', *Historical Journal of Film, Radio and Television* 42, no. 4 (2021): 749–72.

284 Simmons, 'Dear Radio Broadcaster', 444, 450–4. For the gender differences in how listeners sought to 'talk back' to stations, such as to the state-operated WHA station in Wisconsin, see Derek Vaillant, '"Your Voice Came in Last Night . . . But I Thought It Sounded A Little Scared": Rural Radio Listening and "Talking Back" during the Progressive Era in Wisconsin, 1920–1932', in Hilmes and Loviglio, *Radio Reader*, 63–88.

285 Kristine M. McCusker, '"Dear Radio Friend": Listener Mail and the National Barn Dance, 1931–1941', *American Studies* 39, no. 2 (1998): 174.

286 McCusker, '"Dear Radio Friend"', 190.

287 Razlogova, *The Listener's Voice*, 59.

288 Razlogova, *The Listener's Voice*, 59.

289 'What do you want to know?', *Radio Mirror* 2, no. 2 (June 1934), 56–7.

290 Andrea Stanton, 'Dramatic and Literary Programming on the BBC Arabic Service', in *The Wireless World: Global Histories of International Radio Broadcasting*, ed. Simon Potter et al. (Oxford: Oxford University Press, 2022), 188–93.

291 For Argentina, see Claxton, *From Parsifal to Perón*, 6–9, 39–40, 68, 121. For the competition perceived by the British press, see Siân Nicholas, 'All the News that's Fit to Broadcast: The Popular Press versus the BBC, 1922–45', in *Northcliffe's Legacy: Aspects of the British Popular Press, 1896–1996*, ed. Peter Catterall, Colin Seymour-Ure and Adrian Smith (London: MacMillan Press, 2000), 121–47.

292 Paul Rixon, 'The Role of British Newspapers in Framing the Public Perception and Experience of European Radio, 1930 to 1939', *Media History* 26, no. 2 (2020): 153–66.
293 Rixon, 'Radio and Popular Journalism in Britain', 28.
294 Rixon, 'The Role of British Newspapers', 161.
295 Rixon, 'Radio and Popular Journalism', 30–1.
296 O'Dwyer, 'Digitising Context'.
297 Similar rubrics can be observed in the US-based *Radio Mirror*, e.g., Mercury, 'Hot and Airy: New Gossip and Hot News of the Broadcasters', *Radio Mirror* 2, no. 2 (June 1934), 6–7.
298 'Both Sides of the Microphone: Radio News and Gossip by "The Broadcasters"', *The Radio Times* (9 October 1936): 14, https://genome.ch.bbc.co.uk/page/40c4c55bce6d400aae89a32b634e37fd?page=14.
299 Maurice Gorham, quoted in Tony Currie, *The Radio Times Story* (Tiverton, UK: Kelly Publications, 2001), 31.
300 Gorham, quoted in Currie, *The Radio Times Story*, 36.
301 Advertisement for Lux Toilet Soap, *The Radio Times* (9 October 1936): 69, https://genome.ch.bbc.co.uk/page/40c4c55bce6d400aae89a32b634e37fd?page=69.
302 For the modern history of advertising, also in relation to European imperialist imaginaries, see Fred Beard, *Comparative Advertising: History, Theory, and Practice* (Lanham, MD: Lexington Books, 2018), 1–47; David Ciarlo, *Advertising Empire: Race and Visual Culture in Imperial Germany* (Cambridge, MA: Harvard University Press, 2011); Anandi Ramamurthy, *Imperial Persuaders: Images of Africa and Asia in British Advertising* (Manchester: Manchester University Press, 2003).
303 Advertisement for Cadburys Bournville Cocoa, *The Radio Times* (9 October 1936): 53, https://genome.ch.bbc.co.uk/page/40c4c55bce6d400aae89a32b634e37fd?page=53.
304 Davy Burnaby, 'The Stars Come Out', *The Radio Times* (9 October 1936): 3–11, https://genome.ch.bbc.co.uk/page/40c4c55bce6d400aae89a32b634e37fd?page=3.
305 For the advent of illustrated magazines, and the circulation of sketches, photogravures and photographic images, see Thomas Smits, *The European Illustrated Press and the Emergence of a Transnational Visual Culture of the News, 1842–1870* (Abingdon and New York: Routledge, 2019); Habbo Knoch, 'Living Pictures: Photojournalism in Germany, 1900 to the 1930s', in *Mass Media, Culture and Society*

in Twentieth-Century Germany, ed. Karl Christian Führer and Corey Ross (London: Palgrave Macmillan, 2006), 217–33; Sarah Frederick, *Turning Pages: Reading and Writing Women's Magazines in Interwar Japan* (Honolulu: University of Hawaii Press, 2006).

306 While mainly targeting British readers, it was also distributed in France and to British Commonwealth countries, such as Australia, New Zealand, Canada and South Africa. See the publication and distribution details listed in the first issue of the magazine: *Radio Pictorial* 1 (19 January 1934): 36, https://worldradiohistory.com/UK/Radio-Pictorial/Radio-Pictorial-1934-01-19-S-OCR.pdf.

307 'Radio Pictorial' advertisement, *Amateur Wireless and Radiovision* (20 January 1934): 66–7, https://worldradiohistory.com/UK/Amateur-Wireless/Amateur-Wireless-1923-01-20-S-OCR.pdf.

308 'Modern Receiver Design', in *The B.B.C. Year-Book 1934* (London: British Broadcasting Corporation, 1934), 427.

309 S. T., East London, 'What Listeners Think . . .', *Radio Pictorial* 4 (9 February 1934): 22, https://worldradiohistory.com/UK/Radio-Pictorial/Radio-Pictorial-1934-02-09-S-OCR.pdf.

310 See advertisement for *Radio Pictorial* 'star' postcards and album holders in *Radio Pictorial* 49 (21 December 1934): 39, https://worldradiohistory.com/UK/Radio-Pictorial/Radio-Pictorial-1934-12-21-S-OCR.pdf.

311 Writing in his regular *Radio Pictorial* column in 1934, Christopher Stone appealed to his listeners' engagement: 'I shall be deeply interested to see how the special gramophone record programmes, with competitions and money prizes, on Mondays and Wednesdays, appeal to listeners.' Christopher Stone, 'Christopher Stone Calling', *Radio Pictorial* 49 (21 December 1934): 8, https://worldradiohistory.com/UK/Radio-Pictorial/Radio-Pictorial-1934-12-21-S-OCR.pdf. For the development of interactive programmes at the BBC from the mid-1920s, such as the radio drama competition *What Would You Do?* (10 May 1926), in which listeners were invited to suggest an ending to dramatic scenes, see Tim Crook, *Writing Audio Drama* (London: Routledge, forthcoming).

312 Bernard Jones, 'A Personal Word from the Editor-in-Chief', *Radio Pictorial* 1 (19 January 1934): 30, https://worldradiohistory.com/UK/Radio-Pictorial/Radio-Pictorial-1934-01-19-S-OCR.pdf.

313 Julia Taylor, 'From Sound to Print in Pre-war Britain: The Cultural and Commercial Interdependence between Broadcasters and Broadcasting magazines in the 1930s', PhD dissertation, Bournemouth University, 2013, 173–4.

314 Debra R. Cohen, 'Intermediality and the Problem of the Listener', *Modernism/Modernity* 19, no. 3 (2012): 569–92; Debra R. Cohen, '"Strange Collisions": Keywords Toward an Intermedial Periodical Studies', *ESC: English Studies in Canada* 41, no. 1 (2015): 93–104.

315 Asa Briggs, 'The First Broadcasting Critics', in *The Collected Essays of Asa Briggs*, vol. 3: *Serious Pursuits: Communications and Education* (Urbana and Chicago: University of Illinois Press, 1991), 212.

316 Van Puymbroeck, 'Periodical Studies, Intermediality, and Cinema', 61.

317 D. L. LeMahieu, *A Culture for Democracy: Mass Communication and the Cultivated Mind in Britain* (Oxford: Clarendon, 1988).

318 Van Puymbroeck, 'Periodical Studies', 60.

319 Van Puymbroeck, 'Periodical Studies', 64. Van Puymbroeck notes that Lambert not only served on the editorial board of *Sight and Sound*, but also on the board of governors for the BFI, and edited a book for The British Institute of Adult Education. Richard S. Lambert, *For Filmgoers Only: The Intelligent Filmgoer's Guide to the Film* (London: Faber & Faber, 1934).

320 Paul F. Lazarsfeld, *Radio and the Printed Page: An Introduction to the Study of Radio and its Role in the Communication of Ideas* (New York: Duell, Sloan and Pearce, 1940), 319–33. On the strong connection between libraries and broadcasting in the US since the early 1920s, see Cindy Welch, 'Librarians of the Airwaves: Reading in the Ether', in *Radio Cultures: The Sound Medium in American Life*, ed. Michael C. Keith (New York: Peter Lang, 2008), 287–98.

321 Michael Stamm, *Sound Business: Newspapers, Radio, and the Politics of New Media* (Philadelphia: University of Pennsylvania Press, 2011), 4–5.

322 Richard DeCordova, *Picture Personalities: The Emergence of the Star System in America* (Urbana: University of Illinois Press, 2001).

323 Michael Cowan, 'Learning to Love the Movies: Puzzles, Participation, and Cinephilia in Interwar European Film Magazines', *Film History* 27, no. 4 (2015): 30.

324 Cowan, 'Learning to Love the Movies', 29.

325 Daisuke Miyao, 'Before Anime: Animation and the Pure Film Movement in Pre-war Japan', *Japan Forum* 14, no. 2 (2002): 191–209.

326 Hikari Hori, *Promiscuous Media: Film and Visual Culture in Imperial Japan, 1926–1945* (Ithaca, NY: Cornell University Press, 2018), 1.

327 Hideaki Fujiki, *Making Personas: Transnational Film Stardom in Modern Japan* (Cambridge, MA: Harvard University Asia Center, 2013), 44.

328 Chie Niita, 'Japanese Cinema and the Radio: The Sound Space of Unseen Cinema', in *The Culture of the Sound Image in Prewar Japan*, ed. Michael Raine and Johan Nordström (Amsterdam: Amsterdam University Press, 2020), 108.

329 For fan mail in Australia between the 1920s and 2000s, to both public and commercial broadcasters, see Griffen-Foley, *Australian Radio Listeners*, 51–73.

330 For the role of private phone calls, messages and letters as a site of East–West communication in Cold War Europe, including the reading-out of letters on Radio Free Europe and Radio Liberty programming, see Friederike Kind-Kovács, 'Voices, Letters, and Literature through the Iron Curtain: Exiles and the (Trans)Mission of Radio in the Cold War', *Cold War History* 13, no. 2 (2013): 193–219; Christoph Classen, 'Captive Audience? GDR Radio in the Mirror of Listeners' Mail', *Cold War History* 13, no. 2 (2013): 239–54; Rosamund Johnston, 'Listening in on the Neighbors: The Reception of German and Austrian Radio in Cold War Czechoslovakia', *Central European History* 54, no. 4 (2021): 603–20.

331 For East Java in Indonesia in the 1990s and early 2000s, see Bernard Arps, 'Letters on Air in Banyuwangi (and Beyond): Radio and Phatic Performance', *Indonesia and the Malay World* 31, no. 91 (2003): 312–13.

332 Vebhuti Duggal, 'Imagining Sound through the *Pharmaish*: Radios and Request-Postcards in North India, c. 1955–1975', *BioScope: South Asian Screen Studies* 9, no. 1 (2018): 1–23.

333 Duggal, 'Imagining Sound through the *Pharmaish*', 16.

334 Both *pharmaish* requests and the listener magazines were largely male dominated, with some exceptions, such as a girls' radio listener club. Duggal, 'Imagining Sound through the *Pharmaish*', 12, 16, 17, 20.

335 For the selective or limited nature of historical fan letters in existence today, see Simmons, 'Dear Radio Broadcaster', 444–59; Duggal, 'Imagining Sound through the *Pharmaish*'. For radio announcers' disposal of letters after they are read out, see Arps, 'Letters on Air', 304–6.

336 For a critical take on the understanding of so-called 'old' vs. 'new' media, see Lisa Gitelman, *Always Already New: Media, History, and*

the Data of Culture (Cambridge, MA: MIT Press, 2008). On radio's resilient status in contemporary media landscape, see Starkey, 'Radio'.

337 Bertolt Brecht, 'Radio – An Antediluvian Invention?', unpublished typescript from 1927, in Marc Silberman, ed., *Brecht on Film and Radio* (London: Bloomsbury, 2016), 37.

338 LaPlaca, '"Something into Nothing"'.

339 On this point, particularly in relation to print archival sources, see Josephine Dolan, 'The Voice that cannot be Heard', *Radio Journal: International Studies in Broadcast & Audio Media* 1, no. 1 (2003): 63–72.

340 Scannell, *Radio, Television and Modern Life*, 145–6.

341 'The Archers in 70 Objects', BBC, undated, https://www.bbc.co.uk/programmes/articles/1zZryzmc92YYBQyNBxWJl4q/the-archers-in-70-objects.

342 'Why do you listen to The Archers', BBC, undated, https://www.bbc.co.uk/programmes/articles/5Mstn5KJJpgnH4Rd3SYHHSK/stories-and-features-about-the-archers.

343 For life cycles of (de)valuation for sound recordings, see Elodie A. Roy, '"Total Trash": Recorded Music and the Logic of Waste', *Popular Music* 39, no. 1 (2020): 88–107. See also Johannes Müske, 'Constructing Sonic Heritage: The Accumulation of Knowledge in the Context of Sound Archives', *Journal of Ethnology and Folkloristics* 4, no. 1 (2010): 37–47; Lauren Bratslavsky, 'The Archival Value of Television in the "Golden Age" of Media Collecting', *Film & History: An Interdisciplinary Journal* 47, no. 2 (2017): 12–27.

344 Russell W. Belk, *Collecting in a Consumer Society* (New York: Routledge, 1995), 63.

345 Belk, *Collecting in a Consumer Society*, 55.

346 Belk, *Collecting in a Consumer Society*, 55, 66.

347 Marina Bianchi, 'Collecting as a Paradigm of Consumption', *Journal of Cultural Economics* 21 (1997): 278.

348 Belk, *Collecting in a Consumer Society*, 66, 77.

349 On regional radio history collecting practices, see VanCour, 'The Informal Economy'.

350 Some of the examples given by the author from their own collection include autograph books, board games, clocks, jigsaw puzzles, key rings, match boxes, playing cards, and tickets. See 'Memorabilia' (undated), Australian Old Time Radio website, https://www.australianotr.com.au/memorabilia.html.

351 Griffen-Foley, *Australian Radio Listeners*, 12, 20.
352 Griffen-Foley, *Australian Radio Listeners*, 12.
353 See listing at https://www.slsa.sa.gov.au/dont-touch-dial-childrens-radio-club-badges-and-pins.
354 See, for instance, self-published badge guides across the media landscape from the 1930s onwards, such as Mark Taylor, *Australian Radio, TV, Newspapers & Cinema Badges*, 3rd edn (2018), distributed via https://www.facebook.com/AustraliaBadgeGuides/.
355 Belk, *Collecting in a Consumer Society*; VanCour, 'The Informal Economy'; Werner Muensterberger, *Collecting, An Unruly Passion: Psychological Perspectives* (Princeton, NJ: Princeton University Press, 1994).
356 For theatre fan scrapbooks spanning the 1860s to the 1960s, see Sharon Marcus, 'Theatrical Scrapbooks', *Theatre Survey* 54, no. 2 (2013): 283–307. See also Anselmo, 'Bound by Paper'.
357 For example, Susan Tucker, Katherine Ott and Patricia Buckler, eds, *The Scrapbook in American Life* (Philadelphia: Temple University Press, 2006); Ellen Gruber Garvey, *Writing with Scissors: American Scrapbooks from the Civil War to the Harlem Renaissance* (Oxford: Oxford University Press, 2012). While scrapbooking and the swapping of QSL cards date back to the earliest period of radio culture, such circulations are consistent with recent findings about the significance of gifts in fan cultures in helping to 'cement' social connections with each other (as well as radio itself). Karen Hellekson, 'A Fannish Field of Value: Online Fan Gift Culture', *Cinema Journal* 48, no. 4 (2009): 113–18.
358 Scrapbook of Norman S. 'Froggy' Davis, held at the University of Maine Library Archives, https://archives.library.umaine.edu/repositories/2/resources/3032. See also a scrapbook gathered collectively by the members of a radio club: 'Stanford Amateur Radio Club scrapbook', Department of Special Collections and University Archives, Stanford, CA, https://oac.cdlib.org/findaid/ark:/13030/kt996nf8ft/.
359 'Seefred Papers: Lyndon Seefred radio log and scrapbook', History San Jose, https://historysanjose.pastperfectonline.com/archive/D8C1E89C-0A36-4290-8E75-283215813863.
360 For images of creative fan letters combined with station documentation, see, for instance, the 1940s scrapbook made by Cary Simpson, station director at WHUN, Pennsylvania, US, listed for an online sale: https://www.worthpoint.com/worthopedia/1940s-whun-radio-scrapbook-cary-1874365463. The Australian National Film

and Sound Archive (NFSA) has numerous scrapbooks of a more conventional news clipping nature, such as Norma Ferris, 'Scrapbook of press clippings, NFSA, http://colsearch.nfsa.gov.au/nfsa/search/display/display.w3p;page=0;query=radio%20scrapbook%20Format%3A%22Paper%22%20Decade%3A%221930-1939%22;rec=8;resCount=10.

361 'Early New Zealand Radio Personalities', http://www.radioheritage.com/early-new-zealand-radio-personalities/.

362 On American film companies that established clubs affiliated with local radio stations in the years around 1930, such as MGM Radio Movie Club, see Griffen-Foley, *Australian Radio Listeners*, 30.

363 Compiled by Mark Nicholls, an amateur radio enthusiast, it is likely that the material formed more than a media file, since he also served as the editor of an amateur radio magazine. See Mark Nicholls' scrapbooks, https://www.radioheritage.com/mark-nicholls-media-scrapbooks/; 'Mark Nicholls – A Tribute', New Zealand Radio DX League (NZRDXL), https://radiodx.com/articles/dxer-profiles-m-to-q/mark-nicholls-tribute/.

364 James Sawle, http://www.md0mdi.im/scrapbook-of-alec-anderson-gd3hqr/.

365 On the history of the radio building and radio loudspeaker towers in Wrocław across the 1945 divide, see Carolyn Birdsall and Joanna Walewska-Choptiany, 'Reconstructing Media Culture: Transnational Perspectives on Radio in Silesia, 1924–1948', *Historical Journal of Film, Radio and Television* 39, no. 3 (2019): 439–78.

366 Forsyth, 'Small is Big', 423.

367 Michael Curtin, 'Media Capital: Towards the Study of Spatial Flows', *International Journal of Cultural Studies* 6, no. 2 (2003): 202–28.

368 Scott Koga-Brouwes, 'Kyoto City's Public "Radio Towers"', *Ritsumeikan International Studies* 32 (2019): 91–114.

369 'Locals Seek to Preserve Nagoya Park's Wartime Radio Broadcast Tower', *Japan Times*, 6 March 2017, https://www.japantimes.co.jp/news/2017/03/06/national/locals-seek-preserve-nagoya-parks-wartime-radio-broadcast-tower/.

370 Martín Butera, 'A Brief History of the "A Noite" Building', *Radio Heritage*, 5 August 2021, https://www.radioheritage.com/a-brief-history-of-the-a-noite-building/.

371 On the building's significance during the 1964 coup and ensuing dictatorship in Brazil, see Artememoria website, 20 October 2018, http://artememoria.org/artememoria_map_poi/24/.

372 Butera, 'A Brief History'. See also Luiz Carlos Saroldi and Sonia Virgínia Moreira, *Rádio Nacional, o Brasil em sintonia* (Rio de Janeiro: Zahar, 2005), 12–22, 30–3, 67–71, 194–7.

373 For the musical 'auditorium programmes' in the A Noite building, see Bryan McCann, *Hello, Hello Brazil: Popular Music in the Making of Modern Brazil* (Durham, NC: Duke University Press, 2004), 34–6, 181–213.

374 The full name for the radio organization, in operation between 1930 and 1960, was L'Institut national de radiodiffusion (French)/ Nationaal instituut voor radio-omroep (Flemish).

375 These 'newer' facilities at the Auguste Reyerslaan, in use since the 1970s, are currently in the process of being redeveloped as Mediapark Brussels. Ike Picone et al. 'Building mediapark.brussels: At the Crossroads of Media Policy and Urban Development', in *Creative Cluster Development: Governance, Place-Making and Entrepreneurship*, ed. Marlen Komorowski and Ike Picone (Abingdon and New York: Routledge, 2020), 159–71.

376 Nicolas Kenny, 'Saving the Steamship: Brussels' *Maison de la Radio* and the Urban Emotions of a Broadcasting Institution', *International Journal of Heritage Studies* 26, no. 8 (2020): 807–12.

377 Kenny, 'Saving the Steamship', 814–15, 819.

378 See *The Caroline Club* brochure sent to fans in 1964, https://www.offshoreradio.co.uk/list45p.htm.

379 See *The Boat That Rocked* (Richard Curtis, 2009); Ray Clark, *Radio Caroline: The True Story of the Boat that Rocked* (Cheltenham: History Press, 2019).

380 Peters, *Sound, Space and Society*, 69.

381 See http://rcsocietysales.co.uk/.

382 For example, the Transmission Zero website for FM pirate radio (https://www.transmissionzero.co.uk/radio/london-pirate-radio/) or the Brooklyn Pirate Radio Sound Map (https://www.pirateradiomap.com/).

383 Campbell, *The Radio Hobby*, 85–6.

384 Hutchins, 'Poised for the New Millennium'.

385 British Vintage Wireless Society website, https://www.bvws.org.uk/links.php.

386 'Introduction and Brief History of the BVWS', https://www.bvws.org.uk/info/intro.php.

387 Other similar large convention events include the Ham Radio exhibition (Germany), the Ham Fair (Japan) and the Hamvention (United States).

388 See the film at https://www.youtube.com/watch?v=1i2UZBn0pvg&t= 134s. The society also hosts a larger event, RetroTechUK, intended for a more general public, which extends the remit of the society's interest in 'saving' or preserving radio to all kinds of vintage telecommunications items, including hi-fi and audio, televisions, gramophones, telephones, early computers and video games, music recordings and small domestic appliances. For the discourse of collecting as a 'masculine pursuit' in Euro-American contexts, see Geraghty, *Cult Collectors*, 53–71; Roy Shuker, *Wax Trash and Vinyl Treasures: Record Collecting as a Social Practice* (London: Routledge, 2017), 5, 9–10, 34–8, 45–6, 66, 89–90; Will Straw, 'Sizing Up Record Collections: Gender and Connoisseurship in Rock Music Culture', in *Sexing the Groove: Popular Music and Gender*, ed. Sheila Whiteley (London: Routledge, 1997), 3–16; Russell W. Belk and Melanie Wallendorf, 'Of Mice and Men: Gender Identity in Collecting', in *Interpreting Objects and Collections*, ed. Susan M. Pearce (London: Routledge, 1994), 240–53.

389 Geraghty, *Cult Collectors*.

390 Yuling Sun et al., 'Reliving the Past and Making a Harmonious Society Today: A Study of Elderly Electronic Hackers in China', *Proceedings of the 18th ACM Conference on Computer Supported Cooperative Work & Social Computing* (2015): 49.

391 Yuling Sun et al., 'Reliving the Past and Making a Harmonious Society Today', 48–50. The Chinese-language organizations with substantial memberships today include Radio Forum, New World Wireless Forum and Crystal Radio Forum.

392 On the discarding of media, and in-built cycles of obsolescence in contemporary technology production, see, for instance, Charles Acland, ed., *Residual Media* (Minneapolis: University of Minnesota Press, 2007); Kyle Devine and Alexandrine Boudreault-Fournier, 'Making Infrastructures Audible', in *Audible Infrastructures: Music, Sound, Media*, ed. Kyle Devine and Alexandrine Boudreault-Fournier (New York: Oxford University Press, 2021), 3–50.

393 'Becoming a Collector', *Childhood Radio*, https://childhoodradio.com/becoming-a-collector/.

394 See comments in the discussion thread 'Japanese radio – Don't throw rotten eggs at me', Antiqueradios.com, August 2014, https://antiqueradios.com/forums//viewtopic.php?f=1&t=257688&start=20&sid=91415986dc18fc7709a983ea486c9db0.

395 See 'About This Site', *Childhood Radio*, https://childhoodradio.com/about-this-site/. See also Radio Museum, https://www.radiomuseum.org/collection/ron_mansfield.html.

396 Andrew Emmerson, *Electronic Classics: Collecting, Restoring and Repair* (Boston et al.: Newnes, 1998), 203–4.
397 Geraghty, *Cult Collectors*, 163.
398 The arrival of eBay is described as initially causing 'mayhem' from the late 1990s, leading to changes in collector practices of acquisition, which had previously relied on pricing guidebooks. See 'Finding, Buying Transistor Radios', *Childhood Radio*, https://childhoodradio.com/finding-buying-transistor-radios/.
399 Ellis and Haywood, 'Virtual_radiophile (163)'.
400 Ellis and Haywood, 'Virtual_radiophile (163)', 59.
401 Ellis and Haywood, 'Virtual_radiophile (163)', 48.
402 Jason, Pye Radio collector, quoted in Ellis and Haywood, 'Virtual_radiophile (163)', 57.
403 For this emphasis on writing and inscription in Edison's writings, see Lisa Gitelman, *Scripts, Grooves, and Writing Machines: Representing Technology in the Edison Era* (Stanford, CA: Stanford University Press, 1999), 1–3.
404 Karin Bijsterveld and José van Dijck, 'Introduction', in Bijsterveld and van Dijck, *Sound Souvenirs*, 11–21.
405 Thomas A. Edison, 'The Perfected Phonograph', *North American Review* 146, no. 379 (1888): 646.
406 Thomas A. Edison, 'The Phonograph and its Future', *North American Review* 126, no. 262 (1878): 533–4.
407 On the acoustic album promoted in the 1950s and 1960s, see Karin Bijsterveld and Annelies Jacobs, 'Storing Sound Souvenirs: The Multi-Sited Domestication of the Tape Recorder', in Bijsterveld and van Dijck, *Sound Souvenirs*, 25–42. For family photography, see Marianne Hirsch, *Family Frames: Photography, Narrative, and Postmemory* (Cambridge, MA: Harvard University Press, 1997).
408 Eleanor Patterson, 'Capturing Flow: The Growth of the Old-Time-Radio Collecting Culture in the United States during the 1970s', *JCMS: Journal of Cinema and Media Studies* 59, no. 3 (2020): 52.
409 For the 1930–1 presentations at the Radio Olympia exhibition, see Wilson, 'The Olympiads'. The Faye home recorder models could make 6-, 8-, 10- and 12-inch recordings, and came in three models (acoustic, electric, super electric), while the Speakeasie branched from their standard model through to a high end 'De Luxe' and children's 'Junior' model. See *Official Catalogue of the National Radio Exhibition Olympia, Sept 18–26 1931* (London: n.p., 1931), 180, 187, 195, 197. For the local recording studios making off-air

recordings, see Lewis Foreman, 'Revisiting Concert Life in the Mid-Century: The Survival of Acetate Discs', in *The Cambridge Companion to Recorded Music*, ed. Nicholas Cook et al. (Cambridge: Cambridge University Press, 2009), 142–4.

410 For early publications on amateur recording following the advent of radio, see Martin Zimmermann, *Selbstaufnahme von Schallplatten: Selbstbau von Besprechungsanlagen; ausführliche Bauanleitungen* (Berlin: Deutsch-literar. Institut Schneider, 1931); Rudolf Vieweg, *Elektrische Schallplatten-Aufnahme-Anlage: Anleitung zur Selbstaufnahme von Schallplatten u. Baubeschreibung d. dazu notwendigen Apparate; ein Betrag zur Förderung der Handfertigkeit in der Familie* (Leipzig: Beyer, 1932); Heinrich Kluth, *Jeder sein eigener Schallplattenfabrikant* (Berlin: Weidmann, 1932).

411 Friedrich Willi Frerk, *Selbstaufnahme von Schallplatten für Radio- und Gramophonfreunde und Tonfilm-Amateur* (Berlin: Photokino-Verlag, 1932).

412 Erich Schwandt, *Schallplatten-Bastelbuch: Selbstaufnahme- und Wiedergabe-Praktikum*, 3rd edn (Leipzig: Hachmeister und Thal, 1938 [1941]), 14–15.

413 Schwandt, *Schallplatten-Bastelbuch*, 13. For similar envy expressed about the BBC recorded sound archives in Broadcasting House, see Wilfried Goatman, 'In Room 437', *By-Ways of the BBC* (London: P.S. King, 1931), 59–62. On the broader development of national radio archives, see Carolyn Birdsall and Erica Harrison, 'Researching Archival Histories of Radio', *TMG: Journal for Media History* 25, no. 2 (2022): 1–12.

414 On 'audio letter' recordings created during the Second World War by German military personnel, see Thomas Jander, '"Sprechende Feldpostbriefe": Private Propaganda und akustisches Gedächtnis', in *Akustisches Gedächtnis und Zweiter Weltkrieg*, ed. Robert Maier (Göttingen: V&R unipress, 2011), 159–93. For a collection of private audio letters, predominantly from the 1930s onwards, through which people made voice recordings for friends and loved ones, which could be sent by post, see Phono Post (https://www.phono-post.org).

415 On the Peter Huverstuhl collection in Cologne, see Friedrich Dethlefs and Carolyn Birdsall, 'Zur Geschichte der Audiobestände der RRG und ihrer Archivierung', *Rundfunk und Geschichte* 47, no. 3–4 (2021): 15. For early private collections of radio recordings in the US context, see Michael Biel, 'The Making and Use of Recordings in Broadcasting before 1936', dissertation, Northwestern University, 1977.

416 Kate Newbold, 'Captured Live: Cultures of Television Recording and Storage, 1945–1975', PhD dissertation, Northwestern University,

2015, 95. As David Morton has noted, even when the tape recorder became available in the late 1940s, only 'a small fraction of the American public [began] making recordings', suggesting that home recording only really took off in the 1960s, in a new technological and cultural landscape that facilitated the 'tape recorder as a portable entertainment device and tape recording as a low-cost, personalized alternative to commercial records and radio'. Morton, *Off the Record*, 11–12.

417 Tim J. Anderson, *Making Easy Listening: Material Culture and Postwar American Recording* (Minneapolis: University of Minnesota Press, 2006); Pascal Massinon, 'Active Listening: The Cultural Politics of Magnetic Recording Technologies in North America, 1945–1993', dissertation, University of Michigan, 2016; Jean-Baptiste Masson, 'Hunting Sounds: The Development of a Sound Recording Hobbyist Culture in Britain in the 1950s and 1960s', *Unlikely: Journal for Creative Arts* 6 (2020), https://unlikely.net.au/issue-06/hunting-sounds.

418 Karin Bijsterveld, '"What do I do with my Tape Recorder . . .?": Sound Hunting and the Sounds of Everyday Dutch Life in the 1950s and 1960s', *Historical Journal of Film, Radio and Television* 24, no. 4 (2004): 624.

419 For the founding of this organization in 1956, see https://uia.org/s/or/en/1100014890.

420 See http://www.fonoklub.wz.cz/historie.html; Karin Bijsterveld, 'Eavesdropping on Europe: The Tape Recorder and East–West Relations among European Recording Amateurs in the Cold War Era', in *Airy Curtains in the European Ether: Broadcasting and the Cold War*, ed. Alexander Badenoch et al. (Baden-Baden: Nomos, 2013), 101, 116.

421 Milan Haering, personal interview, quoted in Bijsterveld, 'Eavesdropping on Europe', 116.

422 Bijsterveld, '"What do I do with my Tape Recorder . . .?"'

423 For the Dutch NVG (Nederlandse Vereniging van Geluidsjagers, later Nederlandse Vereniging voor Geluid en Beeldregistratie) archives in Wassenaar, see Bijsterveld, '"What do I do with my Tape Recorder . . .?"', 627–8.

424 Tomotaro Kaneko, 'Namaroku Culture in 1970s Japan: The Techniques and Joys of Sound Recording', *Aesthetics* 23–24 (2021): 60.

425 Kazuo Tamai, *Namaroku No Hon* (Tokyo: Kosaido Books, 1977), 22–4, cited in Martyn David Smith, 'Sound Hunting in Postwar

Japan: Recording Technology, Aurality, Mobility, and Consumerism', *Sound Studies* 7, no. 1 (2021): 77. On the emergence of air check fans in Japan during the 1960s FM era, see Shuhei Hosokawa and Hideaki Matsuoka, 'On the Fetish Character of Sound and the Progression of Technology: Theorizing Japanese Audiophiles', in *Sonic Synergies: Music, Technology, Community, Identity*, ed. Gerry Bloustien et al. (Aldershot: Ashgate, 2008), 43.

426 Bas Jansen, 'Tape Cassettes and Former Selves: How Mix Tapes Mediate Memories', in Bijsterveld and van Dijck, *Sound Souvenirs*, 43–54; Andrea F. Bohlman, 'Making Tapes in Poland: The Compact Cassette at Home', *Twentieth-Century Music* 14, no. 1 (2017): 119–34.

427 *Quelle Katalog* (1977–8), 763, quoted in Weber, 'Taking Your Favorite Sound Along', 77.

428 For the Grateful Dead Archive Online project, see https://www.gdao.org about and https://guides.library.ucsc.edu/gratefuldeadarchive. For other examples of off-air taping related to accessing indie and local music, see Zita Joyce, 'Taping Radio: Recording Memories', in Lindgren and Loviglio, *The Routledge Companion to Radio and Podcast Studies*, 389–98.

429 Ken Garner, 'Ripping the Pith from the Peel: Institutional and Internet Cultures of Archiving Pop Music Radio', *Radio Journal: International Studies in Broadcast & Audio Media* 10, no. 2 (2012): 89–111.

430 For an example of an online radio archiving initiative that invites public input, see BBC Genome, https://genome.ch.bbc.co.uk/.

431 Peters, *Sound, Space and Society*, xvi.

432 On the intimacy associated with the Walkman as a personal stereo, see Bull, *Sounding Out the City*, 8–10, 31–42.

433 Jansen, 'Tape Cassettes and Former Selves'. For attempts to crack down on home taping practice during the 1980s, see Andrew J. Bottomley, '"Home Taping is Killing Music": The Recording Industries' 1980s Anti-Home Taping Campaigns and Struggles over Production, Labor and Creativity', *Creative Industries Journal* 8, no. 2 (2015): 123–45.

434 For the 'affective meanings' developed within this community and its focus on the 'Golden Age' of US radio programming, see Patterson, 'Capturing Flow', 47.

435 Charles Seeley, *The Old Time Radio Collector's Handbook* (Atlanta: Rogue Press, 1978), 5, 13–14. See also Patterson, 'Capturing Flow'.

436 Seeley, *The Old Time Radio Collector's Handbook*, 6–8.

437 Seeley, *The Old Time Radio Collector's Handbook*, 9–11.
438 Seeley, *The Old Time Radio Collector's Handbook*, 12.
439 See, for example, the fan periodicals that have been preserved in a UK personal papers collection, which include those devoted to individual performers on BBC radio, such as Tony Hancock, Max Miller and Hattie Jacques, https://archiveshub.jisc.ac.uk/data/gb71-thm/432/thm/432/8. Several of these societies are still in operation and some have collected radio recordings, such as The Tony Hancock Appreciation Society (founded 1976, https://www.tonyhancock.org.uk/episode-guide/radio). See also Seeley, *The Old Time Radio Collector's Handbook*, 12–13.
440 Patterson, 'Capturing Flow', 64.
441 Seeley, *The Old Time Radio Collector's Handbook*, 13. For the national branch contacts, see http://www.thegoonshow.org.uk/page8.html. In addition to The Goon Show Preservation Society's US archives (http://goon.org/), the main website (http://www.thegoonshow.org.uk) gives fans advice on how to access and best order and catalogue recordings of the programme, as well as access to an audio lending library and a newsletter (http://www.thegoonshow.org.uk/page4.html). The location of these fan club branches is also a reflection of the airing of the programme in so-called British 'dominion' countries, such as Australia, New Zealand and Canada.
442 'Radio and TV Nostalgia' entry in Emmerson, *Electronic Classics*, 286. The Vintage Radio Programme Collectors Circle was founded by Roger Bickerton in 1996, but its work was largely taken over by the BBC radio drama-focused Diversity website begun by Nigel Deacon in 2002 (see https://www.facebook.com/DiversityWebsiteRadioDrama), along with an audio drama wiki initiative (https://audiodrama.fandom.com/wiki/Audio_Drama_Wiki) and the Radio Circle group (http://www.radiocircle.org.uk). Another active discussion forum can be found in Digital Spy's 'Radio and Podcasts' section, https://forums.digitalspy.com/categories/radio, along with Radio Survivor, https://www.radiosurvivor.com.
443 In addition to the now-defunct 'Archers Addicts' and 'Archers Anarchists' groups, and the newsgroup uk.media.radio.archers (UMRA), all launched in the 1990s, a more recent formation is the Academic Archers (with a website, Twitter account and regular events) and the weekly podcast Dum Tee Dum (with a website and social media presence).
444 Seán Street, *Crossing the Ether: Pre-War Public Service Radio and Commercial Competition in the UK* (Eastleigh: John Libbey, 2006), 112–15.

445 For the circulation of radio recordings beyond the institutional archive, for instance via YouTube and the Internet Archive, see Carolyn Birdsall, 'Sound and Media Studies: Archiving and the Construction of Sonic Heritage', in *Sound as Popular Culture: A Research Companion*, ed. Jens Gerrit Papenburg and Holger Schulze (Cambridge, MA: MIT Press, 2016), 133–48.

446 Graeme Stevenson, 'Editorial', *Tune Into Yesterday* 83 (Spring 2018): n.p.

447 Email correspondence with Graeme Stevenson, 28 June 2022.

448 See https://www.otrr.org.

449 Michele Hilmes, 'The Lost Critical History of Radio', *Australian Journalism Review* 36, no. 2 (2014): 15. See Audio Drama Wiki, hosted by Fandom.com, https://audiodrama.fandom.com/wiki/Audio_Drama_Wiki.

450 Mary Kidd, Sarah Nguyen and Erica Titkemeyer, 'Subscribe, Rate and Preserve Wherever You Get Your Podcasts', *Journal of Archival Organization* 17, no. 1–2 (2020): 165.

451 Adam Curry, 'The Daily Source Code Archive Project: Bringing The DSC Back', 15 January 2014, http://blog.curry.com/2014/01/15/theDailySourceCodeArchiveProject.html, cited in Jeremy Wade Morris, 'Saving New Sounds: Podcast and Preservation', *FlowTV* (2017), https://www.flowjournal.org/2018/02/saving-new-sounds/.

452 Kidd, Nguyen and Titkemeyer, 'Subscribe, Rate and Preserve'; Jeremy Wade Morris and Eric Hoyt, eds, *Saving New Sounds: Podcast Preservation and Historiography* (Ann Arbor: University of Michigan Press, 2021).

453 Historical radio jingles are a popular object with amateur collectors, which has meant that such informal collections are often more comprehensive and accessible than those preserved by institutional archives. See, for example, Norman Barrington's Radio Pages (https://www.normanb.net/data.htm) or Interval Signals page (http://www.intervalsignals.net), which is maintained in cooperation with the Dokufunk platform in Vienna, Austria (https://www.dokufunk.org).

454 Newbold, 'Captured Live', 118.

455 For example, the active role of private collectors and archiving professionals in the Association of Recorded Sound Collections (https://www.arsc-audio.org/index.php). Recognition that 'amateur' radio archiving may also involve (semi-)professionals, those with knowledge of audio engineering or paid positions in archive or academic institutions can be found in VanCour, 'The Informal Economy'.

456 Dokufunk website, https://www.dokufunk.org.

457 Douglas E. Collar, '"Hello Posterity": The Life and Times of G. Robert Vincent, Founder of the National Voice Library', dissertation, Michigan State University, 1988.

458 Shuker, *Wax Trash and Vinyl Treasures*, 110–12; Amanda Petrusich, *Do Not Sell at Any Price: The Wild, Obsessive Hunt for the World's Rarest 78rpm Records* (New York: Scribner, 2014).

459 Shuker, *Wax Trash*, 53.

460 Roy, *Media, Materiality and Memory*, 118.

461 Jennifer Lynn Stoever, 'Crate Digging Begins at Home: Black and Latinx Women Collecting and Selecting Records in the 1960s and 1970s Bronx', in *The Oxford Handbook of Hip Hop Music*, ed. Justin D. Burton and Jason Lee Oakes (Oxford: Oxford University Press, 2018).

462 See the documentary film *Recorder: The Marion Stokes Project* (2019). For a selection of Marion Stokes' recordings available in the Internet Archive collection, see https://archive.org/details/marionstokesvideo?tab=about.

463 Kathleen Battles and Eleanor Patterson, eds, 'Radio Preservation as Social Activism', *New Review of Film and Television Studies* 16, no. 4 (2018): 415–19.

464 Mitchell, 'Re-Sounding Feminist Radio'.

465 Marie Slocombe, 'The Voice from the Shrine', interview with Madeau Stewart for the BBC sound archive, recorded 25 November 1986, BBC Archive reference number 18SX5546, quoted in Street, *The Memory of Sound*, 118. For a more extensive reflection on 'archival impulses' among broadcast professionals, see Carolyn Birdsall, 'For the Love of Radio: The Archival Impulse in Broadcast Institutions', in *The Oxford Handbook of Radio Studies*, ed. Michele Hilmes and Andrew J. Bottomley (Oxford University Press, forthcoming).

466 'You Have Been Listening to a Recording', Part 3, BBC Forces Programme, 4 April 1942, BBC Archive reference 25SX2915.

467 Madeau Stewart and Craig Fees, 'Marie Slocombe 1912–1995', *Folk Music Journal* 7, no. 2 (1996): 270.

468 Birdsall, 'Divisions of Labour'.

469 David Hendy, 'Biography and the Emotions as a Missing "Narrative" in Media History: A Case Study of Lance Sieveking and the Early BBC', *Media History* 18, no. 3–4 (2012): 363.

470 For the 1938 co-founding of the International Federation of Film Archives (FIAF) on a (Nazi) German initiative, see Rolf Aurich, 'The

German Reich Film Archive in an International Context', in *The Emergence of Film Culture: Knowledge Production, Institution Building, and the Fate of the Avant-garde in Europe, 1919–1945*, ed. Malte Hagener (London and New York: Berghahn, 2014), 306–38.

471 Hans S. von Heister, 'Nur noch auf Schallplatten!', *Der Deutsche Rundfunk* 9, no. 30 (24 July 1931): 3–4.

472 The first series, 'Akustische Weltgeschichte' (Acoustic World History) was launched in late 1929, followed by a series with sound collages of events reported on radio during the previous month entitled 'Rückblick auf Schallplatten' (Retrospective on Record); Birdsall, 'Sound Aesthetics', 261–2.

473 Carolyn Birdsall, 'Sonic Artefacts: Reality Codes of Urbanity in Early German Radio Documentary', in *Soundscapes of the Urban Past: Staged Sound as Mediated Cultural Heritage*, ed. Karin Bijsterveld (Bielefeld: transcript-Verlag, 2013), 147.

474 For the significance of the collection and archive as a site of 'modernist practice' in this period, see Jeremy Braddock, *Collecting as Modernist Practice* (Baltimore, MD: Johns Hopkins University Press, 2012). For more recent efforts at giving radio art a platform and ensuring its preservation and access, see Katrine Pram Nielsen and Jacob Kreutzfeldt, 'The Resonance 107.3 FM Radio Art Collection: Towards an Archive Methodology of Radio as Resonance', *Radio Journal: International Studies in Broadcast & Audio Media* 14, no. 2 (2016): 159–75. See also the radio sound art collections at *Sonophere*, http://sonosphere.org/en/about/this-site.html; *UbuWeb*, https://www.ubu.com.

475 Hans Tasiemka, 'Ein Funkarchiv für die Ewigkeit', *Der Deutsche Rundfunk* 8, no. 30 (1930): 4.

476 For further detail on this development, see Dethlefs and Birdsall, 'Zur Geschichte der Audiobestände'.

477 Lynton Fletcher, Foyles Literary Luncheon, BBC Archive, 30 September 1941, https://www.bbc.co.uk/archive/foyles-literary-luncheon--the-bbc-recorded-programmes-department/z72kf4j.

478 Asa Briggs, *The History of Broadcasting in the United Kingdom*, vol. 3: *The War of Words: 1939–1945* (Oxford: Oxford University Press, 1995), 326–8.

479 *Pieces of Tape*, BBC National Programme, 13 January 1933, https://genome.ch.bbc.co.uk/921fda7f91b247819806cf564ffcb1d8.

480 BBC Genome website, https://genome.ch.bbc.co.uk/.

481 *Twenty Years Ago*, BBC National Programme, Saturday, 4 August 1934, *The Radio Times*, 27 July 1934, 274, https://genome.ch.bbc.

co.uk/page/a34aded09d0246009b1dcde0a795a13a?page=62; George P. Gooch and Harold Temperley, eds, *British Documents on the Origins of the War*, 11 vols (London: HM Stationery Office, 1926–38).

482 A search of *The Radio Times* via the BBC Genome suggests that such scrapbook 'panorama'-style programmes endured from the early 1930s to the mid-1970s, with editions marking special occasions, historical events or general nostalgia for the past, with titles such as *Christmas Scrapbook*, *Armistice Scrapbook*, *Scrapbook of Memories* and *Cinema Scrapbook*.

483 *Scrapbook for 1909*, 20 February 1934, *The Radio Times*, 16 February 1934, 478; https://genome.ch.bbc.co.uk/page/478a8a5a041 5409980d6db4aee6f5d0f?page=38.

484 Leslie Baily, 'How the "Scrapbooks" are Made', *Radio Times*, 4 November 1934, 355, https://genome.ch.bbc.co.uk/page/83d41bd527 c743b19a69e1eec07af824?page=3.

485 Baily, 'How the "Scrapbooks" are Made', 355.

486 Thomas Hajkowski, 'The BBC, the Empire, and the Second World War, 1939–1945', *Historical Journal of Film, Radio and Television* 22, no. 2 (2002): 146. See *Songs from the Scrapbooks*, BBC Forces Programme, 23 May 1943, https://genome.ch.bbc.co.uk/page/e6a7c300503c40238d664a76d7d96c98.

487 *Scrapbook for 1930*, BBC Home Service, 11 February 1940, *Radio Times*, 9 February 1940, 10, https://genome.ch.bbc.co.uk/ dacc7e5514afd1c807333a2e61726cc1.

488 *Room 437*, 18 December 1936, BBC Regional Programme, https:// genome.ch.bbc.co.uk/69871ca426274f2799444a77bb1aea4a; Wilfried Goatman, 'In Room 437'. I would like to thank Elizabeth Darling for sharing this publication with me.

489 *Looking Backwards*, BBC Television, 7 January 1939, *Radio Times*, 1 January 1939, https://genome.ch.bbc.co.uk/page/53c80291ba7547 d8bc78b980c82b1bf9.

490 Carolyn Birdsall, 'Worlding the Archive: Radio Collections, Heritage Frameworks, and Selection Principles', in *Transnationalizing Radio Research: New Approaches to an Old Medium*, ed. Golo Föllmer and Alexander Badenoch (Bielefeld: Transcript, 2018), 197–208.

491 *History Repeats Itself*, BBC Home Service, 15 April 1943, https:// genome.ch.bbc.co.uk/f50245160f0440faa951aa68bd5cdedd.

492 C. Gordon Glover, 'Introducing . . .', *Radio Times*, 21 May 1943, 5, https://genome.ch.bbc.co.uk/page/ac782aba96cf4adeab72ca925a30b 0cb?page=5.

493 'BBC Recording Service – Memo', R45/82 Recorded Programmes / Programmes General, 1941–1942, BBC Written Archives Centre, Caversham; Birdsall, 'Divisions of Labour'.

494 Derek Kompare, *Rerun Nation: How Repeats Invented American Television* (New York: Routledge, 2002), 19–38; Alexander Russo, 'Defensive Transcriptions: Radio Networks, Sound-on-disc Recording, and the Meaning of Live Broadcasting', *The Velvet Light Trap* 54 (2004): 4–17.

495 Patterson, 'Capturing Flow', 52.

496 Cadensa (British Library Sound Archive catalog), http://www.cadensa.bl.uk.

497 For further details of this history, see '40 Years of IASA' (2009), IASA, https://www.iasa-web.org/history.

498 Marie Slocombe, 'The BBC Folk Music Collection', *Folklore and Folk Music Archivist* 7, no. 1 (1964): 12; Western, 'Securing the Aural Border'. For the IFMC and its co-founding of the UNESCO International Music Council in 1949, see Maud Karpeles, 'The International Folk Music Council Twenty-One Years', *Yearbook of the International Folk Music Council* 1 (1969): 14–32.

499 Johannes Müske, 'Dispositives of Sound: Folk Music Collections, Radio, and the National Imagination, 1890s–1960s', in *Music Radio: Building Communities, Mediating Genres*, ed. Morten Michelsen et al. (New York and London: Bloomsbury, 2018), 163–88; Inis Shkreli, 'Communist Politics of Archives: The Case of the Ethnomusicology Archive at the Institute of Folk Culture in Tirana', *Martor* 24 (2019): 73–5; Daniel Gomes, 'Archival Airwaves: Recording Ireland for the BBC', *Modernism/Modernity Print Plus* 3, no. 4 (2019), https://doi.org/10.26597/mod.0084; Sunmin Yoon, 'Remains and Renewals: The Process of Preserving Urtyn Duu in Contemporary Mongolia', *Mongolian Studies* 35 (2013): 119–31; Tom Western, 'Introduction: Ethnomusicologies of Radio', *Ethnomusicology Forum* 27, no. 3 (2018): 255–64.

500 Stefan Fiol, 'All India Radio and the Genealogies of Folk Music in Uttarakhand', *South Asian Popular Culture* 10, no. 3 (2012): 261–72; Atta Annan Mensah, 'Problems Involved in the "Arrangement" of Folk Music for Radio Ghana', *Journal of the International Folk Music Council* 11 (1959): 83–4; Larkin, *Signal and Noise*, 48–72.

501 Marco Roque de Freitas, 'Sounding the Nation, Sounding the Revolution: Music and Radio Broadcasting in Post-colonial Mozambique (1975–1986)', *Journal of Radio & Audio Media* 29,

no. 1 (2022): 80–103. See also the special issue 'Researching (Post) Colonial Broadcasting', ed. Nelson Ribeiro, *Journal of Radio & Audio Media* 29, no. 1 (2022). For an earlier example of how, with a new political regime (National Socialism in Germany), pre-1933 party recordings were retrospectively added to the national radio archive after 1933, see Erica Harrison, '"A Faithful Steward of these Values": The Valorisation of a Translocated German Sound Collection', *TMG: Journal for Media History* 25, no. 2 (2022): 1–25.

502 Moorman, *Powerful Frequencies*, 96–7.

503 Moorman, *Powerful Frequencies*, 112–13.

504 Moorman, *Powerful Frequencies*, 103, 105.

505 Lonán Ó Briain, *Voices of Vietnam: A Century of Radio, Red Music, and Revolution* (Oxford University Press, 2021), 126, 157.

506 On the (sound) archive as a technology of state power, see Carolyn Birdsall and Viktoria Tkaczyk, 'Listening to the Archive: Sound Data in the Humanities and Sciences', *Technology and Culture* 60, no. 2 (2019): S1–S13. For the case of the South Africa Broadcasting Corporation (SABC) archive, founded in 1960, and a recent archival project dedicated to materials that were censored by the SABC prior to 1994, see Lizabé Lambrechts, 'Ethnography of the Archive: Power and Politics in Five South African Music Archives', dissertation, University of Stellenbosch, 2012, 89–111, 202, 219, 222. For the impact of colonial rule on archives related to audiovisual media, see Rakesh Sengupta, 'Towards a Decolonial Media Archaeology: The Absent Archive of Screenwriting History and the Obsolete', *Theory, Culture & Society* 38, no.1 (2021): 3–26; Anette Hoffmann, 'Close Listening: Approaches to Research on Colonial Sound Archives', in *The Bloomsbury Handbook of Sonic Methodologies*, ed. Michael Bull and Marcel Cobussen (New York and London: Bloomsbury, 2021), 529–42.

507 For efforts to hide and later retrieve the recorded sound materials of broadcasters in German-occupied Western Europe during and after the Second World War, see Carolyn Birdsall, 'Tracing the Archival Lives of Radio: Recorded Sound Collections in Belgian and Dutch Radio (1930–1960)', *TMG: Journal for Media History* 25 no. 2 (2022): 1–30.

508 Del Quentin Wilber and Lisa Rein, 'In National Archives Thefts, a Radio Detective gets his Man', *Washington Post*, 2 May 2012, https://www.washingtonpost.com/local/crime/in-national-archives-thefts-a-radio-detective-gets-his-man/2012/05/02/gIQAN1chxT_story.html.

509 For the plans for the music library to be accessible via an online stream, see Howard Campbell, 'JBC Music Library to Come on Stream', *The Gleaner*, 11 March 2010, https://jamaica-gleaner.com/gleaner/20100311/news/news2.html.

510 Bronfman, *Isles of Noise*, 154.

511 For 'Save our Sounds', see https://britishlibrary.typepad.co.uk/sound-and-vision/2015/01/save-our-sounds-15-years-to-save-the-uks-sound-collections.html. For 'Deadline 2025', see https://www.nfsa.gov.au/about/our-mission/support-us/deadline-2025-campaign.

512 Chignell, *Key Concepts in Radio Studies*, 47.

513 On this challenge in the Finnish context, as well as the documentation of tape recordings at the Finnish national broadcaster Yleisradio, see Pekka Salosaari, 'The Audio Legacy of Finnish Radio: An Exploration of Key Factors in the Preservation of Radio Sound Collections', *TMG: Journal for Media History* 25 no. 2 (2022): 1–25.

514 'Gaywaves' (2SER, 1979–2005) set, NFSA Australia, Soundcloud, https://soundcloud.com/nfsaaustralia/sets/gaywaves.

515 For example, Battles and Patterson, 'Radio Preservation as Social Activism'; Amanda Keeler and Josh Shepperd, 'Radio Research as Critical Archival Studies: Cross-Sector Collaboration and the Sound Record', *Journal of Radio & Audio Media* 26, no. 1 (2019): 4–7; Laura Schnitker, 'Archives, Advocacy and Crowd-sourcing: Towards a More Complete Historiography of College Radio', *Journal of Radio & Audio Media* 23, no. 2 (2016): 341–8.

516 Floris Paalman, Giovanna Fossati and Eef Masson, 'Introduction: Activating the Archive', *The Moving Image: The Journal of the Association of Moving Image Archivists* 21, no. 1–2 (2021): 1–25; Cyril Ngoasheng and Ngoako Solomon Marutha, 'Safe and Sound: A Framework for the Preservation of Audio-Visual Records to Support Accessibility for the Radio Broadcasting Stations in South Africa', *Mousaion* 39, no. 3 (2021): 1.

517 Laura Wagner and Ayanna Legros, 'From the Other Side of the Sea: Rasanblaj/Resaasembling Haitian Radio Archives of Exile', *Global South* 15, no. 2 (2022): 154–75; Alejandra Bronfman, '*Face à l'Opinion*: Argentine Activists and the Sound of Solidarity on Radio Haïti-Inter', *Global South* 15, no. 2 (2022): 135–53.

518 Alexander Badenoch, 'Radio Diffusion: Re-collecting International Broadcasting in the Archive of Radio Netherlands Worldwide', in *Transnationalizing Radio Research: New Approaches to an Old Medium*, ed. Golo Föllmer and Alexander Badenoch (Bielefeld: transcript, 2018), 210.

519 See La TopoRadio, https://toporadio.org/index.html. For further background on the work of the Radio Preservation Task Force network that helped to support this project, see Shawn VanCour, 'Locating the Radio Archive: New Histories, New Challenges', *Journal of Radio & Audio Media* 23, no. 2 (2016): 395–403. For a critical account of the 'process of recovery' required to reconnect radio recordings kept separate from the personal papers, see Angela Tate, 'Sounding Off: Etta Moten Barnett's Archive, Diaspora, and Radio Activism in the Cold War', *Resonance: The Journal of Sound and Culture* 2, no. 3 (2021): 395–410.

520 Erik A. Moore and Rebecca Toov, 'Listening to Our Collections: Preserving Records of University-Based Educational Radio Stations in Campus Archives', *Journal of Archival Organization* 17, no. 1–2 (2020): 38–53; Craig Breaden and Laura Wagner, 'Bringing Radio Haiti Home: The Digital Archive as *Devoir de Mémoire*', in *The Oxford Handbook of Musical Repatriation*, ed. Frank Gunderson et al. (New York: Oxford University Press, 2019), 331. For the acquisition of the Anoraks Ireland fan support organization collections, including sounds and print materials, by a higher education institution (and via an online archive initiative), see http://radiowaves.fm/ire/anoraks-ireland-collection; https://pirate.ie/archive.

521 Simon-Olivier Gagnon, 'Archiving Trash Radio in Québec City: The Soundwork of the Coalition Sortons les radios-poubelles', *Resonance: The Journal of Sound and Culture* 2, no. 4 (2021): 636–49.

522 For this longer history across the 1930s to the 1990s in Europe, see Suzanne Bardgett, Friederike Kind-Kovács and Vincent Kuitenbrouwer, eds, 'Transnational Radio Monitoring', special issue, *Media History* 25, no. 4 (2019).

523 David Hendy, 'The Great War and British Broadcasting: Emotional Life in the Creation of the BBC', *New Formations* 82 (2014): 82–99.

524 For important new contributions that explore, among other themes, religious radio archives, non-profit and commercial radio archiving, amateur radio archives of spectrum recordings, and podcast preservation, see Laura J. Treat and Shawn VanCour, eds, Special Issue on Radio Preservation, *Journal of Archival Organization* 17, no. 1–2 (2020).

525 On professionals' 'love' of early radio objects in museum spaces, see Hilary Geoghegan and Alison Hess, 'Object-love at the Science Museum: Cultural Geographies of Museum Storerooms', *Cultural Geographies* 22, no. 3 (2015): 445–65. Tim van der Heijden has pointed to the operations of both 'restorative' and 'reflective'

technostalgia in contemporary memory practices with media technologies: van der Heijden, 'Technostalgia of the Present'.

526 Michelle Caswell, *Urgent Archives: Enacting Liberatory Memory Work* (London: Routledge, 2021).

527 Heikki Uimonen, 'Evening of Sounds: Auditory Cultures in Radio Call-in Programmes', in *Sound, Media, Ecology*, ed. Milena Droumeva and Randolph Jordan (Cham: Palgrave Macmillan, 2019), 261, 262.

528 'Äanien ilta', YLE (Finnish Broadcasting Company), https://areena.yle.fi/audio/1-3073536.

529 Uimonen, 'Evening of Sounds', 262.

530 One interesting exception to the engagement with fans by a public broadcaster is the decision of the BBC to distribute photos of wedding scenes from the radio play *The Archers*, involving cast members, starting as early as the mid-1950s. See https://www.bbc.co.uk/blogs/thearchers/entries/5a28d460-b3d3-3bdd-8f17-664fa6f030f0.

531 Lamerichs, *Productive Fandom*, 200.

532 See the compilation film *Es rauscht der Rhein . . . es strömt das Leben . . .: 40 Jahre aktuelles Zeitgeschehen, 1911–1951* (Filminstitut Düsseldorf, 1996); 'Der Langenberger Sender als Kostüm', *Die Werag*, 10 February 1929, 21, cited in Birdsall, *Nazi Soundscapes*, 76, 193, n. 23.

533 Jason Loviglio, '*Vox Pop*: Network Radio and the Voice of the People', in Hilmes and Loviglio, *Radio Reader*, 90.

534 Loviglio, '*Vox Pop*', 104.

535 Simmons, 'Dear Radio Broadcaster', 450, 451, 453–4.

536 On the phenomenon of bumper stickers, see consumer research during the 1990s: John E. Newhagen and Michael Ancell, 'The Expression of Emotion and Social Status in the Language of Bumper Stickers', *Journal of Language and Social Psychology* 14, no. 3 (1995): 312–23.

537 For the development and expansion of commercial radio in countries that had previously been dominated by public broadcast systems, see Taisto Hujanen and Per Jauert, 'The New Competitive Environment of Radio Broadcasting in the Nordic Countries: A Short History of Deregulation and Analysis', *Journal of Radio Studies* 5, no. 1 (1998): 105–31. On cross-industry branding to radio audiences, see Paulo Nunes and Carolyn Birdsall, 'Curating the Urban Music Festival: Festivalisation, the 'Shuffle' Logic, and Digitally-shaped Music Consumption', *European Journal of Cultural Studies* 25, no. 2

(2022): 679–702. On the multiplatform franchising and merchandise development of 'This American Life' since the 2000s, see Eleanor Patterson, 'This American Franchise: *This American Life*, Public Radio Franchising and the Cultural Work of Legitimating Economic Hybridity', *Media, Culture & Society* 38, no. 3 (2016): 453.

538 For the role of radio websites in station promotion and merchandise sales, see Mary Jackson Pitts and Ross Harms, 'Radio Websites as a Promotional Tool', *Journal of Radio Studies* 10, no. 2 (2003): 270–82. For local and community radio merchandise sales, see Mpolokeng Bogatsu, '"Loxion Kulcha": Fashioning Black Youth Culture in Post-Apartheid South Africa', *English Studies in Africa* 45, no. 2 (2002): 1–11; Charles Fairchild, *Music, Radio and the Public Sphere: The Aesthetics of Democracy* (Basingstoke: Palgrave Macmillan, 2012), 119.

539 While the early decades of radio have been treated from the perspective of class, there has been less explicit discussion in recent scholarship about the relationship of radio to class distinctions (and the contempt of some middle-class listeners for commercial radio). For a recent account for the present music streaming era, see Jack Webster, 'The Promise of Personalisation: Exploring How Music Streaming Platforms are Shaping the Performance of Class Identities and Distinction', *New Media & Society* (2021), https://doi.org/10.1177/14614448211027863.

540 Douglas, *Listening In*, 199.

541 Andrew Stuart Bergerson, 'Listening to the Radio in Hildesheim, 1923–53', *German Studies Review* 24, no. 1 (2001): 83–113.

542 Elizabeth L. Enriquez, interview with meLê yamomo, *Interferenzen: Koloniales Scheitern im Radio* [Interferences: Colonial Failures in Radio], *Deutschlandfunk Kultur*, 11 December 2020, https://www.hoerspielundfeature.de/hoerstueck-ueber-fruehe-radiosender-in-suedostasien-100.html; Enriquez, *Appropriation of Colonial Broadcasting*.

543 Debra Spitulnik, 'Documenting Radio Culture as Lived Experience: Reception Studies and the Mobile Machine in Zambia', in *African Broadcast Cultures: Radio in Transition*, ed. Richard Fardon and Graham Furniss (Oxford: James Currey, 2000), 152, 153.

544 Spitulnik, 'Documenting Radio Culture as Lived Experience', 160–1.

545 Spitulnik, 'Documenting Radio Culture as Lived Experience', 156–7.

546 Weber, 'Taking Your Favorite Sound Along', 71.

547 Weber, 'Taking Your Favorite Sound Along', 74–5.

548 Weber, 'Taking Your Favorite Sound Along', 75–6.

549 Weber, 'Taking Your Favorite Sound Along', 76–7.
550 Jason Loviglio, 'The Traffic in Feelings: The Car-Radio Assemblage', in *The Routledge Companion to Radio and Podcast Studies*, ed. Mia Lindgren and Jason Loviglio (Abingdon and New York: Routledge, 2022), 229.
551 Karin Bijsterveld et al., *Sound and Safe: A History of Listening Behind the Wheel* (Oxford and New York: Oxford University Press, 2014), 73.
552 Dafni Tragaki, 'Acoustemologies of *Rebetiko* Love Songs', in *Music as Atmosphere: Collective Feelings and Affective Sounds*, ed. Friedlind Riedel and Juha Torvinen (Abingdon and New York: Routledge, 2019), 188.
553 Bijsterveld et al., *Sound and Safe*, 17.
554 As the authors note, since the 1970s, one of the most significant developments in the European context is the development of highway noise barriers, with models since the 1990s that restrict the gaze of drivers and have prompted drivers to redirect their attention further by listening to traffic radio and audio books for more 'personal flow *within* the car'. Bijsterveld et al., *Sound and Safe*, 131.
555 Josephine F. Coleman, *Digital Innovations and the Production of Local Content in Community Radio: Changing Practices in the UK* (Abingdon and New York: Routledge, 2021); Arthur D. Soto-Vásquez, M. Olguta Vilceanu and Kristine C. Johnson, '"Just hanging with my friends": US Latina/o/x Perspectives on Parasocial Relationships in Podcast Listening during COVID-19', *Popular Communication* (2022): 1–14; Kate Galloway, 'The Sonic Strategies and Technologies of Listening Alone Together in *The World According to Sound's Outside In: A Communal Listening Series*', *Radio Journal* 20, no. 1 (2022): 85–103.
556 For the significance of overnight talk radio programmes, see Miles Romney, 'The Voice in the Night Unheard by Scholars: Herb Jepko and the Genesis of National Talk Radio', *Journal of Radio and Audio Media* 21 (2014): 272–89.
557 Azmyl Yusof, 'Left of the Dial: BFM 89.9 Independent Radio Station and its Indie Rock-friendly Midnight Programming as a Site of Sustainability', in *Discourses, Agency and Identity in Malaysia: Critical Perspectives*, ed. Ibrahim Zawawi, Gareth Richards and Victor T. King (Singapore: Springer, 2021), 413–28.
558 Liz Gould, 'Cash and Controversy: A Short History of Commercial Talkback Radio', *Media International Australia* 122, no. 1 (2007): 83.

559 Jacqui Ewart, 'Therapist, Companion, and Friend: The Underappreciated Role of Talkback Radio in Australia', *Journal of Radio & Audio Media* 18, no. 2 (2018): 240, 242. For the call-in talk show facilitating a form of listening, see Jonathan David Tankel, 'Reconceptualizing Call-in Talk Radio as Listening', *Journal of Radio Studies* 5, no. 1 (1998): 36–48.

560 Tiziano Bonini and Belén Monclús, eds, *Radio Audiences and Participation in the Age of Network Society* (New York and Abingdon: Routledge, 2014); Jacqui Ewart and Kate Ames, 'Talking Text: Exploring SMS and E-mail use by Australian Talkback Radio Listeners', *Radio Journal: International Studies in Broadcast & Audio Media* 14, no. 1 (2016), 91–107; Maureen Sinton, 'No Longer One-to-many: How Web 2.0 Interactivity is Changing Public Service Radio's Relationship with its Audience', *Journal of Radio & Audio Media* 25, no. 1 (2018): 62–76; Gonen Dori-Hacohen, '"Rush, I love you": Interactional Fandom on US Political Talk Radio', *International Journal of Communication* 7 (2013).

561 A well-known early example of the gathering of the public as a 'radio forum' during a national radio programme is *America's Town Meeting of the Air*, which aired for over two decades starting from 1935: David Goodman, 'Programming in the Public Interest: America's Town Meeting of the Air', in *NBC: America's Network*, ed. Michele Hilmes and Michael Henry (Berkeley: University of California Press, 2007), 44–60.

562 On the BBC radio programme *Music While You Work* (1940–1967), see Keith Jones, 'Music in Factories: A Twentieth-Century Technique for Control of the Productive Self', *Social & Cultural Geography* 6, no. 5 (2005): 723–44. For contemporary study of radio use in the (factory) workplace, see Marek Korczynski, *Songs of the Factory: Pop Music, Culture, and Resistance* (Ithaca, NY: Cornell University Press, 2015). On how radio programmes make explicit reference to their audiences as listening at work, see Grażyna Stachyra, 'Radio in the Workplace: A Liminal Medium between Work and Leisure', *Media, Culture & Society* 37, no. 2 (2015): 270–87.

563 David Goodman, 'A Transnational History of Radio Listening Groups I: The United Kingdom and United States', *Historical Journal of Film, Radio and Television* 36, no. 3 (2016): 437; David Goodman, 'A Transnational History of Radio Listening Groups II: Canada, Australia and the World', *Historical Journal of Film, Radio and Television* 36, no. 4 (2016): 627–48; Lacey, *Listening Publics*, 140–56.

564 During the Great Leap Forward and the Cultural Revolution in China there was a massive expansion of radio loudspeaker systems. State

radio loudspeakers had reached almost 100 million by the mid-1970s, including wired radio loudspeakers in factories, residential courtyards and interior spaces. Jie Li, 'Revolutionary Echoes: Radios and Loudspeakers in the Mao Era', *Twentieth-Century China* 45, no. 1 (2020): 25–45. On public loudspeaker systems in Nazi Germany, see Birdsall, *Nazi Soundscapes*. On radio in Soviet Russia, see Lovell, *Russia in the Microphone Age*; Dmitri Zakharine, 'Electrical Signalling: Radio', in Postoutenko, Tikhomorov and Zakharine, *Media and Communication in the Soviet Union (1917–1953)*, 327–42. For the influence of Soviet Russia's organization of communal, public listening on the British approach to radio in colonial India, see Simon Potter, *Wireless Internationalism and Distant Listening: Britain, Propaganda, and the Invention of Global Radio, 1920–1939* (Oxford: Oxford University Press, 2020), 10.

565 Thokozani N. Mhlambi, 'Sound in Urban Public Space: Loudspeaker Broadcasts in Johannesburg and Durban in South Africa, 1940s', *Cultural Studies* 34, no. 6 (2020): 959.

566 Roar Skovmand, 'De ledende kræfter 1926–1940', in *DR 50*, ed. Roar Skovmand (Copenhagen: Danmarks Radio, 1975), 52, 55, 64, 66, 75, 78, 103–4, 111–12, 114. On the demise of such groups in the 1980s, see Krogh and Michelsen, 'Introduction'.

567 D. L. LeMahieu, '*The Gramophone*: Recorded Music and the Cultivated Mind in Britain between the Wars', *Technology and Culture* 23, no. 3 (1982): 372–91.

568 Christopher Stone, 'Records I like to Broadcast', *Radio Pictorial* 1 (19 January 1934), https://worldradiohistory.com/UK/Radio-Pictorial/Radio-Pictorial-1934-01-19-S-OCR.pdf.

569 'A Recital of Gramophone Records by Christopher Stone', *The Radio Times*, 25 September 1931, 770, https://genome.ch.bbc.co.uk/page/591a7e2c582d4414bd56b3d8779065e1. A comparable effort to introduce listeners to the sounds of the world can be found in the Dutch international shortwave station PCJ's programme *Happy Station* and host Eddie Startz, who from 1928 onwards developed a similarly accessible style and interaction with listeners, particularly across the British Empire; Kuitenbrouwer, '"The Brightness You Bring into Our Otherwise Very Dull Existence"'.

570 The same listing creates a rather sexist comparison: that Stone listens to more records 'even than those young ladies in gramophone factories whose monotonous task it is to sit and listen to records being played through twenty times in succession to ensure that the recording is sound enough to stand the strain of frequent replaying'. See 'A Recital of Gramophone Records'.

571 'Gramophone Shop', *Radio Times*, 12 July 1946, 8, https://genome.ch.bbc.co.uk/page/16a34331843f4bb68145f4c5fa6de063.

572 This interest in radio in visiting spaces of recorded music consumption is suggested by the series, between June 1951 and March 1953, in which the BBC mobile recording unit visited music shops all across the UK. For the first episode, 'A Visit to a Music Shop in Coventry for Interviews with Customers Buying New Records', see the BBC Home Service Midland, 5 June 1951, BBC Genome, https://genome.ch.bbc.co.uk/e5bb003d1afa76241d28784376e930aa.

573 Eva Moreda Rodríguez, *Inventing the Recording: The Phonograph and National Culture in Spain, 1877–1914* (New York: Oxford University Press, 2021), 143–62; Eva Moreda Rodríguez, '*Discòfils*: Notes on the Birth of the Record Club and Record Listening in 1930s Barcelona', in *Phonographic Encounters: Mapping Transnational Cultures of Sound, 1890–1945*, ed. Elodie A. Roy and Eva Moreda Rodríguez (Abingdon and New York: Routledge, 2022), 100–16.

574 Thomas Henry, 'From the Grands Boulevards to Montparnasse: An Essay on the Geohistory of the Phonograph and Sound Recording Business in Paris (1878–1940)', in Roy and Moreda Rodríguez, *Phonographic Encounters*, 251–2.

575 Henry, 'From the Grands Boulevards to Montparnasse', 252–4.

576 See, for instance, the listing for Dalloz's weekly radio programmes *Nouveaux Disques* for RTF's France III national station, as listed in the 'season programme' overview. For 1958–9, see http://www.radioscope.fr/grilles/culture/franceIII1958.htm; for 1959–60, see http://www.radioscope.fr/grilles/culture/franceIII1959.htm.

577 Jean-Jacques Ledos and Lise Mansion, 'Le jazz et la radio, une union durable', *Cahiers d'histoire de la Radiodiffusion* 75 (2003): 14–95. For the private papers of Gédovius held at the INA archives, see Marine Beccarelli, 'Mémoire des ondes: Les archives de la radio française', *Sociétés & Représentations* 49, no. 1 (2020): 189.

578 See the listing for the *Phono-radio-musique* periodical at the Bibliothèque nationale de France (National Library of France): https://data.bnf.fr/en/32839446/phono-radio-musique/.

579 Hennion, *The Passion for Music*.

580 Hosokawa and Matsuoka, 'On the Fetish Character of Sound', 41.

581 Hosokawa and Matsuoka, 'On the Fetish Character of Sound', 41, 44.

582 Shuhei Hosokawa, 'The Swinging Phonograph in a Hot Teahouse: Sound Technology and the Emergence of the Jazz Community in

Prewar Japan', in *Sound, Space, and Sociality in Modern Japan*, ed. Joseph D. Hankins and Carolyn S. Stevens (London: Routledge, 2014), 119–20.

583 Shuhei Hosokawa and Hideaki Matsuoka, 'Vinyl Record Collecting as Material Practice: The Japanese Case', in *Fanning the Flames: Fans and Consumer Culture in Contemporary Japan*, ed. William W. Kelly (Albany: State University of New York Press, 2004), 154–5.

584 Hans Schlee, 'Ein Rundfunk-Museum: Die Neuheit des Berliner Funkhauses', in *Rundfunk Jahrbuch 1931*, ed. RRG (Berlin: Union, 1931), 403–10.

585 Schlee, 'Ein Rundfunk-Museum', 404–5.

586 Schlee, 'Ein Rundfunk-Museum', 405. Already in 1928, a radio historical display for the development of technology was included in the annual German Radio Exhibition in Berlin, along with a memorial display for past inventors including Heinrich Hertz. Bressler, *Von der Experimentierbühne*, 324.

587 Schlee, 'Ein Rundfunk-Museum', 405–7.

588 Schlee, 'Ein Rundfunk-Museum', 407–8.

589 Schlee, 'Ein Rundfunk-Museum', 409–10.

590 *Weekjournaal* [weekly newsreel], Polygoon Hollands Nieuws, 28 February 1948, https://www.openbeelden.nl/media/1151564.

591 Hutchins, 'Poised for the New Millennium'.

592 'Radiolympia Radio Museum', in *Radiolympia: The National Radio Exhibition – Official Catalogue* (London: Radio Manufacturers Association, 1937), 151. It bears mentioning that a much later initiative for a media museum, opened in 1983, was strongly invested in the visual: the National Museum of Photography, Film and Television, which in 2016 became the National Media Museum, and in 2017, the National Science and Media Museum.

593 'Deutsches Rundfunkmuseum in Berlin', *Funk-Technik* 1 (January 1965): 6.

594 'Deutsches Rundfunkmuseum in Berlin'. A similar fascination with displays of computer automation has been described by Lynn Spigel in various plans for television museums in the early 1960s: Lynn Spigel, 'Housing Television: Architectures of the Archive', *The Communication Review* 13, no. 1 (2010): 56–9.

595 Jennifer Rich, 'Sound, Mobility and Landscapes of Exhibition: Radio-Guided Tours at the Science Museum, London, 1960–1964', *Journal of Historical Geography* 52 (2016): 62.

596 Rich, 'Sound, Mobility and Landscapes of Exhibition', 73.

597 The development towards 'authorized' heritage followed shortly after the 1964 Venice Charter (International Charter for the Conservation and Restoration of Monuments and Sites). Laurajane Smith, *Uses of Heritage* (London: Routledge, 2006), 5, 21–34, 85–114.

598 For the interest in radio exhibitions in German-occupied Netherlands, see, for instance, film footage documenting the opening of an exhibition during the 'Dutch radio music festival' in 1942: https://www.openbeelden.nl/media/767293/Muziektentoonstelling_in_Rijksmuseum.nl. For the proposal to prepare a radio museum by the German-occupation era radio direction's board meeting in September 1943, see Gerard van Beek and Kees Cabout, *De lange aanloop: De geschiedenis van het Omroepmuseum* (Hilversum: Stichting Nederlandse Omroepmuseum, 1993), 5.

599 Renso van Bergen, '20 jaar regelen, bellen en praten – Marieke Veen-Bos: afscheid van Omroepmuseum', *Hilversums Historisch Tijdschrift – Eigen Perk* 2 (2006): 81–2.

600 van Bergen, '20 jaar regelen, bellen en praten', 82.

601 van Bergen, '20 jaar regelen, bellen en praten', 31.

602 This phrasing is reflected in the title of Wells' autobiography: Gerald Wells, *Obsession: A Life in Wireless* (London: Gerald Wells, 2002).

603 'Dulwich Wireless Museum – Gerald Wells', in *Collecting: The Passionate Pastime*, ed. Susanne Johnston and Tim Beddow (Harmondsworth, etc.: Viking, 1986), 133–4.

604 'The Story of Gerald Wells and the Vintage Wireless Museum', https://www.youtube.com/watch?v=SJ8JhYDKW_A; 'Dulwich Wireless Museum – Gerald Wells', 136.

605 'Dulwich Wireless Museum – Gerald Wells', 134.

606 'Dulwich Wireless Museum – Gerald Wells', 133, 135.

607 'The Story of Gerald Wells'.

608 'The Wireless World of Gerry Wells', BBC World Service, 20 August 2010, https://www.bbc.co.uk/programmes/p02sbx6h.

609 See the website (https://www.japanradiomuseum.com/gyokuon.html) and blog (https://japanradiomuseum.asablo.jp/blog/). Okabe has a professional background as an employee of an audio equipment manufacturer, and he provides further biographical details at the Radio Museum website, https://www.radiomuseum.org/collection/tadanobu_okabe.html.

610 For the effort to attract visitors by way of special exhibitions, see an article on the special exhibition 'Radio of Burnt Scars', with radio

receivers from the early post-1945 period: https://www.sankei.com/article/20210411-OMQ5IYGX75J3PAMQYDMOZIZMAM/.

611 See the 'Museum Finder' at Radiomuseum.org, www.radiomuseum.org/museum/List_of_museums_science_technical_radio_finder_Museumsliste.html. In a number of cases, a radio exhibition display was incorporated into larger frameworks such as railway or telecommunications museums, including one case of a collection of the HB4FR amateur radio club being incorporated into a military aviation museum in Switzerland: http://www.hb4fr.ch/en-expo-hb4fr—civil-historical-collection.html.

612 This museum display has a strong emphasis on the history of technical devices, which are mainly in glass cabinets, for which the website allows a virtual walk through the space. See https://www.zsmuseum.cn/museum-portal/#gaikuang.

613 Radyo ve Demokrasi Muzesi, https://www.konak.bel.tr/sayfa/radyo-ve-demokrasi-muzesi.

614 For instance, see the 'Experience Broadcast Studio' listed in a floorplan overview for the museum: NHK Museum of Broadcasting, https://www.nhk.or.jp/museum/english/floor_index.html.

615 See https://www.youtube.com/watch?v=8Zb5bjssW6w.

616 The 'Experience' in Hilversum, created in 2006, was closed for renovation in 2020, with the new 'Media Museum' reopened in 2023; see https://beeldengeluid.nl/bezoek/wat-er-te-doen/het-mediamuseum.

617 On the 'script' of multiple elements involved in mediations between exhibition and audience, encompassing 'the location, the architecture and layout of the building, the organization and design of the displays and the means of visitor guidance', see Julia Noordegraaf, *Strategies of Display: Museum Presentation in Nineteenth- and Twentieth-Century Visual Culture* (Rotterdam: NAi, 2004), 14–15. The NHK Broadcast Museum is located at the site of the first broadcast in Tokyo in 1925, whereas the Berlin Rundfunk Museum was located at the foot of the iconic radio tower at the site of the Haus des Rundfunks and exhibition grounds used for national radio exhibitions prior to 1939.

618 'National Radio Museum', Taiwan Ministry of Culture, https://museums.moc.gov.tw/EN/MusData/Detail?museumsId=f3bc85f3-3ead-4ad6-9742-4b99123e097d.

619 Huang Shan, 'Taiwan Radio Museum holds exhibit of intercepted broadcasts', China.org.cn, 31 October 2008, http://www.china.org.cn/english/China/230300.htm.

620 See https://radiophonic.space/html/exhibitions.html.
621 This set-up can be viewed in a film for the 'Radiophonic Spaces' exhibition: https://heritageinmotion.eu/himentry/radiophonic-spaces. A similar spatialized set-up was also adopted in a recent exhibition entitled 'Radio Activities', curated by Alfredo Thiermann, with small transistor devices suspended from the ceiling. However, in this case the sounds used were allowed to resonate in the museum space, as a means of exploring the 'architecture of radio' constructed in the contested radio space of a divided Berlin. See https://www.e-flux.com/announcements/426984/radio-activities.
622 The Media Archaeology Fund (Medienarchäologischer Fundus), founded by Wolfgang Ernst at the Humboldt University in Berlin, was intended to establish a collection of working obsolete media technologies, which are organized according to their technical proximity (rather than conventional categorizations). Lori Emerson, '"Archives, Materiality, and the Agency of the Machine": An Interview with Wolfgang Ernst', Library of Congress, 8 February 2013, https://blogs.loc.gov/thesignal/2013/02/archives-materiality-and-agency-of-the-machine-an-interview-with-wolfgang-ernst/; Anthony Enns, 'Foreword: Media History versus Media Archeology', in Wolfgang Ernst, *Chronopoetics: The Temporal Being and Operativity of Technological Media* (London: Rowman & Littlefield, 2016), xxiii.
623 For a consideration of radio within the 'sound history' of mental health treatment and in contemporary exhibition spaces, see Carolyn Birdsall, Manon Parry and Viktoria Tkaczyk, 'Listening to the Mind: Tracing the Auditory History of Mental Illness in Archives and Exhibitions', *The Public Historian* 37, no. 4 (2015): 47–72.
624 The exhibition went on tour to a second location in Leicester: https://archive.ica.art/ica-off-site/touring-exhibitions/ica-touring-programme/touring-venues/potteries-museum-art-gallery-1/.
625 For the AM/FM online archive, see https://www.amfm.org.uk/.
626 A selection of these objects can be seen in this news coverage: https://www.theguardian.com/artanddesign/gallery/2015/may/22/london-1980-pirate-radio-scene-in-pictures.
627 Zita Joyce, 'Alternative Radio: Exhibiting Radio and Music Heritage after the Christchurch Earthquakes', *International Journal of Heritage Studies* 24, no. 3 (2018): 230–42.
628 Joyce, 'Alternative Radio', 230–1. See also the four-part radio series *A History of Student Radio*, Radio New Zealand (2014–15), https://www.rnz.co.nz/national/programmes/a-history-of-student-radio.

629 Joyce, 'Alternative Radio', 235, 236.
630 Bijsterveld and van Dijck, *Sound Souvenirs*.
631 Joyce, 'Alternative Radio', 240.
632 For the live performances from the museum exhibition, see 'RDU40 – Feeding the Natives', RDU, 29 April 2016, RDU.org.nz, http://rdu.org.nz/rdu40-feeding-the-natives/.
633 This signature tune or call sign, and other clips from the station, can be heard via 'The Voice of Peace', BBC Radio Four, 1992, posted on YouTube by 'The Radio Programme', https://www.youtube.com/watch?v=3FtoE4oYfPw.
634 See, for instance, the displays on the history of radio documented for the Museum of Communications, located at Reichman University, near Tel Aviv: https://www.runi.ac.il/en/schools/communications/museum/. For the previous exhibition set-up in the same space, see the photos at https://www.alamy.com/stock-photo-radio-museum-at-the-interdisciplinary-center-herzliya-israel-132654193.html.
635 For the significance of touch in museum narration and visitor experiences, see Elizabeth Pye, ed., *The Power of Touch: Handling Objects in Museum and Heritage Contexts* (London: Routledge, 2016).
636 Uimonen, 'Evening of Sounds', 280.
637 José van Dijck, 'Remembering Songs through Telling Stories: Pop Music as a Resource for Memory', in Bijsterveld and van Dijck, *Sound Souvenirs*, 118.
638 Esther Hammelburg, 'Live Event-Spaces: Place and Space in the Mediatized Experience of Events', in *Locating Imagination in Popular Culture: Place, Tourism and Belonging*, ed. Nicky van Es et al. (London and New York: Routledge, 2020), 215–29.
639 Hammelburg, 'Live Event-Spaces', 117.
640 Brian Fauteux, '"Songs You Need to Hear": Public Radio Partnerships and the Mobility of National Music', *Radio Journal: International Studies in Broadcast & Audio Media* 15, no. 1 (2017): 47–63; Christopher Cwynar, 'Brick, Mortar, and Screen: Networked Digital Media, Popular Music, and the Reinvention of the Public Radio Station', *Journal of Radio & Audio Media* 27, no. 1 (2020): 74–92.
641 For example, Göran Bolin, 'Passion and Nostalgia in Generational Media Experiences', *European Journal of Cultural Studies* 19, no. 3 (2016): 250–64; Ben Green, '"I Always Remember that Moment": Peak Music Experiences as Epiphanies', *Sociology* 50, no. 2 (2016):

333–48; Lauren Istvandity, *The Lifetime Soundtrack: Music and Autobiographical Memory* (Sheffield: Equinox Publishing, 2019).

642 For an overview of the top 10 selections since the start of the programme, see https://en.wikipedia.org/wiki/Top_2000.

643 Frederik Dhaenens, '"Timeless" Rock Masculinities: Understanding the Gendered Dimension of an Annual Belgian Radio Music Poll', *Feminist Media Studies* (2021), https://doi.org/10.1080/14680777.2021.1939402.

644 For memory practices with recorded music, see William Howland Kenney, *Recorded Music in American Life: The Phonograph and Popular Memory, 1890–1945* (Oxford and New York: Oxford University Press, 1999); Elodie A. Roy, 'Worn Grooves: Affective Connectivity, Mobility and Recorded Sound in the First World War', *Media History* 24, no. 1 (2018): 26–45.

645 The introduction of recordings to capture radio programming was not only motivated by ideals of historic preservation, but in some cases led to the 'time-shifting' of programmes, for instance, of sporting events at a later hour or on another day. Such practices were made easier with the widespread introduction of magnetic tape recording, but recording for short-term uses predominated and the high cost of tape led to the practice of recording over tapes with programming content, rather than preserving these for future reuse. Salosaari, 'The Audio Legacy of Finnish Radio'. For music's significance in radio history, see Christina L. Baade and James A. Deaville, eds, *Music and the Broadcast Experience: Performance, Production, and Audiences* (Oxford: Oxford University Press, 2016).

646 For *Tunes We All Know*, see the first episode on 26 June 1933, BBC National Programme on BBC Genome: https://genome.ch.bbc.co.uk/550b4ba095be429e90338a8e60d4ebc1. For *Memories*, Radio Luxembourg, 2 September 1934, see Stephen Williams 'Logbook', 11, 387/7/1, Radio Luxembourg collection, Sheffield University Library.

647 *Time for a Tune*, 25 April 1939, BBC National Programme, https://genome.ch.bbc.co.uk/36975e5325034cbd9b1d29a87c8ce831.

648 See episodes of *Saturday at Nine-Thirty* from 9 December 1939 and 20 April 1940 at https://genome.ch.bbc.co.uk/.

649 https://genome.ch.bbc.co.uk/.

650 See the listing for *New Songs for Old*, 18 April 1940, BBC Home Service, https://genome.ch.bbc.co.uk/c1f596d424354a829587e5bcff4c800f.

651 Christina L. Baade, *Victory through Harmony: The BBC and Popular Music in World War II* (Oxford and New York: Oxford University Press, 2013), 13, 57–8, 87, 103.

652 See https://genome.ch.bbc.co.uk/.

653 Alexander Russo, '"Selling Station Personality": Managing Impending Change in Postwar Radio, 1947–1952', in *Making Media Work: Cultures of Management in the Entertainment Industries*, ed. Derek Johnson, Derek Kompare and Avi Santo (New York: New York University Press, 2014), 222.

654 Roy Shuker, *Understanding Popular Music Culture*, 4th edn (Abingdon and New York: Routledge, 2013), 121–2, cited in Andreas Lenander Ægidius, 'Music Radio as a Format Remediated for Stream-Based Music Use', in *Music Radio: Building Communities, Mediating Genres*, ed. Morten Michelsen et al. (New York and London: Bloomsbury, 2018), 291; Jody Berland, 'Radio Space and Industrial Time: Music Formats, Local Narratives and Technological Mediation', *Popular Music* 9, no. 2 (1990): 179–92; Heikki Uimonen, 'Beyond the Playlist: Commercial Radio as Music Culture', *Popular Music* 36, no. 2 (2017): 178–95.

655 For examples from Brazil, Canada, Israel, Portugal and the US, see the contributions to the following special issue: Christopher Cwynar and Brian Fauteux, 'Introduction to Public Radio and Music in the Streaming Era Symposium', *Journal of Radio & Audio Media* 27, no. 1 (2020): 4–7; Bottomley, *Sound Streams*, 144–72.

656 Tim Wall, 'Finding an Alternative: Music Programming in US College Radio', *Radio Journal: International Studies in Broadcast & Audio Media* 5, no. 1 (2007): 35–54; Tal Laor, 'Alternative Broadcasting? Maybe! Music Programming in College Radio in Israel', *Journal of Radio & Audio Media* (2020): 1–24, https://doi.org/10.1080/193765 29.2020.1833886.

657 For example, Emily W. Easton, 'Unpredictable Programming: A Freeform Approach to Building Audiences', in *Radio's Second Century: Past, Present, and Future Perspectives*, ed. John Allen Hendricks (New Brunswick, NJ: Rutgers University Press, 2020), 119–33; Micaela di Leonardo, 'Grown Folks Radio: US Election Politics and a "Hidden" Black Counterpublic', *American Ethnologist* 39, no. 4 (2012): 661–72; Dolores Inés Casillas, *Sounds of Belonging: US Spanish-language Radio and Public Advocacy* (New York: New York University Press, 2014), 152; Matthew Van Hoose, 'On the Tropical Counterpublic: Infrastructure and Voice on Uruguayan FM Radio', *Popular Music and Society* 39, no. 3 (2016): 301–16; Maria Sonevytsky, 'Radio Meydan: "Eastern Music" and the

Liminal Sovereign Imaginaries of Crimea', *Public Culture* 31, no. 1 (2019): 93–116.

658 For example, Daniel Fisher, 'Intimacy and Self-abstraction: Radio as New Media in Aboriginal Australia', *Culture, Theory and Critique* 54, no. 3 (2013): 372–93; Lori Kido Lopez, 'Mobile Phones as Participatory Radio: Developing Hmong Mass Communication in the Diaspora', *International Journal of Communication* 10 (2016), https://ijoc.org/index.php/ijoc/article/view/4530.

659 For the post-war resurgence of record sales and the popularity of spoken word formats in the US context, see Jacob Smith, *Spoken Word: Postwar American Phonograph Cultures* (Berkeley and Los Angeles: University of California Press, 2011), 5. For the consolidation of US record companies and radio in the late 1920s, see Kyle Barnett, *Record Cultures: The Transformation of the US Recording Industry* (Ann Arbor: University of Michigan Press, 2021), 1–40.

660 Kompare, *Rerun Nation*, 34; Russo, 'Defensive Transcriptions'.

661 For the David Goldin collection, now held at the Marr Sound Archives, University of Missouri, Kansas City, see https://library.umkc.edu/archival-collections/goldin; 'The Man Who Saved Radio', RadioGOLDINdex, https://radiogoldin.library.umkc.edu/Home/About.

662 Erich Czech-Jochberg, *Vom 30. Januar zum 21. März: Die Tage der nationalen Erhebung.* (Leipzig: Verlag Das neue Deutschland, 1933); Birdsall, 'Radio Documents', S110–S112.

663 Due to anti-Semitic pressure, Koch went into exile in 1935. While taking a business trip to Switzerland, he decided to flee to England, where he went on to work for the BBC and also helped in producing a number of sound books. Joeri Bruyninckx, 'For Science, Broadcasting, and Conservation: Wildlife Recording, the BBC, and the Consolidation of a British Library of Wildlife Sounds', *Technology and Culture* 60, no. 2 (2019): S188–S215.

664 Colin Symes, *Setting the Record Straight: A Material History of Classical Recording* (Middletown, CT: Wesleyan University Press, 2004).

665 Nicholas Jones, 'The Fourth Format: How Audiobooks have become a Standard Format for General Publishers alongside Hardback, Paperback, and E-book', in *Contemporary Publishing and the Culture of Books*, ed. Alison Baverstock, Richard Bradford and Madelena Gonzalez (London: Routledge, 2020), 264. For a chronological listing of the 'BBC Radio Collection' releases, see

https://www.discogs.com/label/58734-BBCRadio-Collectio?sort=year&sort_order=asc.

666 See the listings for the follow-up to BBC Radio Collection, BBC Audiobooks, which was sold to AudioGo (that folded in 2013): https://www.discogs.com/label/57367-BBC-Audiobooks?sort=year&sort_%20order=asc.

667 Richard Berry, 'Radio, Music, Podcasts – BBC Sounds: Public Service Radio and Podcasts in a Platform World', *Radio Journal: International Studies in Broadcast & Audio Media* 18, no. 1 (2020): 63–78.

668 Jeremy Wade Morris, 'Infrastructures of Discovery: Examining Podcast Ratings and Rankings', *Cultural Studies* 35, no. 4–5 (2021): 728–49, https://doi.org/10.1080/09502386.2021.1895246.

669 Bolter and Grusin, *Remediation*.

670 Birdsall, 'Sound and Media Studies'.

671 For example, Cooper, *Radio's Legacy in Popular Culture*; Alexander Badenoch and Berber Hagedoorn, 'TV on the Radio/Radio on Television: European Television Heritage as a Source for Understanding Radio History', *VIEW: Journal of European Television History and Culture* 7, no. 13 (2018): 97–113.

672 Ariane Holzbach, 'MTV and the Remediation of FM Radio', in *Music Radio: Building Communities, Mediating Genres*, ed. Morten Michelsen et al. (New York and London: Bloomsbury, 2018), 273–90.

673 Lopez, 'Mobile Phones as Participatory Radio'; Lori Kido Lopez, 'Challenges of Accessing and Preserving Hmong Radio', *New Review of Film and Television Studies* 16, no. 4 (2018): 489–93.

674 Kristine Ringsager and Sandra Lori Petersen, 'Voicing Otherness on Air: Theorizing Radio Through the Figure of Voice', in *Music Radio: Building Communities, Mediating Genres*, ed. Morten Michelsen et al. (New York and London: Bloomsbury, 2018), 77.

675 John L. Sullivan, 'The Platforms of Podcasting: Past and Present', *Social Media & Society* 5, no. 4 (2019), https://doi.org/10.1177/2056305119880002; Laurie Clarke, '"It's the way the industry is going": How YouTube is transforming podcasting', *Guardian*, 3 September 2022, https://www.theguardian.com/media/2022/sep/03/video-podcasting-youtube-joe-marler-mrballen-tiktok.

676 Hilmes, 'The New Materiality of Radio'. See also Christian Mortensen and Vitus Vestergaard, 'Embodied Tuning: Interfacing Danish Radio Heritage', *Journal of Interactive Humanities* 1, no. 1

(2013): 23–36; Laurence Cliffe et al., 'Materialising Contexts: Virtual Soundscapes for Real-world Exploration', *Personal and Ubiquitous Computing* 25, no. 4 (2021): 623–36; 'Visualising a Radio of the Past Using Technology of the Future', *Beeld en Geluid*, 2 June 2020, https://www.beeldengeluid.nl/en/knowledge/blog/visualizing-radio-past-using-technology-future.

677 See https://radio100.moeb.ca/en/. This exhibition is a collaboration between radio and phonograph collector groups and heritage institutions and funding partners. For a print-based timeline on this same occasion, see Anne F. MacLennan, 'Celebrating a Hundred Years of Broadcasting – An Introduction and Timeline', *Journal of Radio & Audio Media* 27, no. 2 (2020): 191–207.

678 See https://resistanceradio.online/. Since this exhibition took place during the COVID-19 pandemic, the exhibition was moved online, but a temporary low-power FM was set up during live events, along with an online webcast, both of which were shut down following the exhibition.

679 See https://pirate.ie/archive/.

680 Robert Barnet Riter et al., 'Preserving the History of Birmingham Black Radio: A Discussion of Preservation, Outreach and Collaboration', *Global Knowledge, Memory and Communication* (2021), https://doi.org/10.1108/GKMC-04-2021-0062.

681 Peter Lewis and Caroline Mitchell, 'The Radio Garden: Private Pleasures and Public Benefits', *Interactions: Studies in Communication & Culture* 12, no. 1 (2021): 39–50.

682 Uimonen, 'Evening of Sounds', 261; Freire, 'Remediating Radio'.

683 Paddy Scannell, 'For-Anyone-as-Someone Structures', *Media, Culture & Society* 22, no. 1 (2000): 5–24.

684 Larkin, *Signal and Noise*, 50.

685 Alasdair Pinkerton and Klaus Dodds, 'Radio Geopolitics: Broadcasting, Listening and the Struggle for Acoustic Spaces', *Progress in Human Geography* 33, no. 1 (2009): 10–27.

686 Berlant, *Desire/Love*, 2–3.

687 Arjun Appadurai, *Modernity at Large: Cultural Dimensions of Globalization* (Minneapolis: University of Minnesota Press, 1996), 83.

688 Mia Lindgren, 'Personal Narrative Journalism and Podcasting', *Radio Journal: International Studies in Broadcast & Audio Media* 14, no. 1 (2016): 23–41; John Biewen and Alexa Dilworth, eds, *Reality Radio: Telling True Stories in Sound* (Chapel Hill: University of North Carolina Press, 2017).

689 Appadurai's position on affect leans more towards a social constructivist position, noting that affect 'is in many important ways learned: what to feel sad or happy about, how to express it in different contexts, and whether or not the expression of affects is a simple playing out of inner sentiments (often assumed to be universal) are all issues that have been richly problematized. This body of work has gone far to show that emotion is culturally constructed and socially situated and that universal aspects of affect do not tell us anything very revealing' (Appadurai, *Modernity at Large*, 147). Berlant's work is situated more squarely in affect theory, arguing that its contribution is in helping to reveal 'the contradictions and ambivalences in our projects and attachments . . . Clearly, affect theory is central to the history of our concepts of ideology (the relation of explicit to affective attachment) but it is also a way of describing the force of the unsaids in collective life that shape how what can be said is thought and transmitted. These problems of finding form for the empiricism of the unsaid aren't limited to feminist and queer theories. But feminists and queers are especially interested in affect because desire is unruly and induces intensities of attachment outside of calculation.' Lauren Berlant, 'Affective Assemblages: Entanglements & Ruptures – An Interview with Lauren Berlant', *Atlantis: Critical Studies in Gender, Culture & Social Justice* 38, no. 2 (2017): 13–14.

690 Lauren Berlant, *Cruel Optimism* (Durham, NC: Duke University Press, 2011).

691 Berlant, *Desire/Love*, 8–9.

692 Berlant, *Desire/Love*, 13, 16–17.

693 Appadurai, *Modernity at Large*, 35.

694 Appadurai, *Modernity at Large*, 8.

695 Appadurai, *Modernity at Large*, 7.

696 Appadurai, *Modernity at Large*, 7. For productive work in radio/media history on the 'entanglements' between and across such scales and geographies, see Marie Cronqvist and Christoph Hilgert, 'Entangled Media Histories: The Value of Transnational and Transmedial Approaches in Media Historiography', *Media History* 23, no. 1 (2017): 130–41; Michele Hilmes, 'Entangled Media Histories: A Response', *Media History* 23, no. 1 (2017): 142–4.

697 Berlant, *Desire/Love*, 17.

698 Loviglio, *Radio's Intimate Public*, xviii

699 Berlant, *Desire/Love*, 2–3.

700 Adi Kuntsman, 'Introduction: Affective Fabrics of Digital Cultures', in *Digital Cultures and the Politics of Emotion: Feelings, Affect and Technological Change*, ed. Athina Karatzogianni and Adi Kuntsman (Basingstoke: Palgrave Macmillan, 2012), 1–17; Joanne Garde-Hansen, Andrew Hoskins and Anna Reading, eds, *Save As . . . Digital Memories* (Basingstoke: Palgrave Macmillan, 2009).

701 For a critique of this reading of affect within the 'ontological turn' in sound studies, see Brian Kane, 'Sound Studies without Auditory Culture: A Critique of the Ontological Turn', *Sound Studies* 1, no. 1 (2015): 16; Marie Thompson, 'Whiteness and the Ontological Turn in Sound Studies', *Parallax* 23, no. 3 (2017): 266–82.

702 Steingo and Sykes, 'Introduction'.

703 Steven Feld, 'I Hate "Sound Studies"' (2015), https://steven-feld-a936.squarespace.com/s/I-Hate.pdf.

704 For example, Susan J. Douglas, 'Radio and Sound Studies: How we got here', in Lindgren and Loviglio, *The Routledge Companion to Radio and Podcast Studies*, 40–9; James Mansell, 'Historical Acoustemology: Past, Present, and Future', *Music Research Annual* 2 (2021): 2. For an important exception, see Timothy D. Taylor, Mark Katz and Tony Grajeda, eds, *Music, Sound, and Technology in America: A Documentary History of Early Phonograph, Cinema, and Radio* (Durham, NC: Duke University Press, 2012).

705 For an early reflection on this question, see Michele Hilmes, 'Is There a Field Called Sound Culture Studies? And Does It Matter?', *American Quarterly* 57, no. 1 (2005): 249–59.

706 Hills, 'From BBC Radio Personality to Online Audience Personae', 68.

707 Papacharissi, *Affective Publics*. This argument is in line with a broader and much-needed recentring of media history and theory to recognize that radio is 'foundational for understanding the emergence and evolution of modern mediation and, indeed, mediatization'. See Lacey, 'Up in the Air?', 118.

708 See also Birdsall and Carmi, 'Feminist Avenues for *listening in*'.

709 Akrofi-Quarcoo and Gadzekpo, 'Indigenizing Radio in Ghana'.

710 For example, Lori Kido Lopez, *Micro Media Industries: Hmong American Media Innovation in the Diaspora* (New Brunswick, NJ: Rutgers University Press, 2021); Coleman, *Digital Innovations and the Production of Local Content in Community Radio*.

711 Wetherell, Smith and Campbell, 'Introduction'.

INDEX

Note: References in *italic* refer to figures. References followed by "n" refer to notes.

activism 11, 20, 130, 141–2
advertising 17–8, 20, 33, 38, 54, 60–1, 78, 85–8, 100, 102, 138, 174
affect 3–10, 13–32, 41–2, 47, 89–90, 92, 105, 107, 111–2, 132, 143, 189–97
    theory 25, 28, 30–1, 189–92
affective practice/process 15, 24–32, 57, 72, 79, 89–94, 119, 122, 149, 152, 176–82, 186, 189–97
affective publics 4, 195, 201n12, 202n15, 270n707
African(s) 20, 60, 139, 152–3, 157
African American(s) 56, 130, 184–5, 205n38, 220n205, 221n206, 228n273, 246n461
age(ing)/life cycle 6, 27–8, 34, 99, 113–5, 163, 177–8, 189–90, 189, 193, 196
    children/childhood 95, 98–100, 103–4, 113–4, 125, 147, 152–3, 165–8, 177, 193, 196
    older age 23, 99, 113–5, 152, 163, 177, 193, 196, 210n85, 239n390
    teenager(s) 1–2, 17, 23, 98–100, 103–4, 110–1, 147, 152–3, 182

amateur(s)/amateur radio 8, 11, 16–7, 24, 41–57, 63–4, 65, 72, 78, 86, 92–3, 97, 100, 103–5, 112–4, 116–27, 142–4, 148, 159, 162–3, 165–8, 182, 193–6
    recorded sound collecting 116–30
    as 'fans' 46
    knowledge practices 43–57, 72–4
    QSL cards 48–9, *49*, *50*, 50, *51*, 97, 100, 103, 144, 194, 236n357
    scrapbooks 103–4
    self-build/tinkering 42, 44–7, 52, *53*, 54, 56, 65, 113, 166
    as technical hobby 10, 42, 44–55, 96, 112, 122, 128, 144
    women in *51*, *53*, 54–6, 92
Angola 43, 139
Appadurai, Arjun 189–92, 215n145
archive(s)/archivist(s) 8, 11, 24, 38–40, 95–8, 102–3, 118–46, 148, 171–3, 178–9, 181–5, 187, 194
Argentina 44, 81, 208n64, 251n517
audiophile 5, 134, 159, 186

audiovisual(ity) 32, 74, 77–92, 182–5
Australia 1–2, 50, 69, 70, 72, 91, 100, *101*–2, 112, 123, 137, 141, *151*, 155–6
Austria 63, 128

Belgium 74–5, 107, 110, 227n260, 227n263, 250n507, 264n643
Berlant, Lauren 189–92
Bijsterveld, Karin 39–40, 200n7, 202n14, 242n418, 242m420, 255n551
Bonini, Tiziano 200n8, 201n12, 211n91, 256n560
Brazil 105, 107, *108*–9, 200n7, 208n67, 265n655
British Broadcasting Corporation (BBC) 7, 20, 72, 74, 81–8, 96, 110, 121, 123–6, 131–8, 157–8, 178–83
Bronfman, Alejandra 140, 218n186, 251n517

Canada *51*, 69, 72, 123, 137, 142, 184
car 1, 14, 21, 23, 65, 66, 154–5, 193
 bumper stickers 8, 99, 150, 154, 186
China 43, 69, 113, 157, 169–71, 210n90
cinephilia 6, 88, 89
class 23, 34, 38, 44, 54, 56, 78, 80, 87, 95, 130, 145, 155, 157, 163, 180
clothing/fashion 11, 18, 34, 87, 148–50, *151*, 173, 185, 194
collector(s)/collecting 4–6, 10–1, 24, 38–40, 95–103, 112–30, 138–40, 143–5, 159–60, 166–9, 179, 182, 194, 196

pins/badges 100–2, *101*, *102*, 144
music 4, 128–30, 139, 157–60
'old time radio' recordings 10–11, 39, 76, 122–30, 145, 181
colonial(ism) 7, 43, 49–50, 57–9, 62–3, 79, 93, 139, 170–1, 186, 196–7
consumption/consumer culture 5, 14, 17, 21, 23, 32–5, 37, 39, 51–2, 58, 77–8, 81, 85, 89, 96–101, 112–3, 120, 129, 150–4, 158–9, 168, 186, 189–92
curation 11–2, 96–9, 121, 140, 148–9, 157, 176–87
Czechoslovakia (former) 119, 156

decolonization 7, 139, 145, 196
Denmark 157, 257n566, 267n676
digital audio/media 2, 4, 11–2, 15, 19, 39, 121, 124, 126–8, 140–1, 154, 174, 176, 180, 182–5, 187, 190, 192, 194–5, 200n7
digital radio 3–4, 8, 39, 127, 141, 143, 180, 182–5, 190, 192, 194–5
Dijck, José van 39–40, 176–7, 202n14
disability 33–4, 155, 210n87, 213n123
Douglas, Susan 205n43, 205n45, 270n704

eBay 95, 102, 115–6
emotion(s) 4–16, 19–20, 24–33, 36–7, 41–2, 50, 54, 61, 76, 94, 103, 107, 110–2, 116, 122, 132, 142–3, 145, 150, 154, 172, 185, 190, 194, 197, 205n38
 affect and 9, 25–31

INDEX

history of the emotions 15, 25, 28–31, 197, 207n61
encyclopaedia 10, 42, 59, 72–7, 93, 127
ethnicity 23, 34, 180
exhibition(s) 10, 11, 15, 42, 59, 60, 62–9, 71–2, 76, 92–3, 112, 148, 160–75, 181, 184, 186, 193, 196–7

family 2, 16, 18, 22–3, 43, 54, 61, 80, 116–7, 153, 163, 166–7, 186, 193, 196
fan(s)/fandom(s) 4–10, 13, 15, 20, 24–8, 31–2, 35, 40–94, 95–116, 118, 120–8, 142, 144, 149–52, 157–60, 173–5, 179, 182, 184–7, 191, 194–6
  affect/attachments 6, 25–7, 31, 41, 77, 83
  creativity 5–6, 83–4, 96, 103, 149–50
  crossover 10, 42, 51, 90–2, 128, 152, 157–60, 186, 194, 196
  letter(s) 10, 22, 71, 77–81, 86–8, 91–4, 150, 194
  magazines 5–6, 9, 10, 78, 80–1, 85–90, 92, 94, 122, 158
  music 4–6, 35, 119–20, 129, 145, 157–60, 176–7, 179, 186, 195–6
  pathologies 25, 46–7
  pedagogy 42, 89–90
  performance/play 6, 26, 77, 83–5, 89–90, 149
  scrapbooking 6, 8, 10, 103–4, 144
  studies 6, 9, 15, 25–6, 31–2, 35, 40, 195–6
feminism 7, 55, 130, 196, 205n38, 214n138, 215n150, 220n204, 269n689

film/cinema 6, 10, 15, 17, 18, 34–5, 42, 51, 59–62, 65, 76–8, 80–2, 85, 87–93, 118, 123, 129, 157, 161–2, 183, 192–7
Finland 147–8, 176, 185, 251n513, 264n645
First World War 43–4, 51, 112, 135
France 49, 51, 63, 69, 72–3, 119, 158–9
Frevert, Ute 28

gender 2, 7, 16, 23, 34, 38, 54–6, 87, 103, 130, 132, 145, 155, 159–60, 163, 177, 180, 190, 191, 196
Germany 2–4, 45, 51–2, 55, 57–8, 60–9, 71, 74–5, 93, 104, 112, 118–20, 123, 133, 149, 153, 156, 157, 160–4, 182
Ghana 72, 139, 208n67
gramophone/phonography 34–5, 51, 54, 60, 75, 90–1, 116–8, 134, 157–9, 178
Grossberg, Lawrence 25–6

Haiti 142
hams, see amateur(s)/amateur radio
headphone/headset 18, 47, 88, 119, 152, 154, 161, 163, 171
hearing 14, 20, 32–4, 110, 154
heritage 10–1, 15, 21, 38–40, 62, 96–9, 103–7, 110–2, 133, 138–41, 144–6, 163–4, 174–8, 187, 197, 216n156
  institution(s) 8, 99, 104, 121, 130, 141, 146, 160–4, 184–6, 197
  professional(s) 107, 110, 144, 197, 245n455 252n525
  studies 10, 15, 38, 39, 197

Hills, Matt 5, 26–7, 202n20, 203n23, 203n24
Hilmes, Michele 200n6, 201n11, 206n50, 207n61, 221n214, 229n274
hooks, bell 13, 15, 40, 205n38, 205n39
Hoskins, Janet 37–8
Hungary 74–6

Indonesia 43, 75, 91
imagined community 19, 61, 77, 80
India 43, 50, *50*, 79, 91–2, 139, 192
infrastructure(s) 12, 24, 32, 36, 55, 93, 95, 104–5, *106*, 107, 112, 127, 139, 142–44, 180, 183, 186, 196–7. *See also* radio – buildings, radio – towers
interactivity 6, 10, 59, 65, 71, 76, 78–80, 82, 85, 90, 93, 97, 142, 155–6, 163–4, 169, 171, 176, 185, 186, 230n282
intermedial(ity) 9, 15, 18, 32–40, 42, 57, 59–60, 74, 77–93, 134, 157, 159, 182, 183–4, 212n101, 214n132. *See also* audiovisual(ity), remediation
intersectional(ity) 23, 34, 205n38
intersensorial(ity) 9, 15, 32–40, 59, 195. *See also* sense(s)
Ireland 43, 139, 142, 184
Israel 174–5, *175*, 265n655, 265n656
Italy 16, 44, 75, 201n12, 229n273

Jamaica 140
Japan 52–4, *53*, 57, 58, 69, 72, 90–1, 105, *106*, 120, 123, 159–60, 167–70

Joyce, Zita 174, 243n428, 262n627

Kenya 72
knowing/knowledge 5–6, 10, 28–30, 41–94, 115–16, 122, 194
  amateur knowledge of radio 10, 43–57
  authoritative/epistemic authority 10, 42, 59, 93
  institutional knowledge practices 10, 57–77, 160–2
  intermediality 77–92
  popularization of radio 57–77
  related to print media 77–92
  Western epistemologies 10, 195, 204n33, 204n34
Korea 17

Lacey, Kate 200n6, 204n34, 206n53, 229n278, 256n563, 270n707
Lamerichs, Nicolle 27, 212n101
language 7, 19, 20, 43, 51, 65, 73, 79, 81, 91, 124, 130, 139, 142, 152, 175, 180, 183, 195, 197, 204n34, 207n63, 207n64, 223n231
LaPlaca, Laura 95–6, 98
Latina/o/x 130, 208n64, 246n461, 255n555
library 45, 62, 81, 103–4, 120, 122–7, 129, 131–2, 137–42, 159, 178–9
listener(s)/audience(s)
  as community 58, 155, 176
  radio's appeal for 16–25, 192
  as readers 33, 77, 80–3, 88–91
listening 4, 21, 42, 44, 75, 147, 152–60, 176–87, 193, 194, 197

as 'addiction' 4, 16, 24, 25, 47, 116, 165, 193
attention vs. distraction 14, 21, 24, 29, 35, 153, 193
collective/group listening 21–3, 147, 152–60, 176–8, 186–7, 192–4
commuting/travelling 21, 152–4, 186, 207n57
as embodied 42, 149, 176, 194, 195
to enemy radio 11, 23–4, 142, 143, 170–1, 210n90, 252n522
exploratory 16, 47
publics 77–8
in public space(s) 152–3, 156–60, 174–5, 186, 193
love/loving 2–3, 5–7, 13–40, 79, 89–90 97, 102–3, 123, 139, 143, 148–9, 159, 185, 189–92, 195, 201n13, 202n14, 205n38. *See also* radiophilia
affects and 25–32
appeal of radio 16–25
emotions and 25–32
material culture and 5–6, 32–40, 97, 111, 123, 144, 159, 165–6
Loviglio, Jason 200n6, 229n274, 253n533, 255n550
Luxembourg 20, 86, 124–5, 158, 178

magazine(s) 1, 5–10, 15, 17, 22, 32, 34–5, 42, 44, 45–6, 52, 53, 54, 56, 69, 71–3, 76–92, 94, 102, 104, 123, 134–5, 157–9, 161–2, 195
Malaysia 155
material culture 4–6, 8, 10–1, 15, 32, 36–40, 46, 95–9, 104–13, 123, 161–2, 171–4, 181–3, 186, 195, 197
loving/love and 5–6, 32–40, 97, 123, 159, 258n581
memory and 6, 8, 11, 95–6, 105–15, 113, 148, 197
neglect/decay 97, 99, 100–2, 131, 132, 142, 145
studies 15, 37, 197
media studies 5, 33, 196, 172, 197, 204n33, 245n445, 250n506, 262n622
memory 4, 11, 15, 20, 22, 34, 37–40, 95–7, 103–16, 134–7, 144, 147, 148, 164, 173–82, 187, 194, 197, 209n76
and forgetting 39, 96, 105–10
heritage and 38–9, 163, 176–7, 184, 197
musical 176–82
nostalgia and 4, 6, 34, 39, 164, 176–82
objects 11, 15, 39, 95–7, 144, 164, 174
public 148, 174, 178, 186
as a social activity 38, 147, 176–82, 187
and sound technologies 39–40, 134, 174, 202n14, 216n153, 240n404, 240n407, 243n428
studies 10, 15, 39, 197
merchandise 5, 8, 100, 112, 148, 150–1, *151*, 185–6, 194
Mexico 142
migrant/diasporic 20, 38, 80, 183, 191
military 43, 49, *50*, 54, 57–8, 63, 112
modernism 18, 107
modernity 7, 43, 47, 49–50, 58, 69, 156
Mongolia 139

Morse code 16, 41, 43, 47, 55, 63, 74
Mozambique 43, 139
museum(s) 11, 15, 38, 40, 62, 104, 112, 148, 160–75, 184–6, 193, 197
music 1–6, 15, 17–9, 21, 24, 27, 35, 39, 65, 74,–5, 91, 107, 110–2, 116–20, 129–30, 135, 139, 151, 153–5, 157–60, 172, 174, 176–82, 183, 186, 194, 195
   cafés 159–60, 186, 193
   collecting as male-dominated 130, 159, 160, 196
   fans 4–5, 6, 35, 157–60, 179, 196
   passion for music 4, 159, 177
   on radio 21, 24, 27, 50, 60, 86, 135–7, 154, 157–8, 176–82, 186
   recording 4, 15, 17, 39, 63, 77, 129, 140, 157–9, 174, 176–82
   shops/stores 11, 59, 129, 158–60, 186, 193

national(ism) 7, 44, 58, 62, 185–6, 192
Netherlands 50, 61–4, 64, 65, 66, 74–6, 118–9, 142, 156, 162, 164, *165*, 169–70, 176–7, 181
New Zealand 104, 112, 123, 172–4
newspaper(s) 15, 17, 35, 61, 69, 77, 81–2, 85, 91, 103–4, 107, 135, 164, 195
niche/narrowcasting 24, 94, 150–1, 194
Nigeria 139, 209n78, 215n142
noise 19
nostalgia 4–6, 34, 39–40, 94, 111, 113–4, 135, 137, 144, 164, 177–82

paper 15, 38, 77, 91, 98, 100, 103–4, 144
participatory culture 88–90, 150
Patterson, Eleanor 240n408, 246n463
Philippines 20, 43, 152, 206n55
photograph(y) 15, 20, 35, 51, 56, 71–4, 80, 85–90, 117–8, 161, 169, 172, 195
podcast(ing) 2–4, 8, 19, 24, 33, 39, 96, 127–8, 155–6, 180, 182–4, 190, 193–5
   studies 3–4, 24, 127, 195
Poland 24, 69, 75, 104, 139
Portugal 49, 207n59, 217n165
postcard(s) 32, 48, 69, 86, 91–2, 93, 100, 103, 144, 194
postcolonial/decolonial approaches 195, 204n33, 250n506, 254n542
practice theory 25–31
print culture 72–3, 77–92, 93, 103, 196

race 23, 34, 56, 58, 92, 130, 180, 200n6, 221n214. *See also* African(s), African American(s), white/whiteness
radio
   building(s) 10, 32, 36, 68, *68*, 69, *70*, 71, 93, 98, 104–10, 133, 137, 144, 148, 160, 162, 164, 166, 170, 193. *See also* infrastructure(s)
   call-in/talkback 23, 147, 155, 176, 185, 194
   campus/college 142, 172–4, 180
   club 5, 43–6, 51, 54–6, 65, 92, 100–2, 111, 122–3, 126–7, 144, 172, 193, 196
   comedy/humour 17, 83–5, *84*, 124, 182, 194

INDEX

commercial 33, 52, 86, 124–5, 143, 150–1, 155, 172, 175, 179–80, 183, 190, 197
contests/competitions 78, 81, 89, 102, 150
as democratizing 17, 54, 92, 156
design 18, 32–4, 36–7, 38, 45, 60, 65, 71, 80–5, 107, 113, 144, 153, 166, 174
dial/tuner 33, 36, 149, 213n121
disc jockey (DJ) 20, 86, 111, 157, 178–9, 183
dislike, aversion to 3
domestication/as furniture 2, 7, 16–8, 20–3, 33, 36–8, 43–4, 46, 54–5, 60, 65, 66, 75, 83, 89, 97, 104–5, 116–7, 132–3, 152–4, 160, 165–7, 186, 193, 196
drama 60, 74, 91, 124, 126, 127, 133, 147, 169, 171, 194
education/schools 21, 54, 61, 81, 87–9, 135, 155, 193
as ephemeral 4, 10, 24, 38–9, 94, 95–7, 128, 130, 143–4, 194
genre 14, 17, 19, 35, 42, 74, 90, 124, 128, 145, 151, 155, 171, 192
ident(s)/theme songs 174, 182–3
and illness 4, 14–6, 24, 155, 193
interval signal(s) 74, 128, 174
intimacy 3–4, 18, 23, 80, 83, 92, 175, 180
inventor(s) 58, 63, 69, 71, 74, 78, 116, 161–3, 196
jingle(s) 20, 128, 147, 183
liveness 18–20, 39, 60, 71–2, 133, 147, 177–8, 185
monitoring 11, 143, 170–1
news 21, 23
non-users 3, 43

offshore/pirate 56, 110–2, 121–2, 129, 142, 143, 172, 174–5, 184
prison 24, 184
public broadcasting 131–3, 138, 151, 155, 169–70, 172, 177, 180
in public space(s) 21–2, 24, 152–3, 156, 193, 196
reportage 60, 68, *68*, 69, 74, 85, 88, 119, 120, 133, 178
receiver/set 18, 22–3, 33–4, 36–8, 47, 50, 52, *53*, 54, 60, 63, *64*, 65, 66, 68, 71, 86, 98, 104, 112–5, 144, 149–50, 153, 161, 164, 166, 168, *168*, 169, 189–90
schedule 9, 17, 81–4, 88, 90, 96
serial/soap opera 20, 89, 96, 107
shortwave 50, 57, 170
star(s)/celebrity 6, 10, 20, 25, 35, 72–3, 78–81, 83, 85–90, 99, 100, 103–4, 128, 136, 171, 178–9, 196
studies 3–4, 76, 93, 195, 197
studio 20, 74, 81, 107, 112, 125, 138, 156, 161, 169, 184, 193
tower(s) 32, 36, 69, *70*, 93, 104–5, *106*, 149, 163, 166, 193
transistor 8, 18, 21–3, 25, 52, 71, 72, 104, 105, 113–4, 144, 152–4, 168, 193, 196
voice(s) 19, 71, 91, 129
in workplace 21, 49, 83, 155, 157, 184, 193
radiogenic 17
radiogram 36, 38, 60, 144
radiophilia (the love of radio) 6–15, 18, 22, 24, 32, 34, 37–41, 44, 50, 77, 79, 91–2, 96–9, 105–12, 132, 138, 143–5, 148, 153, 176, 191–7

definition of 2
sharing and displaying 148–87
virtual radiophiles 115–6
Razlogova, Elena 80
reading 33, 35, 42, 75–7, 80–83, 88–91
recording
    cassette 1, 36, 120, 121, 123–6, 149, 154, 182, 186
    copying (tape) 1, 120, 122, 126, 129, 141, 189
    home recording 36, 97, 117–9, 121, 129, 138, 144, 157, 189, 196
    illicit (bootleg) 117–22, 127, 129
    mixtape 120, 122
    radio (off-air) 1, 97–8, 117–22, 128–9, 131–4, 138, 178, 189
    transcription disc 117, 180, 182
    vinyl 11, 140, 149, 181, 182, 187
    voice(s) 71, 116, 117–8, 129
    wire 118–9, 144
religion 17, 21, 23, 49, 61, 157, 180
remediation 35, 88, 137, 179, 183
Russia 17, 44, 72, 156–7

Scheer, Monique 29–30
scrapbooks/scrapbooking 6, 8, 10, 103–4, 118, 135, 144
Second World War 23, 54, 61–2, 74, 75, 93, 110, 118, 136–7, 145, 159, 164, 168, 170, 179, 181–2
sense(s) 9, 11, 15, 32, 40, 76, 90, 186. *See also* intersensoriality
    anthropology of the senses 34
    haptic 9, 33, 34, 90
    hearing/auditory 32, 42, 59

    smell/olfactory 32, 33–4, 42, 115
    taste 32–3, 42
    touch 22, 33, 42, 59, 90, 174–5
    vision/visual 32, 35, 42, 76, 86, 90
sexuality 141, 180, 190, 191, 251n514
Slocombe, Marie 131, 133–9
social media 127, 155, 177, 184–5, 187,
sound
    effects 19, 60
    quality 79, 117, 119–22, 153, 161
    studies 4, 37, 194–5
sound hunters 119–20, 129, 145
South Africa 20, 50, 123, 157, 207n63, 232n306, 250n506, 251n516, 254n538
Spain 158
sport(s) 6, 17, 21, 75, 105, 128, 152, 155, 171, 176, 182, 192–4
Sri Lanka 91
Stoever, Jennifer Lynn 200n6, 221n214, 246n461
Stone, Christopher 86, 137, 157–8, 178–80
Switzerland 75, 119, 139, 156

Taiwan 72, 170, *170*, 171, *171*, 186
taste preferences 43, 87, 132, 145, 157, 177–9
technology
    audio cassette 11, 120, 121, 123–6, 149, 182
    computer 22, 47, 163, 190, 195
    (hi-fi) stereo 1, 22, 36, 56, 71, 72, 114, 190

loudspeaker(s) 18, 21, 47, 65, 68, 104, 156–7, 161, 164
maintenance/repair 54, 57, 112–5, 166
microphone 65, 71, 135, 161
miniaturization 105
mobile/smartphone 105, 149, 155, 180, 190, 194, 195
obsolescence 112, 142
wireless 41, 59, 105
technological imperialism 58
technostalgia 40, 112–4, 144, 165–6, 181–2, 216n154
telegraphy 16, 51, 55, 58, 63–4, 160
telephony 22, 34, 35–6, 105, 149, 155, 166, 180, 190, 194
television 1, 6, 15, 18, 22, 65, 71, 76, 102, 123, 128, 130, 143, 164, 168, 177, 183, 192, 195, 197
time/temporality 22, 27, 97, 147, 155, 190
transnational/global 6, 34, 50, 58, 176, 185, 189–92, 196
Turkey 169

United Kingdom (UK) 7, 19–20, 23, 49, 61, 64–5, 67, 68, 72–3, 81–8, 96–7, 110–3, 115–7, 119, 121, 123–6, 130–1, 133–8, 141–2, 145, 162, 165–7, 172, 178–9, 181–3

United States (US) 6–7, 43–4, 48, 54–5, 57, 59, 63, 73, 78, 80–1, 89, 112, 117–8, 124, 128, 130, 134, 138, 145, 150, 152, 157, 182–4
Uruguay 208n64, 265n657

value/valuation 38, 82, 97–9, 101, 110, 112–4, 116, 121, 152
VanCour, Shawn 213n125, 216n151, 245n455, 252n519, 252n524
Van Puymbroeck, Birgit 214n133, 233n316, 233n319
Vietnam 43, 140
visual culture 32, 59, 65, 80–7, 90, 195

Walkman 1, 21, 22, 36, 72, 105, 120, 121, 154, 168, 193
Wetherell, Margaret 30–1, 216n156
white/whiteness 59, 113, 118, 130, 145
women 53, 54–6, 86–7, 92, 103, 130, 138, 155, 159, 160, 163, 196
writing 42, 48–9, 80, 85, 91–2, 93–4

Zambia 152–3, 196, 214n131
Zimbabwe 221n208

www.ingramcontent.com/pod-product-compliance
Ingram Content Group UK Ltd.
Pitfield, Milton Keynes, MK11 3LW, UK
UKHW021854170226
468125UK00005B/103